G000090102

Regional French Cookery

THE INTERNATIONAL WINE AND FOOD SOCIETY'S GUIDE TO

Regional French Cookery

Kenneth Toyé

COLOUR PHOTOGRAPHY BY KENNETH SWAIN

THE INTERNATIONAL WINE AND FOOD PUBLISHING COMPANY
DAVID & CHARLES

A publication of
The International Wine and Food Publishing Company,
Marble Arch House, 44 Edgware Road, London, w2

© Kenneth Toyé, 1973

All rights reserved. No part of this publication may
be reproduced, stored in a retrieval system, or
transmitted, in any form or by any means, electronic,
mechanical, photocopying, recording or otherwise,
without the prior permission of The International
Wine and Food Publishing Company.

This book was designed and produced by
Rainbird Reference Books Limited,
Marble Arch House, 44 Edgware Road, London, w2

Editor: Betty Shepherd

ISBN   07153 6327 1

Text printed by
A. Wheaton & Co, Exeter, Devon
Bound by A. Wheaton & Co, Exeter, Devon

au peuple francais
avec l'hommage de l'auteur

Contents

List of Colour Plates

Acknowledgments

I would like to thank my wife, Cynthia, for her invaluable help in the preparation and testing of dishes.

Also, Betty Shepherd, for her painstaking work on my manuscript, and Rosemary Wadey for preparing the food for photography. And, 'brothers and sisters of the kitchen', with whom I have cooked and tasted, argued and agreed: Mme. Bergant, Mme. Francou, Mme. Benoît, Mme. Troin, Leo Evans, Claude de Ville, Josef Bettini, M. Culoz-Vilars, and Jean Bentley.

K.T.

Introduction

The tremendous variety found in the regions of France makes one hesitate to attempt an analysis of regional French cooking. Just consider the boundaries: the Channel, the Atlantic, Spain, the Mediterranean, Italy, Switzerland, Germany, Luxembourg, Belgium. There is a world of cooking within these limits. At any given moment, in France, a legion of cooks are preparing a host of dishes. Glistening mussels open invitingly in a kitchen by the sea in Normandy. Golden trails of cheese escape the fork emerging from a *fondue* cooked for hungry climbers in the Savoie. In St. Raphael, a long-married couple sample the overpowering richness of an *aioli*. Even to mention such dishes is to invite us to enter this world and explore it.

France has always been a country of many divisions. Richelieu, and later the Revolution, worked for uniformity under strong central government. We ordinary mortals, who tend to distrust state intervention in our affairs, are mightily relieved to perceive that it was all of no avail. The character and customs of the different regions that go to make up the country are just as firmly defined. The *beret basque* flutters at the Spanish border and the Breton mother continues to name her children exactly as she likes.

So France is not merely one state, but many states, where people eat, sleep and dream – of what they are going to eat tomorrow at that reunion of old classmates, at Uncle Achille's birthday party, or simply for lunch in the cafe round the corner where the pâté is so good. Yes, food is of vital importance to the Frenchman. He is as proud to have good food at his table as his wife is to prepare it. This is not to say that in these scurrying days the 'food to take away' from the local *charcuterie* is not in evidence. But then, wonder of wonders, any citizen of France is quite likely to show pride in that fact that he, or she, managed to find such a magnificent source of food.

This pride is touching in its simplicity and intensity, and it is the feeling that gives quality to the French cuisine. Madame de Sevigny provided a fitting memorial to this sense of the importance of food when she described how Vatel, the *maître d'hôtel* of the Duke of Burgundy committed suicide because the last table among many was not well enough served – not well enough served in his own opinion!

The importance of food in France, and the comradeship among cooks, is illustrated by one event that happened in a French kitchen. Once upon a time in a little town in the Var a group of people stood waiting for a *bouillabaisse* to come to fruition. We had looked forward to this magic moment for three weeks. At last the mistral had relented and the boats could go out to fish. The glistening creatures gurgled in the pot. The garlic-laced *rouille* gently insinuated its aroma into the room. The *croûtons* stood stiffly to attention. Then Grandmère took me quietly aside and, after administering an oath of secrecy, whispered to me the final *tour de main* that would set the seal on a perfect dish. The others were eager to learn the secret, but were turned aside with: 'But it is just a little something between cooks. Now, if you will excuse us mesdames'. And Grandmère knew that I would never divulge her secret.

This book has been compiled in the spirit of that 'little something between cooks'. This comradeship of the kitchen stems from a certain sense of equality, for we are all equally beset with difficulties. Anyone confronted with some vegetables and a piece of meat has the same problems as those experienced by the great chef *Carême*, who so gloriously overcame them.

Brittany

The influence of the sea is everywhere in the peninsula of Brittany. It is the sea that gives soft, almost Mediterranean, winters. It is the sea that brings the rain, so that Brest has a downfall every other day and most other places every third day. From the sea came the Celts, who gave their language and customs to the country, and added a few strange bumps in the ground and some even stranger isolated rocks. The sea attracts the Bretons themselves, so that the large settlements are all on the coast, and it draws the holiday-maker to marvel at the vast beaches of the Arvor and the deep rocky inlets of the Morbihan.

But the sea and the tourist trade reveal only one side of Brittany; another is shown in the cooking of the area. The *galette* and the pancake suffer strange transmutations under the onslaught from abroad; but traditionally the former has always been eaten salted on farms and in fishing villages, and the latter is as broad as a buckler, crisp and substantial and rarely made of wheat flour; more usually from buckwheat. Fish is eaten grilled over furze twigs or gently simmered in stock. Cured hams swing in the kitchen, and the cider barrel stands solidly in the corner.

The interior of Brittany is strange and isolated and gives the impression that it wants to stay that way. The *Landes*, the hill and heathland, is rugged and yet soft. Granite outcrops spill out onto the fragant furze, gorse and heather. Cottages crowd together for protection and send out as their lines of communication sunken roads between hedges. Each field seems to be a little private world of its own with its hidden crop of oats or buckwheat. Potatoes nestle deep in the ground, just as the people draw deep into the ingle-nook fireplaces in the depths of winter.

The animals are allowed more space than the plants as they prepare for the last great voyage to the market towns. Places like Uzel greet beasts to provide meat for the table; Ploeuc specialises in the pig and the calf; Rostrenen is the market for cows and sheep. Everywhere, the cow and the hen provide produce for the larder. Butter is still churned by hand in the dairy, and the skimmed milk left in the churn is used in the kitchen. The smells of milk and cider blend in many a Breton kitchen.

Of course the coast does not only mean tourists; it means fishing and market gardening. Fishing has changed over the centuries. Larger boats with engines now carry the fishermen to Iceland in the North and Portugal to the South. Sardine, tunny, hake and cod flow in glistening masses from the holds, some to be eaten fresh but many more to be canned, dried, salted, or frozen, and packed away for the future. Even the shellfish – lobster, crab, mussel and oyster – are now plucked from their native home; transported, and cosseted in beds tended and chosen for them.

Market gardens came very early to the north coast of the Arvor; in the eighteenth century strawberries were cultivated, to be exported for the enjoyment of those strange people, the English. Now this has become an important industry, and early potatoes, artichokes, onions, broccoli, cauliflower, and asparagus flood into city markets all over Europe. Strange names like Plougastel-Daoulas, or St. Pol de Léon, appear on bunches and boxes of produce. People have to eat all the year round, and Brittany can help to balance the diet for places where the climate is not so kind.

But let it not be said that Brittany is a land of milk and honey. The sea and the land give their plenty; but it is only by the stamina, courage and ingenuity of the people that the produce can be harvested. Breton cooking is the result of the difficulties of fishing and farming; it is frugal, careful, and takes full advantage of the stuff available. Nourishing it must be, for work on the land or at sea is hard. So at once we have a cooking lesson. Good, nourishing food can be prepared at a reasonable cost, with local products, but only as the result of planning and effort. Surely, it is worth the effort to eat well.

PANCAKES AND GALETTES

The pancake has, with the *galette*, pride of place in the Breton kitchen. Piled high on their own shelf, these can provide sustenance for a whole day, and a special treat for early risers the next morning. Perhaps it would not be a bad idea to linger a moment over the pancake and *galette*, for then we will have a basis for cooking in the Breton style.

PANCAKES. Hanging next to the pancake shelf, and never to be washed with soap and water (let alone detergent), is the pancake pan. This one is heavy, of black iron, a present from Marie Rose. It could be light, and of aluminium; it will still work if rubbed lightly with a piece of bacon fat while sizzling hot, before and after cooking. Pancakes in this land of Celtic tradition are sometimes made of ordinary flour but more often of buckwheat flour.

8 servings (2 6-inch pancakes each):

6 oz. (1 full cup) plain flour	**1 oz. (2 tablespoons) melted butter**
3 eggs	**1 tablespoon (1¼) cooking oil**
¾ pint (scant 2 cups) milk	

We'll not use sugar in the mixture, then we can eat the pancake as savoury or sweet. Let us discuss this later. Sift the flour into a large mixing bowl. Nowadays flour scarcely needs sifting, but make sure there are no lumps in the mixture. Break in one egg and mix into the flour, then mix in the other two. You should have a very thick, sticky paste. With experience you will know whether to add more flour or an extra egg to get the right consistency. All the mixing is done with a wooden spoon. Now mix in the milk. Add this drop by drop, stirring hard. When you have poured in enough to make a soft paste, continue to work with a whisk. When all the milk has been added you will have a runny mixture that will just coat the back of a spoon. Whisk in the oil and butter. You don't have to let this mixture stand, but if you do your pancakes will be lighter.

Now the cooking. If the pancakes are to be eaten as a savoury, fat from pork or even bacon can be used. For the sweet dish I always use oil. Pour plenty of oil into the pan then pour it out again so that the pan is oiled all over with no surplus. Heat until a light vapour appears. Scoop up some of the pancake mixture with a ladle and pour a thin jet gently into the centre of the pan, rocking it with a circular motion so that the mixture spreads quickly and evenly; make sure that the pan is covered all over. The pancake cooks very quickly. Heat until bubbles begin to form on one side and then flip over with a palette knife. Cook again until golden brown. Stack the pancakes – the Breton name is *pillig-du* – on a warm plate, and cover; but they are at their best served straight from the pan.

The pancake is a very versatile product of the kitchen. Simply sprinkled with sugar it is delicious, or we could add lemon juice, jam, honey or syrup. We could stuff them with a creamy cheese sauce, or with fish sauce and shrimps. The possibilities are endless, but first make your pancake. Experiment with any flour you like.

GALETTES. It is said that the growing of buckwheat[1] saved agriculture in Brittany. For the first time these hardy country folk had a cereal crop that they could depend upon. The *galette* was evolved as the ideal way to use this crop as food. The recipe is simplicity itself, and it is nearly always eaten salted.

1 lb. (3 cups) plain flour	**2 teaspoons (2½) salt**
½ lb. (1 cup) butter	**milk**

Rub the butter into the flour. Add the salt, and with milk make a soft dough. Let this stand. Roll out very thin and cut into rounds. In Brittany these are fried like pancakes, but you may prefer to bake them in the oven, brushing with salted milk. The *galette* is cooked when it is golden brown. As with pancakes, use your own ideas. Crush anchovies into butter and spread on the *galette*, or sprinkle on sliced fried onions or mushrooms.

MENU

Our friend Marie Rose often has a dozen people to dinner in the evening but still has to get on with her own work about the farm during the day. She cannot spend a long time preparing the meal, and it is a joy to see her flitting about the kitchen, stirring here, inspecting, prodding, shaking a pan and then laying a simple but well arranged table. What a lesson I learned from one meal! Here is her menu.

SOUPE	SOUP
CÔTE DE PORC	PORK CHOPS
POMMES DE TERRE AU PETIT SALÉ	POTATOES WITH SALT PORK
SALADE	SALAD
POMMES AU FOUR	BAKED APPLES

[1] Buckwheat (*fagopyrum*), probably for 'beechwheat', because its three-cornered seed is like beechmast. It is not a true cereal, and will grow on much poorer soils.

MEAT AND VEGETABLE SOUP. Soup can be a meal in itself. It does not need long preparation and it is a good way of using up odd scraps of meat and vegetables. Most soups are started by cooking onions, and Marie Rose's was no exception. Chopped onions were softened in butter, and then cold vegetables and minced scraps of meat, together with a good handful of chopped parsley (don't ever throw the stalks away) were placed in the pot. Now was the time to add pepper and salt, and garlic. All this was gently shaken to absorb the butter and to heat. A few stalks of thyme came next and then, quite simply, water. This was left to simmer gently.

POTATOES WITH SALT PORK. The potatoes were cooked on top of the oven with small onions and strips of salt pork; Marie Rose wanted to cook them quickly so she added water, but they could be cooked slowly in butter. This used to be the staple diet in farmhouses in Brittany. The great steaming cauldron would gently swing over the fire as the children helped themselves with, or without, permission.

BAKED APPLES. PORK CHOPS. SALAD (LETTUCE). Next our good friend cored large apples, put them on a greased oven-sheet and stuffed them with sugar, raisins and cinnamon, popped one clove in each, and roasted them in the oven. The pork chops were fried in a heavy iron frying pan, using butter, salt and many twists of the pepper-mill. Lettuce dressed with oil and vinegar rounded off the preparation. A few fresh dandelion leaves, well washed, with the tender roots carefully scraped, were a tasty addition to the salad. Why do we always rely on lettuce for salads? In France the dandelion is considered a delicacy, and tender young thistles, shredded cabbage, and young spinach are all treated with respect.

COFFEE. The whole meal took scarcely an hour to prepare. The cider barrel in the corner did valiant service that night, as the stories went round of mysterious lights in the deep sheltered ways of the *bocage* and the astounding skill of the old players of *palet*, who skimmed their flat stones to within centimetres of the distant mark. After two of the fragrant baked apples, with an attendant mug of sweet cider, the kitchen bed in its open cupboard with gay curtains looked so inviting that I asked to be woken up with coffee. The resulting discussion on taking coffee at night was laced with a mixture of Breton folklore and mediaeval medicine. In spite of this I had my coffee, prepared in the old way of the countryside. The ground coffee, plenty of it, was poured into a linen cylinder with one end sewn up, and hot water was dripped through it.

MENU

The sea is never very far away wherever you are in Brittany. Jeannine's mother and father live in Lorient and so, for her important *fête* day Marie Rose, her godmother, together with her family and close friends, made the union of the two Brittanies; the inland farm came to the sea. Jeannine's father works for a firm that salts and freezes the fish, particularly hake, caught by the deep sea fishers of Lorient, and he made sure that the dinner was plentifully supplied from the harvest of the sea. These are the dishes of that wonderful meal.

HUITRES DE BELON	OYSTERS
CREVETTES MAYONNAISE	SHRIMPS MAYONNAISE
HOMARD GRILLÉ	GRILLED LOBSTER
GIGOT D'AGNEAU FLAGEOLETS	LEG OF LAMB WITH KIDNEY BEANS
SALADE	SALAD
FAR BRETON	FAR BRETON

Lorient is not very far away from the Loire, whose northern banks produce the crisp white wine, Muscadet, that goes so well with shellfish; indeed, with all the dishes of that fête of fêtes.

OYSTERS. This menu takes a long time to prepare, but there is not one complicated dish, and it is all easy to serve. I always thought that the Portuguese oyster was cheaper than the native because it took time, nerve and skill to open. (In fact, it is easier to tend, and multiplies quicker than the other varieties). Test the oysters by knocking them together. They should make a sharp, hollow sound and remain tight shut, sealing in the liquid that means freshness and flavour. They are opened just before the meal by inserting a knife blade in the division of the two shells and twisting firmly. My old wounds have healed up since I acquired an oyster knife that has a short blade and a broad guard, preventing the point from slipping through the shellfish. Take away one half of the shell and serve the oyster flat on the other half, full of the natural juice. A squeeze of lemon is all that is needed. The shrimps are boiled and shelled, served on a bed of cucumber rounds with an attendant bowl of mayonnaise (see page 85).

GRILLED LOBSTER. The lobster presents us with a problem. Should we stun it, and split it alive to grill; or shall we plunge it in boiling water with sliced carrot, onion and herbs, to cook first? The first method gives the tastier dish but seems brutal. However, is the second way any less brutal? If the lobster is to be split in two along the back and tail, a stout knife will accomplish this. The whole creature can be eaten, but the stomach bag is usually, and easily, detached. In the head is a dark green paste that should be taken out and used as a sauce. The halves are grilled, flesh up, sprinkled with herbs, pepper and salt, and a little oil. (Always remember that butter gives a strong flavour to a dish but that ground-nut oil imparts little or no extra taste). If the lobster has been boiled first it will not need so much grilling. The claws should be taken from the body before grilling, cracked, and grilled separately. The only way that I know to eat a lobster is to take hold of it with your hands!

LEG OF LAMB WITH KIDNEY BEANS. Cooking leg of lamb is simplicity itself. The leg should be trimmed of superfluous fat. Make a few slits in the flesh to hold several cloves of garlic. If you like, lay thyme and bay leaves on top. Twenty minutes to the pound, in a hot oven (mark 7; 425°F.), is ample to cook the meat, which should be quite pink towards the bone. Kidney beans are simmered gently in water with a *bouquet* of herbs and an onion studded with cloves. Jeannine's mother used parsley, thyme and bay leaf, tied to a stick of celery, for her *bouquet*. The *gigot* was lifted into the festival class by the added glory of a glass of *calvados* – apple brandy from Normandy – poured over it just before serving.

FAR BRETON.   This is the only dish of this wonderful meal that needs a full recipe.

1 lb. (3 cups) flour	½ lb. (½ cup) sugar
1½ pints (3¼ cups) milk	1 tablespoon (1¼) cognac
4 eggs	orange water

Mix the flour with a cup of the milk. Separate the eggs. Add the egg yolks, and then the whites, lightly beaten. Mix in the sugar, the rest of the milk, the orange water and cognac. Pour into a greased tin and cook for 10 minutes in a hot oven (mark 7; 425°F.), then for a further 30 minutes at moderate (mark 4; 350°F.).

Serving a fruit bowl at the end of a long meal refreshes the guests and renews the flow of conversation. Again aiming at something special, Jeannine's father offered a basket of strawberries from Plougastel-Daoulas. Over coffee Grandpère gave the speech of thanks for the dinner, and sent round the table his offering to the guests, an old pottery flask of apple brandy.

COTRIADE

In the same friendly town of Lorient we could sample this fish dish that is a meal in its own right. The dish can be quite cheap to prepare, a true fisherman's meal, and we shall try the cheapest of fish, mackerel.

6 servings:

6 mackerel	parsley
1 onion	white wine
1 leek	3 oz. (full ½ cup) flour
1 clove garlic	4 oz. (½ cup) butter
fennel	croûtons
celery	

Clean the fish. Make a stock with the heads and tails, with water, wine, finely sliced onions and leeks and a *bouquet* made of fennel, celery, and parsley. Chop garlic finely and add, with pepper and salt, to the stock. Simmer the fish in this stock for about 15 minutes. Remove the fish and keep warm. Make a white sauce with the butter, flour and the stock in another pan. (To make 2 pints (5 cups) of sauce, melt 4 ozs. (½ cup) of butter and stir in flour until the butter is all absorbed. Add the stock a little at a time, whipping slowly with a whisk.) The mixture will at first make a paste, which will gradually thin into a thick cream. Always cook the sauce very well so that the taste of flour disappears. It will take at least another 2 pints (5 cups) of stock to make a slightly creamy soup. Season to taste. Dry out slices of the stale bread in a cool oven (mark 1; 300°F.) with a little garlic and salt. Pour the creamy soup onto these croûtons in a soup tureen, and serve. The fish will be eaten after this soup, slightly moistened with stock. This makes a substantial meal but it could perhaps be rounded off with another Breton favourite, the *beignet*. (Illustrated on page 65.)

BEIGNETS

9 oz. (full 1½ cups) flour   **water**
2 eggs   **butter**
salt   **4 apples, peeled and sliced**
3 teaspoons (4) sugar

To make a batter, add a pinch of salt and the sugar to the flour, and mix in the eggs. Use enough water to make a very thick creamy mixture. Beat in the softened butter. Heat a pan of deep fat until just steaming. Dip apple slices into the batter and sizzle in the oil until a golden brown. Drain and serve on a white napkin.

BAKED COD

Winter had come since the trip to Lorient. It was a soft, friendly day when we made our way along the sunken road from the tiny village to the stone farmhouse. Marie Rose had asked us to bring one of the enormous loaves of rye bread so beloved in this country. The cows gave a low friendly greeting from behind the safety of thick hedges, and the clatter of the butter churn ushered us into the warm kitchen. We came to talk about food, or rather to look at recipes, for our helpful friend had unearthed an old notebook of her grandmother's. In careful, round script there lay before us household events, shopping lists, addresses and recipes. A wealth of life that had unfolded nearly a hundred years ago.

Why people turn their noses up at cod I can never understand! Marie Rose had a dish of this honest fish tucked away in the oven that would grace any table. As we ate she told me how to make it.

4–6 servings:

1½ lb. fresh cod fillets   **oil**
1 large onion, sliced   **cream or milk**
½ lb. bacon slices   **1 oz. (2 tablespoons) butter**
1 lb. potatoes, thinly sliced   **salt and pepper**

Cook the sliced onion lightly in butter. Oil a fairly deep oven-proof dish. Cover the bottom with a layer of bacon slices, the onion, and slices of potato. Place the fish, cut into manageable pieces, on top. Add salt and pepper. Top up the dish with more potatoes, onions and bacon, add cream or milk to cover and dot with butter. Season again, until the liquid has a good flavour. Cook in a moderate oven (mark 4; 350°F.) for about 1 hour.

BRETON RECIPES

Grandmother's book was a storehouse of good things. Here are a few of the dishes she noted down.

ARTICHAUX (Globe artichokes).   Trim right across the top of the leaves before cooking and the artichoke will open out like a flower. Cook in boiling, salted water, until the heart at the base is soft. They are eaten leaf by leaf. Eat only the tender tips that join onto the heart. Dip in vinaigrette dressing (see page 82), or eat hot with melted butter, when they are delicious – tear away all the inside leaves to the heart, leaving only a fringe that forms a sort of crown and pour melted butter into the crown.

CONCOMBRES FARCIES (Stuffed cucumbers).   Cut the cucumber into one-portion lengths, split lengthwise and scoop out pith and seeds. Stuff with the following mixture: chopped, cold, cooked vegetables (carrots, beans, potatoes and peas are good for this), hard boiled eggs (cook the eggs for about 15 minutes then cool them quickly in cold running water), and shrimps richly mixed with mayonnaise (see page 85).

COQUILLES ST JACQUES (Scallops St Jacques).   Wash the scallops, dry, and allow to open in the heat of a warm oven. Keep the deep shell. Carefully scrape out the fish, including the pink piece called the coral. Make a stock as you do for a *cotriade*, (page 18) but minus the fish heads, and gently poach the scallop flesh in this. When it is tender remove from the stock, with which you make a white sauce following the *cotriade* method. Slice the fish and place the coral on top, fill into the shell, top with the sauce, very well seasoned, dot with butter, and brown in a hot oven (mark 7; 425°F.) or under the grill.

Marie Rose and I agreed that here were three dishes that would be a joy at the start of any meal. Our plates were washed and we sat down to the 'stocking' coffee that she had made before.

CHICKEN FRIED WITH HERBS.   By chance a page of the well-worn notebook came open at a method of cooking chicken. Simply cooking chicken pieces in hot oil and butter with a few herbs gives a dish full of flavour; the herbs and the seasoning flavour every piece of chicken. Grandmère added a Breton touch. The chicken is cut in pieces, dipped in egg and rolled in breadcrumbs, then tossed in the oil. The pan seems to sing as the chicken gently turns a golden brown.

BRETON BAKED EGGS.   Why not try this recipe for the children's supper? As with many country dishes it is wholesome and sweet, the type of dish that usually meets with plenty of youthful enthusiasm.

4–6 servings:

5 eggs	pinch of salt
5 ozs. (full ½ cup) sugar	1 pint (2½ cups) of milk
1 tablespoon (1¼) of flour	vanilla essence

Beat eggs and sugar together and slowly sift in the flour. Add a pinch of salt. Whisk in the milk slowly and flavour with the vanilla. Lightly oil a deep oven dish and pour in the mixture. Cook in a moderate oven (mark 4; 350°F.) for about 40 minutes. When the mixture is just beginning to set you could stir in a handful of raisins. Serve hot or cold. Marie Rose's children ate the lot very readily!

You will see that in Brittany – as in other kitchens all over France that I hope we shall visit together, on rolling hill, beside deep forest or racing stream, overlooking ocean or broad river – food is prepared simply, using the products of the surrounding countryside. The country-woman is just as busy as her sister of the city. She has her part to play in her husband's work on farm or in fishing port. Her house is usually very difficult to keep clean and she has fewer of the appliances that have become essential to the city-dweller. She has visits to make, conversation to maintain, letters to write, children to look after; in fact, she has to cope with all the thousand and one events that make up a life.

The day is full; there is not time to spare on extensive preparation; and meals must be prepared. This challenge is met and dealt with in thousands of homes in the regions of France. Perhaps we can learn to do likewise.

There is an important footnote to all this. In France the men of the household are usually fully committed to what goes on in the kitchen. This commitment extends from encouragement to active participation. Diminutive footballers not only eat every scrap on the plate, but are known to stir a sauce or string the beans.

Poitou-Charante

Between the Rivers Loire and Charente lies a region of great diversity. To the north is Vendée, divided into the granite hills of the Gâtine and the rolling agricultural land about Poitiers. To the south are the marshes of the coast with the old port of La Rochelle; and inland there is ample opportunity to sample the great product of the area, cognac.

From time immemorial people have lived poorly in this place. It has the difficulties of Brittany, and a few extra for good measure. The salt water marshes have been drained and utilised, and now farm houses perched on any available high ground overlook the constant activity of market gardening, and the greener, broader areas of cereal. The monks started the work, Dutch engineers finished it, at the same time bringing the strange art of distilling to the inland wine-growing area.

The hills of the Gâtine, tucked up against the Loire, seem to be a continuation of Brittany. Here gorse and heather grow on the rocky slopes with, here and there, the deep shadowy mass of trees. In the valleys the humans group together behind high hedges, to care for their live-stock and coax wheat, vegetables and fodder crops from the ground. To the east the land relents a little. The red earth is good. Wide rolling fields produce beef, and the fodder crops. The slopes of the Layon give refreshing wine, while north of the Charente vine-growing becomes more serious, and the high-walled, sturdy-gated *chais* give forth nearly 50 million bottles of distilled wine a year; though for all this green crops interlace with the vineyards and walnut trees flower in the fields. There is a balance of activity which comes from the old farming recipe of the Charente: take a field of cereals to feed animals; a little grazing and the beasts will feed man; add some vine to give that little extra money that we all seem to need, and you have contentment.

If the hills of the north of this region seem to continue Brittany, this does not hold true for the coast. The cliffs and bays of the coast become lower from north to south, ending in the salt marshes of the Poitou coast. However, human activity remains much the same. Fishing – tending the mussel and oyster beds around Marenne, going about in small craft to seek lobsters, sea perch and lampreys, or voyaging far across the ocean for cod, hake, sardine and tunny – supplies the needs of the people of the coast and others beside. La Rochelle, with its guard-towers and walled gardens, is a fishing port for local fishermen; larger ships go to La Palice.

Just notice what a variety of products are available in the Poitou-Charente region: wine and brandy, deep sea fish and shell-fish, cereals and market garden produce, the fowl of the farmyard and the wild game of hill and marsh, cattle for milk and beef. And there is the omnipresent pig. What a useful animal he is! Perched on hill farm or grunting in the valleys he is always there to serve us.

All this produce, with some fair-sized centres of population, means a certain amount of industry. Much of the 'working blue' clothing of the French comes from Cholet in the Gâtine, as do half the country's shoes. The salt industry of the marshes has virtually disappeared, but the coast thrives on preserving and canning. Poitiers looks to the future by providing higher education. Such a diverse region shows very clearly the attitude of the French to food. However large the towns, however great the effort of producing so many million bottles of wonderful cognac, the Frenchman never loses contact with the countryside and the type of cooking that has gone on there for centuries and goes on still.

EGG DISHES

The French draw a nice distinction between the hen's egg from the factory-like battery, and the egg fresh from the farm; the former is designated as fit for cooking and omelets, and the latter as fit for everything. The farms that crowd this region give a plentiful supply of fresh eggs, so if we demote a few of them to the omelet variety it would, perhaps, be not inappropriate to start our cooking in this part of France with one or two egg dishes.

THE OMELET. One great French cook said that to cook an omelet one needed eggs, butter, a pan – and a lifetime of experience. I like to think that he was throwing up that smoke screen of mystique that the expert hides behind. An omelet is a simple dish but one that is much ill-used.

We could use the same pan as we used for the pancake. This is a good idea because it should not be washed, just wiped with a cloth or kitchen paper. Whatever the pan, expensive steel and copper, or cheap aluminium – even tin – it will not stick if it is never washed, and is rubbed over from time to time with a piece of bacon fat. Either butter or oil can be used to cook omelets, but butter does give its distinctive flavour to food. Let's use oil. Oil the pan well and heat until just smoking. Oil that sizzles the food on contact will not penetrate the surface and the food will not absorb too much. In the meantime mix the eggs, using three or four per person. Season well. Pour the mixture into the centre of the smoking pan and as the eggs begin to set, draw a fork or spoon through them, touching the bottom of the pan. This is to lift the cooked egg away, and let the fresh egg come into contact with the hot surface. In this way the omelet builds up thickly and the bottom does not burn. When the top is still just runny, fold in half with a spatula and slide onto a warm plate.

That did not seem very difficult to me. The variations are endless. Just before folding, we could sprinkle on grated cheese, sliced cooked mushrooms, cooked tomatoes, even chopped cooked bacon. Why not cooked fish, shrimps, or even, luxury of luxuries, finely sliced lobster? The best omelet I ever tasted had simply a few sliced truffles!

23

MENU

Let's think of the omelet in a meal. The menu might be:

SALADE DE TOMATES	TOMATO SALAD
OMELETTE NATURE	PLAIN OMELET
CAROTTES A L'ÉTUVÉE	SLICED CARROTS
TARTE TATIN	FRUIT TART

TOMATO SALAD. SLICED CARROTS. Here we have a nourishing menu without meat. Slice the tomatoes as thinly as possible with a very sharp knife. Sprinkle with finely chopped onion and parsley and a little vinaigrette (see page 82). Season well. Don't prepare too long in advance as the tomatoes quickly lose their freshness. The omelet we've dealt with; you can whip the eggs in advance and season them, if you like. Slice the carrots thinly, into little sticks, and cook them in a pan with very little water, about a ½ inch in the bottom, and a knob of butter. Season well, adding a sprinkle of sugar. Cook until they are soft, but with a crispness still in them.

FRUIT TART. SHORTCRUST PASTRY. *Tarte Tatin* is the simplest fruit tart possible. Into an ovenproof dish slice a thick layer of apples. Sprinkle them with sugar and add a few dots of butter. (The apples will cook without water). Now cover over with a layer of shortcrust pastry. Let's just check the pastry. Two parts of flour and one part of fat rubbed together. (For 4 people, 8 oz. (1½ cups) flour to 4 oz. (½ cup) butter and margarine mixed). Flavour with a little sugar. Add a little water and mix to form a firm paste, not moist. Do not use too much water. (You can always dry the mixture out with some extra flour if it's not firm enough). Roll out, and cover the apples with pastry, sprinkle with sugar and bake in a fairly hot oven (mark 6; 400°F.) until the pastry is brown. When cooked, pour any excess liquid from under the pastry, and turn over so that the pastry is underneath. Cooking time about 25 minutes.

OEUFS POCHÉS AU GRATIN (Poached eggs with white sauce). We shall now promote the fresh egg back to its own rank. Freshness is essential for eggs boiled in the shell, or fried in the pan. Here is a slightly different way. Poach some eggs. Drain them; put into an ovenware dish, season, and cover with white sauce (see page 95). Sprinkle a little cheese over the surface and dot with butter. Pass under the grill until the top is just turning brown.

BASS BAKED WITH HERBS

The Dumas family live not far from Niort and often drive to the coast to enjoy the sands of Olonne. M. Dumas, a keen fisherman, is friendly with many of the fishermen who earn a living along the low-lying coast of the Poitou marsh. If he brings home a fish for Sunday lunch he has to deal with it himself, for Madame cannot bear to touch fish. 'You be the fish chef and I'll do the rest'. There is an added satisfaction in cooking something you've caught yourself. On the Saturday he brought home some splendid bass. Oncle Bibert promised to come to lunch on the Sunday and bring some sorrel with him to add to the fish dish. Annie, the Dumas' eldest daughter, was very eager to see her father and Oncle Bibert prepare the fish, and also to taste, when nobody was looking, the *Pineau de Charentes* that the grown-ups were taking as an aperitif. Bibert came early with the sorrel, a great bunch of succulent leaves. There was enough to make a soup as well.

They worked round an old marble table outside the kitchen door, leaving Madame Dumas in full possession of the kitchen. First the fish were scaled by scraping with a sharp knife. After Father had cleaned them, taking care to scrape out the gills, Oncle Bibert cut right along the backbone and prised it out, taking out most of the other bones at the same time. Soon the fish, one for each grown-up and one for the children to share, were ready for stuffing.

6 servings:

6 bass	**a bunch of herbs**
1 lb. spinach	**2 oz. (4 tablespoons) butter**
¼ lb. shallots	**dry white wine**
sorrel	**3 eggs**

Madame washed the spinach very well and cooked it with a little salted water, and butter, keeping the leaves whole. (This could be done the night before). Then she chopped and lightly cooked the shallots in butter and added the spinach, finely chopped, plus a few leaves of sorrel, put in the herbs tied in a bundle (see page 17), and moistened with the wine. She simmered the mixture for 10 minutes, took it from the stove, and blended in three eggs. There was enough stuffing for the six fish.

Annie was sent to fetch the stuffing and soon the fish were full of the piquant mixture, and tied round with fine twine. They looked fine and fat in the flat oven dish, well salted and sprinkled with oil. They would be cooked in a fairly hot oven (mark 5; 375°F.) for 15 minutes to the lb. Father and Oncle Bibert sat and tasted the smooth Pineau, while Annie went to see if her mother needed any help.

MENU

6 servings:

BAR FARCI	STUFFED BASS
RÔTI DE PORC AUX AROMATES	ROAST PORK WITH HERBS
POMMES SAUTÉES	SAUTÉ POTATOES
HARICOTS VERTS	FRENCH BEANS
SALADE	SALAD
FROMAGES	CHEESE
SOUFFLÉ VANILLÉ	VANILLA SOUFFLE

ROAST PORK. Madame Dumas had chosen loin of pork on the bone because she wanted to use her own herbs. She had cut the meat from the bone and was trimming it when Annie came in. 'Just in time to help, Annie'. Sprigs of fresh thyme, bay leaves, parsley, and two cloves of garlic were laid on the meat and then Madame made a roll of the joint with the fat outside. The tying is not difficult and after the first few times you feel like an expert. Annie tried. First she put a lassoe-loop over one end and drew it tight. With the fat side facing down she looped round again and passed the end back through the loop. She continued looping like this and tied off near the other end. Not bad for a first attempt.

FRENCH BEANS. SAUTÉ POTATOES.   Tante Marie came in all of a rush from church and prepared the young green beans. She left them whole, and cooked them quickly in well-salted water. The pork was already in the hot oven under the dish of bass, and Maman had started the *pommes sautées*. She peeled the potatoes and cut them into small squares, then literally made them jump in the hot pan with a little oil. She salted as she went along and added a sprinkle from her bunch of fresh thyme. The potato cubes browned quickly and soon cooked. She popped them in the oven to keep hot. The cooking times, in a hot oven (mark 7, 425°F). are: bass 15 minutes to the lb.; pork 1 hour 20 minutes for a medium-sized loin.

The fish were ready and Annie and her aunt laid the table. The bread pannier, with a long fresh crusty loaf, stood on a side table, for Madame Dumas always liked to cut the bread as it was needed. 'Monsieur Charles and Patrick are late'. Charles was a young teacher at the Lycée who was living with the family.

VANILLA SOUFFLÉ.   While waiting for her son and the young teacher, Madame Dumas showed Annie how to make the soufflé; most soufflés are simply a tasty sauce made with egg yolks folded into the beaten whites.

6 servings:

6 eggs	**a few sticks of angelica**
1 tablespoon (1¼) cornflour	**⅓ pint (scant 1 cup) of milk**
3 oz. (3 tablespoons) sugar	**vanilla essence**

It is useful to have a jar of sugar with a few vanilla pods in it always on hand in the kitchen. Madame separated the whites of the eggs and put the yolks into a saucepan. She mixed in the vanilla sugar and the cornflour then, while gently heating, added the milk, whipping gently. Slowly the mixture thickened and made a vanilla custard. She added a little of the vanilla essence, and the angelica, finely chopped. The soufflé was not cooked until the main course of the meal had been eaten. Then Madame quickly whipped the egg whites until solid, and added the remaining yolks to the sauce. The whites and the sauce were folded together, and turned into a deep soufflé dish, greased with softened, clarified butter. They were sprinkled with vanilla sugar and put into a fairly hot oven (mark 5; 325°F.). 25 minutes later the top had domed up and the inside was cooked. A tablespoon of flaming cognac over the top gave the finishing touch.

But now they are waiting for Patrick and his friend. Just in time to prevent the fish from overcooking they rush in. Monsieur Charles had gone into Niort to look for some wine as a gift. Chilled bottles of *Coteaux de Poitou* were already on the table and this red wine from Saintes would be very welcome with the cheese.

BEURRE BLANC.   Oncle Bibert had made a little *Beurre blanc* sauce by softening chopped shallots in butter, adding white wine and a little vinegar, and when the liquid was nearly reduced, adding cream and more white wine. It went well with the fish. They ate the meat first with a few potatoes, and the vegetable afterwards. Salad, just a leaf or two, and then the cheese: rich, deep yellow Port Salut, made by the Trappist monks, and soft creamy St Maure. At this stage Madame Dumas went to finish the soufflé.

Needless to say the men finished off with a glass of brandy while Oncle Bibert, who owned a small *chais*, explained to Charles the names *Grande Champagne, Petite Champagne, Fins Bois, Bona Bois* and *Bois ordinaires,* and their significance in the Cognac. "Your chef at the Lycée is a great connoisseur! He really knows about cognac".

MENU

Monsieur Blanc had the very important job of preparing the banquet for the 'Friends of the Lycée'. All through the year thousands of school meals were served under his supervision. But for the *Amicale* he would send the cooks away and cook himself. That he would really enjoy!

16 servings:

MOUCLADE	MUSSELS IN CREAM SAUCE
HUITRES DE MARENNE AU GRATIN	POACHED OYSTERS AU GRATIN
FAISAN FARCI	STUFFED PHEASANT
POMMES PAILLES	STRAW POTATOES
ÉPINARDS	SPINACH
SALADE	SALAD
FROMAGES	CHEESE
FRUITS	FRUIT

One of the young *commis*, Henri, wanted to help him so, in fact, everyone but the *plongeur*[1] could have the rest of the Saturday free. Sixteen were invited to the meal, including the Mayor, so he would need two brace of pheasants, and his friend of the marshes, Ficelle, would probably have a damaged bird for next to nothing so that he and Henri could have a good supper as well. Blanc ordered the birds three weeks in advance; one week to find them, and two weeks to hang.

PHEASANT, HANGING. Hanging any game, particularly birds, is very important. Monsieur Blanc showed Henri the difference between the cock and the hen. The cock was longer and had a fine long tail and greeny-blue tinges to its plumage. The hen looked brown and plump. He wanted the birds hung until the tail feathers pulled off easily. It was, in fact, about ten days after shooting that they were ready. Ficelle had calculated exactly for this was two days before the *Amicale*. On the Friday morning they had two cock pheasants and two hens, plus two damaged hens. They would have a feast!

PHEASANT, DRAWING AND PLUCKING. On Friday night they got to work. First the birds were drawn and plucked. Henri thought it was rather like cleaning chickens but the feathers were a nuisance. The wings were useful to hold on to as they worked

---

[1] The *plongeur* does the washing up.

round the birds. They tried to pull the feathers in the direction of the quill so that the skin was not broken. The whole birds were quite easy but it was impossible not to damage the skin of the imperfect ones.

PHEASANT, STUFFING AND ROASTING

4½ oz. breadcrumbs soaked in milk	¼ lb. goose liver
¼ lb. shallots, chopped	¼ lb. veal
4 tablespoons (5) parsley	¼ lb. bacon

Monsieur Blanc minced the veal and chopped the liver and bacon finely. Starting with the breadcrumbs in a large bowl, everything was gradually mixed together. It made one mass as it was bound together with the dampened breadcrumbs. Henri helped his chef to stuff the birds and tie with bacon fat round them. They were now ready to be put into a hot oven (mark 6; 400°F.) and roasted for 60 minutes.

POACHED OYSTERS AU GRATIN. MUSSELS IN CREAM SAUCE. On Saturday, Henri could hardly wait for the day to pass and soon after lunch he started scrubbing the mussels and opening the oysters. The potatoes had already been peeled and lay in salted water. The spinach was washed, dried and arranged carefully with all the stalks together. Henri scraped away at the gleaming mussel shells, being careful to pull away the weed that the mussel had been feeding on.

Monsieur Blanc nodded approvingly as he took up the first oyster shell and twisted it open. He detached the fish from its shell and carefully kept the juice in a large pot. The oysters were gently poached in this juice, with white wine added. The chef cooked them for about ten minutes then removed the fish, dried them, and put each one back in its own shell.

Henri already had his orders so he went ahead, taking a good handful of mussels for each person and heating them quickly in a large pot with a sprinkle of white wine. He turned them now and again with a wooden spoon to make sure they were all open. He drained off the juice and waited for further instructions. Monsieur Blanc showed him how to make a white sauce with the mussel juice (see page 18). Before serving, the thick creamy sauce would be poured over the mussels, still attached to one half of the shell. 'We'll add some fresh cream to bring the sauce to perfection'.

M. Blanc was determined to show what food could be like in the Charente. He cut the potatoes into the finest sticks, and made Henri carefully wash and dry the salad. They had a magnificent fruit tray with melons, halved and sprinkled with cognac, grapes, apples, pears, and walnuts collected from the trees of a local vineyard.

At 6.30 sharp Monsieur l'Intendant began pouring the aperitifs and greeting the guests. The Directrice was there early and so was the Mayor. At seven the word came down to the kitchen, and Henri was shown how to run some cream into the oyster shells, to sprinkle butter and cheese over each plump oyster and then to pass them for a few minutes under the hot grill. The mussels were finished off in the manner prescribed and the two men, aided by four pupils, entered with their steaming trays to well deserved applause.

The pheasants had been put on at aperitif time, and were now ready. The dark, well-hung meat cut beautifully, and soon the stuffing was giving forth its delectable aroma.

STRAW POTATOES. SPINACH. The potatoes had been already plunged in to deep hot oil and would only need to be re-dipped in steaming oil. Henri had carefully tied the deep green spinach leaves into bunches before cooking them in a little water. They were now just simmering in butter. Soon the pheasant was being appreciated with a wine from the Bordeaux region, *Léoville Poyferré*, and the assembled company felt relaxed and well-cared for.

LEMON SABLÉS. Meanwhile Monsieur Blanc and Henri were making some lemon sablés, in case the ladies wanted to nibble something with the coffee and the *Grande Champagne* cognac that the Intendant had taken from his private cellar.

6 oz. (¾ cup) butter	**salt**
1 oz. (1 tablespoon) sugar	**juice and zest of large lemon**
12 oz. (2¼ cups) flour	**milk**
yolk from 2 eggs	

Rub the butter and sugar together. Add the salt, egg yolks, lemon juice and grated zest. Sift in the flour, mixing all the time. Mix with a little milk to make a pliable mixture. Roll out ⅛-inch thick, cut in circles, and bake on an oiled baking tray until brown. Be very careful not to overcook. The sablés will be brown but still pliable. They go crisp if left to cool on a wire tray.

The feast was judged perfect by the company but, for Henri, the best time was to come. For Monsieur Blanc's wife and sister-in-law came to share their dinner. The two bottles of champagne donated by the *Directrice* were much appreciated.

RECIPES, POITOU-CHARENTE

After the meal Monsieur Blanc and his wife, who had been in hotel service together, told tales of the kitchen and of wonderful dishes. Here is a selection that Henri was careful to note down.

OEUFS BELLE ANGEVINE

4 servings:

12 eggs	**4 oz. (½ cup) butter**
½ tablespoon (¾) parsley, chopped	**1 pt. (2½ cups) béchamel sauce**
½ tablespoon (¾) chives, chopped	**2 tablespoons (2½) cream**

Hard-boil the eggs (12 minutes). Cool them, cut in half and take out the yolks. Mix the yolks with chopped parsley, chives, the softened butter, and the cold béchamel sauce (see page 95). Fill the whites with this mixture. Add the egg mixture left over to hot béchamel, together with the cream. Place the stuffed eggs on an ovenware dish, and cover with the enriched white sauce. Put in a fairly hot oven for 15 minutes (mark 5; 375°F.).

CHOUX AUX LARDONS

1 cabbage
1 large onion
1 tablespoon (1¼) butter
1 tablespoon (1¼) oil
½ lb. bacon, sliced

1 cup water
1 glass wine *or* 1 tablespoon wine
    vinegar in 1 glass of water
garlic
salt and pepper

Roughly chop a crisp cabbage. Finely slice the onion and soften it in a little oil and butter. Add the cabbage. Stir well and add a good handful of small bacon slices. The mixture is gently frying; add a cupful of water and a glass of wine, chopped garlic, pepper and salt. Simmer until the cabbage is tender but still crisp.

CHAUDRÉE

6 servings:

4½ lb. fish, conger eel, whiting, plaice
2 glasses dry white wine
5½ pints (13½ cups) water
1 small onion

1 small carrot
bouquet garni
4 oz. (½ cup) butter

This is one of the many fish dishes to be found round the coast of France. For each person you will need 1 small whiting (about ¼ lb.), ½ a plaice (¼ lb.) and 1 slice of conger eel (¼ lb.). Leave the plaice on the bone, and cut it in half before cooking.

Make a *court-bouillon*. Plunge in the conger eel, sliced, and cook for five minutes, then add the other fish. Cook for a further 15 minutes. Take out the fish and keep warm. Add butter to the *bouillon*, season, and use as soup. Moisten the fish with the hot soup.

COURT-BOUILLON. Let us remind ourselves of how to make this. Simmer together; water, white wine, finely sliced onion, carrot, *bouquet garni*. Add butter and season well. Cook for 20 minutes.

GOGUES (Sausages)

The last dish Henri wrote down was perhaps the most interesting. It is the simplest method of making *saucisson* (sausage) that he had ever seen. Chop equal quantities (½ lb.) of onion, bacon pieces, spinach, lettuce leaves and beet. Toss them in oil or lard until well softened. Now the only difficult thing to acquire – pig's blood. Pour in pig's blood, and mix until you have a wet mixture. Either stuff pieces of pigs' caul with the stuffing and tie firmly, or wrap in thin slices of beef, hammered out very thinly and tied in the shape of a bag. In both cases the Gogues are poached in water for 2½ hours. You will have about 10 4-oz. sausages. Both varieties are cooled, but the sausage type is eaten with no more attention, while the beef one is sliced and browned in a little oil.

Henri was glad when Monsieur Blanc's sister-in-law began to talk of Limousin for he was going to stay for a week during the holiday with a cousin who had fled from Algeria during the Civil War to settle near Limoges. Perhaps he would have a chance to sample the beef and veal of the 'slopes of a thousand cattle'.

Limousin

Monsieur Halimi, Henri's cousin, had hated his new home in Limousin to begin with. It was a cold, wet, windy place after Algeria. However now that his shop in Limoges was flourishing and he was beginning to make friends, he began to appreciate the peace of the place and the very varied countryside. Like the old established Limousins he began to be proud of the old craft, porcelain-making in Limoges, and even prouder of the great beef cattle of the plateau, the source of the new wealth of the region.

Like any visitor or holiday-maker he coaxed his *deux chevaux*[1] over the length and breadth of Limousin, the Marche and into Perigord in the South. It was on the vast tranquil spaces of the plateau that he found peace of mind after the tragedies of his old homeland. The wide fields and open prairie with regular clumps of sweet chestnut trees attracted him, and led him on to plunge into the deep-cut valleys with foaming streams. At Brive the valley opened out to reveal neat fields of vegetables and fruit trees. About Correze steep gorges crowded in, perhaps to hide the salmon and trout in the streams.

It was from the rich valley of Brive that he first dared to climb up to the *Montagne*. The *deux chevaux*[1] whirred up to the high places with its top rolled back to catch the fresh morning air. Surprisingly here was no mountain slope but another, higher, plateau. Here were the 'Plateaux des Mille Vaches',[2] They seemed desolate and strange; cut by the occasional peak; mirrored here and there in isolated stretches of water. But the herds were there to keep nature company; many more than a thousand.

His first friend was a fisherman on the Vienne. Halimi sold rods in his sports shop, and after patient application to a book on the subject decided that he must try his luck. The rod seemed like a telegraph pole, his boots were too big and slippery with newness – and in he went. His friend-to-be fished him out and took him home to dry. Over a bowl of steaming soup, Jean Pierre told Halimi of the way of the trout and salmon, and how to cook them. 'If I'm hungry I eat the fish, if not I put him back for sport in the future'. Halimi was invited to supper and from that day he felt at home in the Limousin.

Jean Pierre's family had always lived in the region. Far back, his ancestors had been

[1] 'Two Horse.' The nickname for the small tinny Citroën car.
[2] Plateaux of a thousand cattle (or cows).

men-at-arms to the counts of Ventadour. Perhaps they had been companions to the great poet, Bernard of Ventadour, whose father worked in the kitchens of the château. Up to fifty or sixty years ago life had been hard in this region; witness the innumerable relations of Jean Pierre far away in Paris, Grenoble, or even Alsace.

But since the advent of artificial fertilizers, and the development of the science of stock-rearing, things had been better. The sheep had diminished in numbers, and beef and dairy cattle had taken over the upland pastures. Market towns began to flourish; Bourganeuf, Eymoutiers, Ussel. The refrigerated lorries now trundle along roads to Paris, Lyon and even further afield. Milk and its products are important.

Now for the first time, Limousin grows many crops. Apart from the fertile valley of Brive where vegetables grow in abundance, wheat covers a large part of the lower Limousin. The sweet chestnut still gives its valuable crop. Industries have sprung up in the deep-cut valleys, and hydro-electricity, so abundant in this place of swift flowing streams, supplies power for manufacturing, and work for many people. Jean Pierre himself had forsaken the skill of his forbears and taken to the new skills of the electricity plant.

Soon, married to his friend's favourite sister, Halimi was enjoying the very distinctive local dishes. Accustomed to looking after himself, he would often add an Algerian dish to his wife's menu. The rich searing *Hariza* sauce went well with the mutton dishes which are a speciality of the region. Algeria and France met and were in harmony.

Beef rearing is the great industry of Limousin, and in kitchens throughout the region beef is used in all its forms. Grilling is probably the best way to taste the quality of the meat, but more interesting dishes are to be prepared from the cheaper cuts. The first soup that Halimi had with Jean Pierre was made from rich stock, and it is a dish that he never forgot.

BEEF AND VEGETABLE SOUP (*Boeuf à la mode*)

8-10 servings:

2 lb. shin of beef	bouquet of herbs
1 lb. mixed carrots, turnips and	garlic, chopped
parsnips	seasoning
3 leeks	beef knuckle *or* split calf's foot
large onion, studded with 2/3 cloves	

Chop the vegetables and scald the bones and meat. Put them into a large pan with seasoning, herbs, and the onion. Cover well with water and bring to the boil. Skim. Cook for five hours. Skim and strain.

The soup can be served clear, or the vegetables cooked in it can be added. If the meat cooked in the stock is of good enough quality it can be served as a dish, with the vegetables as a garnish. Cook four or five pounds of top rump or silverside with the stock and you have *boeuf à la mode*. This dish can be served hot, or cut into slices and set in the jelly that will be formed by the stock when cold.

LARDING. All beef boiled in a piece in this way tends to be dry. Larding will obviate this. You must have a larding needle. Strips of salt pork $\frac{1}{4}$-inch wide and about 4 inches long are threaded into the needle. With the pork strips, make stitches across the meat about a $\frac{1}{2}$-inch deep. When you have stitched one strip, start again 2 inches away, and make a parallel line of stitches. This larding is a little extra trouble but makes all the difference to the dish.

RAGOÛT OF BEEF

In our Limousin kitchen let us make a ragoût of beef. With regional variations, it is to be found all over France. We'll keep this one simple, as it's the first one we've cooked. A large ovenware dish, plenty big enough for the family, is a necessary piece of equipment. This can be of earthenware, enamelled iron, or aluminium. Even an old pot with no handle will do, as long as it will fit into the oven. But it must have a lid that fits.

4–6 servings:

2 lb. chuck or other steak　　**2 teaspoons ($2\frac{1}{2}$) flour**
1 lb. small onions　　**1 tablespoon ($1\frac{1}{4}$) tomato purée**
1 lb. carrots　　**salt and pepper**
bouquet garni

Cut the beef into manageable pieces. (Almost any cut of meat will do but chuck is perhaps the best for this dish). Sear the pieces in a frying pan. This serves two purposes; the meat will be an appetizing colour after cooking and the searing forms a cooked, protective layer round the meat. Treated in this way the meat will stay juicy and hold together well. Place the meat in the oven dish with the whole onions and carrots. Season well and add a *bouquet* of herbs (see page 17). Add the flour and the concentrated purée of tomato and stir well. Cover with water and check the seasoning. Cook in the oven until the meat is soft; probably for a dish for six, this will be about 3 hours in a moderate oven (mark 4; 350°F.).

RAGOÛT OF BEEF, VARIATIONS. As with most simple dishes it is the variations that are exciting. In Burgundy the dish is cooked in red wine, and mushrooms are added in the last hour of cooking. In Provence white wine is often used, and a few strips of bacon added when the meat is seared. The Dauphiné cook will add sliced potatoes to the dish, with some crushed filet of anchovy as an extra seasoning. Why not use beer as the cooking agent, as they do in Flanders? Monsieur Halimi's wife serves the dish with a special garnish of braised chestnuts.

A DINNER MENU

Consider the ragoût of beef, and how we can fit it into a dinner menu. There is plenty of sauce with the dish so I don't think we need to have soup. Think of the taste of the dishes on the palate before deciding on the menu. We need a cool, refreshing flavour before the steaming luscious dish of beef, and a not-too-sweet, crisp, fruit dish afterwards. In the mouth we imagine a cool tangy flavour, then comes a richly-sauced dish, and we round off with a sweet acid flavour with a sponge or crust consistency. As we decided in the beginning, we must think of the dishes as complimentary to each other. So don't cook all your best dishes for one special menu. Take one good dish and support it with other dishes. The same goes for the wine. Serve one wine that is really good, and build to it with good, honest, ordinary wines. Here is our menu:

POINTES D'ASPERGES VINAIGRETTE	ASPARAGUS VINAIGRETTE
RAGOÛT DE BOEUF	RAGOÛT OF BEEF
MARRONS BRAISÉS	BRAISED CHESTNUTS
(SALADE)	(SALAD)
(FROMAGES)	(CHEESE)
CLAFOUTIS DE PRUNES	SPONGE WITH PLUMS

For a serious meal, salad and cheese courses are nearly obligatory, and are served in order after the vegetables.

We are installed in Jean Pierre's kitchen on the Limousin Plateau one rainy afternoon. The sound of rushing water is all about us and the air smells good. We might very well be in the Scottish highlands.

ASPARAGUS VINAIGRETTE. The ragoût is, of course, put in the oven early, about 5 o'clock as we are eating at 8. The asparagus is scraped carefully and the woody ends cut off. It is tied into portions of ten pieces, (more or less if you wish), and cooked for 20 minutes in plenty of well-salted water. We can just try the stems with a knife to see if they are tender. They will be served with a vinaigrette sauce (see page 82).

BRAISED CHESTNUTS. The sweet chestnuts need some attention, but make such an unusual garnish that we think they are worth it. First a slit is made in the hard skin; then they are put into a hot oven. After a little while they can be taken out and skinned. The light hairy inside cover is removed at the same time. The nuts are then cooked with very little water in a covered dish with a *bouquet* of herbs. There will be vegetables cooked in the ragout, and with the chestnuts this will be enough.

CLAFOUTIS. This is a type of light sponge cooked with fruit, usually cherries or plums.

5 oz. (full ¾ cup) flour	pinch of salt
2 eggs	nearly ½ pint (1 full cup) milk
4 oz. (¼ cup) sugar	½ lb. plums

Mix the eggs and the flour as for a pancake. Beat in the sugar, salt and milk. Butter an oven dish and line with the plums. Cover this with the mixture and cook in a moderate oven (mark 4; 350°F.) until brown.

Jean Pierre came home tired out after work at the hydro-electric station, but the smell of the ragoût cooking in the oven did wonders for his powers of recovery. Soon he was dealing with the aperitif and thinking about the wine. In fact he took the two together, for he served a white wine from the Coteaux du Berry as an aperitif. The red he had picked up from the *supermarché*. It came without pretention in litre bottles but tasted good with the beef, rich in its sauce. There was some white left to go with the *clafoutis*.

TERRINE OF LIVER

While buying the wine he had thought to get the makings of a terrine.

1 lb. chicken livers	some bacon
1 lb. calves' liver	1 tablespoon ($1\frac{1}{4}$) mixed herbs,
$\frac{1}{2}$ lb. fresh lean pork	chopped
$\frac{1}{2}$ lb. lard	Salt and pepper
$\frac{1}{4}$ lb. (2 cups) breadcrumbs	bay leaf

After supper he showed us how to make the terrine that his mother always made. He minced all the meat and chopped the liver as finely as possible, mixed the pork and calves' liver, and added half the lard and the breadcrumbs. Two rashers of bacon were laid in an earthenware dish, and on top a layer of the mixed meat, liver and breadcrumbs. Then came a sprinkle of herbs and seasoning, followed by the chopped chicken liver. He continued with alternate layers until all was used up, then he covered the top with the rest of the lard and a bay leaf. The terrine would take about three hours in a warm oven, (mark 3; 325°F.).

While the terrine cooked in the oven we finished the wine and chatted about the Common Market, the Tour de France and the difference between a pâté and a terrine. 'There really is no difference now. In the old days a pâté used to be cooked in a pastry crust, and the terrine in its earthenware dish. Now a pâté with a crust is called *pàté en croûte*. The omnipresent *pàté de campagne* is really a terrine. A terrine can be turned out of its dish or eaten from the dish.' Jean Pierre turned out his terrine by plunging the bottom of the dish into boiling water for a few moments and up-ending it onto a plate. It soon set hard again in the refrigerator.

CABBAGE AND BACON SOUP

Once a month Monsieur Halimi and his friend went on a weekend fishing trip along the River Vienne. They stayed with an old chap nicknamed Fiston, in his stone cottage above Eymoutiers. Bread and cheese or cold meats were the order during the day; but their suppers were famous. Indeed, it was not surprising that friends of Fiston would often call at the cottage round about aperitif time, and end up by staying for a meal.

They often spoke of the supper on their first fishing trip, shortly after Halimi had taken a tumble in the river. They had caught four good trout, and the trudge to their haven in the hills sharpened the appetite. No apertif was needed. Fiston had made a cabbage and bacon soup. Cabbage is often much maligned and ill-treated by the Anglo-Saxon race, but the fragrant aroma that came from the soup pot as the two friends entered would have turned anyone into a cabbage addict.

8 servings:

1 lb. stewing lamb	$\frac{1}{4}$ lb. leeks, washed and sliced
$\frac{1}{4}$ lb. of lean bacon	1 lb. firm cabbage, cut into 8 pieces
4 oz. carrots, finely sliced	potatoes
4 medium onions, sliced	5 pints ($12\frac{1}{2}$ cups) water
1 parsnip, sliced	

Boil the meat and the bacon in a large pot. Skim, and add the vegetables, except the cabbage and potatoes, first sticking a clove into one of the onions. Cook for one hour or until the meat is cooked. Cut the cabbage into four, clean the potatoes and add to the soup. The dish is ready when the potatoes are cooked.

FRIED TROUT

The rich soup warmed them through, and set the seal to their appetite. After, they ate three of the trout, cleaned, floured and fried in butter in an iron pan. The subtle flavour of the fish was brought out by a squeeze of lemon. Then came the meat, cabbage and vegetables. At the end came the washing up; three pairs of hands made short work of it.

MIQUES (Dumplings)

On one memorable occasion they had caught a salmon. Fiston added some *miques* to the soup, for a celebration, and three large steaks were cut from the glistening fish. They called the meal 'The feast of the Salmon'.

Make a dough with ½ lb. (1½ cups) corn meal plus ½ lb. (1½ cups) ordinary flour, 1 tablespoon (1¼) of pork fat or lard, salt, and warm water. This dough is made into small balls, floured, and poached in water for about 25 minutes. When they are cooked the *miques* rise to the surface. They are eaten with the soup. 'This used to be the peasant bread of the region', remarked Fiston.

SALMON STEAKS, SAUCE RAVIGOTE

The steaks of fish were poached gently in a *court bouillon* (see page 30) and eaten with a *sauce ravigote*: chopped tarragon, watercress, chives, and parsley, mixed with a little mustard, wine vinegar and oil. If it had been a warm evening they might have grilled the fish over the barbecue fire that Fiston often made outside. There did remain one problem, the remaining salmon. On the old man's advice the rest of the fish was poached at once in a *court bouillon*. Not having a fish kettle presented a problem, but this was overcome by cutting the fish into three pieces, and then poaching in Fiston's largest pot.

MENU

On Sunday night Madame Halimi was confronted with three large pieces of disintegrating salmon. For a Limousine this was no problem. 'Tomorrow we shall have *quenelles*'. The Monday menu, in honour of the left-over salmon was:

QUENELLES DE SAUMON GRATINÉES	SALMON QUENELLES
SALADE	SALAD
FROMAGES	CHEESE
PROFITEROLS AUX FRAISES	STRAWBERRY PROFITEROLS

36

This is a good example of an interesting meal made from one basic preparation and some left-overs.

SALMON QUENELLES. A quenelle is a kind of fish ball simmered in water. This time Madame was going to make them with salmon, but they could be made of trout or, most famous of all, pike. This is the way she went to work. To hold the dry crumbling fish together she needed a type of pastry. Remember the *miques* were cooked in water. Her pastry for the quenelles was the same as for making cream puffs, *pâte à choux*. The fish would be mixed with this.

$\frac{1}{4}$ lb. ($\frac{1}{2}$ cup) butter	pinch of salt
$\frac{1}{2}$ pint (1$\frac{1}{4}$ cups) water	4 eggs
4 oz. ($\frac{3}{4}$ cup) flour	1$\frac{1}{4}$ lb. salmon

Melt the butter with the water in a saucepan. Add the salt. When the mixture foams up, add all the flour and beat in with a wooden spoon. Mix thoroughly until you have a mass of pastry that will cling together. If it is at all runny, dry it out over a low heat. Now remove the pan from the heat and add the eggs, one by one.

The pastry was left to cool and then divided in half. Half was set aside. Madame Halimi mixed the fish, minced finely, with the other half, and seasoned the mixture well. She formed little cylinders with the mixture, and poached them in very gently boiling water until they rose to the surface, continuing the cooking for a few moments more.

The quenelles need some type of creamy sauce, a plain white sauce will do (see page 95). Before serving they were coated in the sauce, sprinkled with a little cheese and browned under the grill.

PROFITEROLS

What about the other half of the pastry? This was made into small cream puffs known as *profiterols*. The mixture is shaped into balls, with two spoons, and baked on an oiled tray in a moderate oven (mark 4; 350°F) for about 40 minutes, until golden brown, and dry in the middle. To check whether they are cooked, just look on the surface of the puffs. When all the beads of moisture have disappeared, the profiterols are cooked.

CHOCOLATE SAUCE. Usually profiterols are filled with cream and coated with chocolate sauce. For this sauce, melt some chocolate in a saucepan (any plain chocolate will do) and add a little water. The liquid chocolate will turn dark and shiny when you add the water. Pour in a teaspoonful of oil, this will help the chocolate to coat the pastry shell. (Madame Halimi preferred to use a strawberry syrup as a sauce, to which she would add a little lemon juice to make it less sweet).

CHOUX PASTRY. (See QUENELLES, above). *Pâte à choux*, and all pastry mixes, are very useful basic preparations. From the *pâte à choux* Madame Halimi could have made a cheese savoury by pressing a tiny cheese cube into a ball of mixture, and rolling it in grated cheese. This cheese preparation is baked in the oven and rises to be light and fluffy. There was a little pastry left, which she mixed with an equal quantity of mashed potato and cooked in deep, steaming oil. Potatoes prepared in this way are called *pommes dauphines*.

GÂTEAU DE CHÂTAIGNE (Chestnut Gâteau)

There were great preparations in the Halimi home, for Henri, a young cousin, was coming to visit them from Niort. He had met Madame Halimi at the wedding, but had gone straight back to cookery school in Marseille. The young couple felt rather responsible for him, for both his parents had been killed during the Civil War.

It was November and the chestnuts were ripe, so Madame would make one of her *Grandmère's* specialities, *Gâteau de Châtaigne*. (The sweet chestnut tree is a 'châtaignier' in French, but its fruit are nearly always called 'marrons'. Here the fruit is given its correct name).

1 lb. chestnuts	**3 egg-whites**
1 pint (2½ cups) of milk	**caramel**
8 oz. (½ cup) sugar	**3 tablespoons (4) sugar**
vanilla essence	**3 tablespoons (4) water**

Pierce the chestnuts and put them in a hot oven (mark 7; 425°F.) to split. Skin them, as *marrons braisés* (p. 34). Simmer in the milk and sugar for one hour. Crush, with remaining liquid, and press through the strainer (or liquidise with electric mixer). Add a few drops of vanilla essence, and cool. Fold the egg-whites, well beaten, into the chestnut purée. Melt the 3 tablespoons (4) of sugar to a brown caramel mixture with a little water, and run into a mould. Cook in the pan of water in a moderate oven (mark 4; 350°F.) until set; about 40 minutes. Turn out and serve with cream.

MENU

Henri was very excited to set out in the direction of Limoges. His cousins were waiting for him with open arms and soon he was telling them about his work at the Lycée and his apprenticeship with Monsieur Blanc. The history of the meal cooked for the *Amicale* drew forth an observation from his cousin's wife that now he was just with the family, and they ate like any other family in Limoges. Later Henri was to think that if everyone ate as they did that day the families of Limoges were extremely fortunate!

MOUSSE AU SAUMON	SALMON MOUSSE
CHAMPIGNONS VINAIGRETTE	MUSHROOM VINAIGRETTE
PAUPIETTES DE VEAU	PAUPIETTES OF VEAL
POMMES PERSILLÉES	BOILED POTATOES
CHICORÉE EN SALADE	ENDIVE SALAD
FROMAGES	CHEESE
GÂTEAU DE CHÂTAIGNE	CHESTNUT GÂTEAU

MUSHROOM VINAIGRETTE. First the mushrooms were simmered in water with a little vinegar, sliced carrot and onion, well seasoned. When chilled, Madame Halimi dressed them with chopped parsley and a vinaigrette dressing (see page 82).

SALMON MOUSSE. Salmon because of its colour and delicate flavour is particularly good in a mousse.

2 lb. salmon, minced finely	**salt**
5 whites of egg, whipped	**white pepper**
1 pint cream, whipped	**mixed spice**

Mince the fish very finely and force through a sieve, seasoning with pepper, salt and mixed spice. Mix in the cream and then fold in the beaten egg whites. Turn into a mould (which should be about ¾ full) and cook in a moderate oven (mark 4; 350°F.), standing the mould in water, for 1 hour or until set. Cool, and turn out onto a plate.

CRAYFISH. The mousse looked a truly regal dish, garnished with two crayfish that Fiston had sent along for the feast. Crayfish are easy to prepare. The intestines are cleaned away from the centre of the tail. They are washed well, and plunged into a boiling *court bouillon* for 10 minutes.

PAUPIETTES DE VEAU (Paupiettes of veal). The French are very particular about the quality of veal. The calves are taken at three months and should be milk fed. Any solids in the animal's diet will show up as redness in the meat. The meat should have a fresh smell and a shiny surface. Beware of meat that is too young. This will show, in cuts like the shoulder or breast, by a great deal of transparent foamy substance. Halimi chose veal cut from the leg and flattened into *escalopes* by his butcher. Madame was very pleased with the meat.

6 servings:

¼ lb. pork, finely minced	**3 oz of breadcrumbs**
1 medium onion, chopped	**1 egg**
1 teaspoon (1¼) parsley chopped	**salt and pepper**
1 teaspoon (1¼) thyme, chopped	**6 veal escalopes**
cloves of garlic, chopped	**6 rashers of bacon**

To make the stuffing, chop onion finely and mix with the pork, parsley, thyme, garlic, breadcrumbs. Bind with the egg (1 egg binds about ½ lb. of the mixture).

Cut rough squares of veal about 4 inches across. On each square put some of the mixture, and roll the veal and its stuffing into a cylinder. Wrap round with a piece of bacon and secure with thread. Braise in a pan on top of the stove, with chopped onions and a little carrot softened in oil. Colour the paupiettes for ten minutes, and then add enough water to cover the bottom of the pan. Do not cover the meat with liquid. Simmer on top of the stove for about 1 hour, until the veal is well done.

ALGERIAN HARIZA SAUCE. In fact the paupiettes took longer than an hour, so there was time for an extra aperitif, and the table was a bit merrier as a result. Halimi jumped up after the second *pastis* and burst into the kitchen, intent on making a *hariza* sauce for his cousin's enjoyment. He cooked some chopped onions in a saucepan, added fresh tomato purée and some sliced red chili pepper, with lots of garlic, then added water. Cooked for a few minutes, he had a sauce that burnt everyone's mouth and recalled to Henri the old days in Algeria.

Jean Pierre had never tasted a better white wine from Sancerre and told his friend so. The fragrant, pale yellow liquid went well with the delicate salmon dish. The red wine came from well within the Bordelais area, Château Cheval, *premier grand cru classé*. First the fragrance warmed them, then the rich, dry flavour. They could well believe the oath sworn before the mayor of St. Emilion, part of which says: 'Do you swear to uphold the fame of your city and its vineyards, to forget your own interest to this end, and to serve the common good by word and deed?' This great wine was a monument to the oath of the *vignerons*.[1]

[1] This oath, which had existed for eight hundred years, was revived in 1948. It is sworn by members of the association of vine-growers and crop growers.

Aquitaine

The oath of allegiance sworn to the vine and its great product, wine, reminds us that the wealth and fame of Aquitaine has long been dependant upon this plant. A plant that is so hardy and yet needs so much attention.

All over the plain and into the foothills, people tend the vine. It must be protected and cosseted against the wind, the rain, the frost and against various diseases. The Phylloxera of the nineteenth century nearly dealt a death blow to the wine industry of the Aquitaine and of the rest of France. By determination and, most happily, with the help of their cousins far across the Atlantic, the vine-growers prevailed, and the great wines of the Bordelais still aid the digestive processes and ease the cares of the peoples of the world.[1]

The struggle to produce the grapes for wine-making has always been great because this plain, with the *Massif Central* on one side, the Pyrenees to the south, and the ocean to the west, does not have an ideal climate for the growing of vines. Although it is a region with a constant warm climate, being open to the Atlantic it has a high rainfall and suffers from strong winds. The influence of the Mediterranean does not help; winds and storms burst into the area from the south-east at moments that are not always opportune for the harvest. Perhaps the difficulties of cultivation give the grapes a richer flavour.

It is, however, a fertile land. The river Garonne in its middle course meanders through green fields and rich, dark soil. Nearly all the vegetables imaginable are grown in the river valley, and much fruit, some strange to the north, like melons, peaches and aubergines. The more tender crops are grown under glass. The people live by an old saying of the region, that if the weather is fine a farmer must get to work and never put off until tomorrow what he can do today.

In the Bordeaux lands wine is far and away the most important product but even here, (and immigrants from Algeria have had a great influence), other crops are grown side by side with the vine. In the middle valley of the Garonne, besides vegetables, wheat and maize are grown; and more and more important is the rearing of stock. It is said that Aquitaine feeds itself; and to this end the creatures of the farm yard and pasture do their full share.

---

[1] A disease-resistant strain of vine was brought from California to replace the plants killed by the phylloxera between 1858 and 1863.

While working on the dishes of this region we must not forget the Landes, that strange, low sandy forest region by the Atlantic coast, with the lower hills of the Pyrenees to the south and the *Massif Central* to the east. From the Landes, and the coast in general, we can use fish and shellfish direct from the sea. From the hills of the south and east lamb is readily available; and ewes' milk that makes that king of cheeses, Roquefort.

The word 'truffle' sounds strange and mysterious. To the cook anywhere it is a word that is synonymous with a rich aroma and even richer flavour. Truffles, as if the people of this great plain were not spoilt enough by the wines of Bordeaux, are plentiful in the hilly region of Perigord. So too are mushrooms of many varieties, and that other product available to the kitchen, and so neglected by many people interested in cooking, the sweet chestnut.

All around the fertile plain, prehistoric remains are to be found in caves and grottos in the hills. This rim of prehistory is made up of rocky cliffs, wild plateaux, and foaming, racing streams. The water seems to be making a dash for the rich haven below just as the ancient peoples gravitated to this garden land.

Garden it may have been, but peaceful it certainly was not, at least until recent times. First the English had to be driven off, after they had organised the vineyards to produce gallon upon gallon of *gros rouge*. Then the finer taste of Paris was catered for, and the *vin de qualité* came into being.

As the climate is affected by the south, so too is the kitchen. Oil is used as a cooking agent all over the area, and garlic has its special influence over many of the dishes. Sun-loving fruit, like melons, and vegetables, like aubergines, are freely used. A word about garlic. If you can't stand it, don't use it. But remember, many a dish will not be as it is cooked in Aquitaine if you leave it out. Perhaps the best way round the difficulty would be to use a little and to make sure it is well cooked into the dish. If you have any sneaking fear about the effect of garlic on your social life, only use fresh, crisp pieces of garlic, and use a garlic press to minimise the hazard. And now into the kitchen.

TRUFFLES

Most truffles are black, and because of their rarity they are known as the black diamonds of the kitchen. Like the diamonds that are worn, truffles add a never-to-be-forgotten distinction to what they embellish. They grow underground and are, in fact, the parasitic growth of a certain type of holm oak; they are usually found by pigs on the look out for a tasty morsel, or dogs seeking a reward. (In passing, it might be added that dogs of most disreputable descent seem to be the most successful truffle hunters).

Chicken with a little chopped truffle sprinkled into the stuffing, and terrines enriched in the same way, acquire a new and exciting flavour. The truffles fresh from the fields are washed, peeled and used raw as a flavouring. Sliced and gently cooked in butter, with a little wine sprinkled over at the end of cooking, they may be used as a garnish for meat and hors d'oeuvre dishes.

In Perigord truffles have been cooked, over the centuries, in the embers of the fire. The truffle dish, *truffes en chausson*, takes some of its particular taste from the embers, but may be cooked in the oven. A whole truffle, or a very large one divided, is wrapped in a slice of streaky bacon and folded into a pastry case. An ordinary shortcrust pastry (see page 24) will do very well for this. It is then baked in the oven for about 20 minutes. To cook in the embers of a fire, the pastry will have to be of flour and water only, and will be cracked open and discarded at the end of the cooking. (You could experiment, using the usual pastry and covering it with cooking foil).

MENU

Let us move away from the exotic and expensive, and prepare some very simple dishes as they would be prepared in the Aquitaine. We are in the main vineyard area, not far from St. Estephe and our house is on a gentle, rounded hill, looking out onto the plain. Our wine is of the best and our cultivated mushrooms prolific. After the work of the day a soup is a good idea. What about this for a simple working supper?

TOURIN	ONION SOUP
CHAMPAIGNONS BORDELAISES	MUSHROOMS COOKED IN GRAPE JUICE
TARTE AUX RAISINS	GRAPE TART

ONION SOUP. Onions are made into soup all over France and the Tourin is the Aquitaine variety. Slice $1\frac{1}{2}$ lb. onions finely, and soften them in some oil until they start to turn brown. Add 3 pints ($7\frac{1}{2}$ cups) of boiling water and cook for 15 minutes. Season with salt, pepper and garlic. Thicken this soup with eggs; for three pints of soup we need 4 egg yolks. Serve with slices of bread roasted in the oven in a baking dish in a little oil.

The *tourin* can also contain tomatoes. Skin the tomatoes by boiling in water for 2 minutes. The skins can then be gently pulled off. Chop and add to the soup.

TO THICKEN WITH EGG-YOLKS. Thickening with egg yolks is a very useful method in the kitchen and, in principle, it is always the same. Mix the egg yolks together and gently whip in some of the hot soup, a drop at a time. The mixture will thicken as the eggs cook. Add soup until a large part of it is with the eggs, then mix unthickened and thickened soup together. Stir over gentle heat for 15 minutes. Be very careful not to boil the soup when you reheat.

MUSHROOMS IN GRAPE JUICE. Mushrooms should not be washed, and the cultivated variety need no skinning. Take off the stalks; slice and toss the caps in oil. Chop the stalks and cook in oil with chopped shallots. Flavour with garlic and parsley. Add to the caps and warm gently. In this area, a delicious addition is made to the dish: natural grape juice. The juice is added when the mushrooms are sizzling in the pan. As a variation, we can pour béchamel sauce over cooked mushrooms, sprinkle with cheese, and brown them under the grill. Or add white wine instead of the grape juice, fry the mushrooms with tiny squares of bacon and sprinkle with parsley. Once more, experiment!

GRAPE TART. As with many other fruit, grapes can be put fresh into a cooked tart case. The pastry case is made with short crust pastry and cooked empty in the oven. Line a tart tin with pastry (see page 24), cover with paper or foil, and weigh this down with white beans. Cook until light brown. Fill the cooked pastry case with grapes, and cover with a jelly – or apricot syrup, easily prepared by heating apricot jam with a little water.

FRUIT JELLY. Flavoured jellies already made up are easily procured, but why don't we make our own fruit jelly with fruit and gelatine. Make a juice by cooking the fruit in very little water with sugar added. Gooseberries are very good for this. Taste the juice to check the flavour and sugar content. Sieve. Dissolve 2 oz. powdered gelatine in 2 tablespoons of warm water and heat gently, stirring all the time until the liquid is clear. Slowly add 1 quart (5 cups) of warm fruit juice, whipping gently all the time.

MENU

Monsieur Culas had a birthday coming up and he was allowed to choose the main dish for the festive occasion. Henriette Culas thought it would be better to have the dinner on Saturday. She knew before she was informed what the favourite dish would be. When they took their holidays in the Lande district her husband would constantly be on the look-out for a restaurant that had burbot on the menu. 'But Monsieur, we have lamprey cooked in red wine or roast woodcock'. Their pride in these specialities would be hurt by his quiet, 'But no burbot'. With the main dish decided for her she began to plan her menu.

Her husband would take great delight in choosing the wine. The only problem was to find a Graves dry enough for the fish dish. Like so many people in his region, Monsieur Culas was in the wine trade and, being very proud of the wines of Bordeaux, liked to choose local wines for a special occasion.

HAM, BOILED AND BAKED

They lived in Agen, on the River Garonne, and whatever the activities going on in the stone-built farm-houses of the area, one thing was sure; there would be pigs rooting about in the low-lying fields. Madame Culas always cooked her own ham and her dream was one day to have a kitchen with beams on which she could hang the cured bacon. She would begin her menu with sliced ham.

Her young sister Denise wanted to learn the way to cook ham, so she came on Friday afternoon from Tonneins. A local butcher always had very good smoked hams and that day was no exception. Denise was given the job of preparing the vegetables for the pot. She peeled onions and shallots and scraped some large carrots. Madame tied the ham round with string and put it into a great pot full of water. The butcher always chose her a mild-cured joint so that there was no need to soak it. Next, the vegetables went into the pot together with half a clove of garlic, peeled, one large onion stuck with cloves, plenty of freshly crushed pepper and a *bouquet garni*. The pot was covered, the water brought to the boil and then the heat was set for simmering. The gammon weighed 13 lbs. and would take 20 minutes to the pound. 4½ hours later the ham was drained, the rind removed. Madame sprinkled plenty of breadcrumbs over the steaming meat then browned it in a moderate oven (mark 4; 350°F.) for 15 minutes.

MENU

Supper that night was to be a special occasion for it was the actual day of Monsieur Culas's birthday. There would be plenty of ham for supper as well as for the celebration on Saturday. Here is the supper menu.

OEUFS SUR LE PLAT	EGGS SUR LE PLAT
JAMBON	HAM
POMMES SARLADAISES	POTATOES WITH TRUFFLES
PETITS POIS	GARDEN PEAS
FROMAGES	CHEESE
GÂTEAU ST HONORÉ	GÂTEAU ST HONORÉ

Needless to say Monsieur managed to find some champagne with which to supplement the birthday supper.

GÂTEAU ST HONORÉ. As soon as the ham was cooked Henriette started to work on the cake. Gâteau St Honoré is the typical gâteau produced for birthdays the length and breadth of France. It is assembled, rather than made, from crisp cream-puff balls fashioned from *pâte à choux* (see page 37). She made the *pâte à choux* in the morning so that it would have time to cool.

On an oiled oven tray she placed about 20 small (walnut sized) balls of the pastry and baked them in a fairly hot oven (mark 5; 375°F.). On a second tray Denise made a circle of pastry, forcing the mixture through a bag fitted with a wide nozzle. The long sausage of pastry was about 1 inch thick and made a circle 9 inches in diameter. Both were baked until crisp and golden brown and, most important, completely dry.

Madame made a syrup with water and sugar; 12 oz. ($\frac{3}{4}$ cup) sugar to $\frac{1}{4}$ pint (full $\frac{1}{2}$ cup) of water. She heated this mixture until all the sugar was dissolved and foamy bubbles formed on the surface. The puffs when baked and cooled were dipped in this syrup and left to cool on an oiled board. The gâteau was assembled when the balls were cool. They were stuck round the top of the ring, using some of the syrup. The centre was filled with whipped, sweetened cream and decorated with chopped nuts and angelica. A birthday candle was stuck to each pastry ball. 'Then he can't be more than twenty', remarked Denise.

POMMES SARLADAISES. The next job was the vegetables. Denise peeled potatoes and sliced them thinly. She lined a large frying pan, sizzling with oil and butter, with a layer of potatoes, sprinkled a few chopped truffles on top then added another layer of potatoes. This was repeated until a thick mound of potatoes stood six layers high. When the bottom of the 'cake' was brown she turned it over and browned the other side. Denise could never flip them over like her sister, who managed easily, so she covered the frying pan with a large tin, turned it upside down so that the browned layer of potatoes was on top and slid the uncooked side into the pan. One or two potatoes stuck and she quickly scraped these off before sliding back the potato cake. When the other side was brown she slid the potato cake into an oven dish, sprinkled it with butter, and finished it off in the oven. As the truffles began to cook, a rich, almost sweet scent filled the kitchen, the house, and spilled over into the street.

GARDEN PEAS. Madame Culas saw to the peas. All along the river Garonne fresh vegetables are grown, and the small, sweet, garden peas are famous. Madame did not just cook them in salted water, but used a method that is common to all French kitchens.

4 lb. peas	cup of water
2 oz. (4 tablespoons) butter	sugar
12 small onions	salt
1 lettuce	bouquet garni

All the ingredients were put into a covered pan and cooked very slowly for one hour. The sauce that is formed during cooking should taste of sugar, so if necessary some must be added during cooking. Small cos lettuces are ideal for this dish.

EGGS *sur le plat*. The family was soon round the aperitifs. Even the children were allowed a small glass of Montbazillac, a soft-flavoured wine from the town of that name in the Aquitaine. 'I've forgotten the eggs', whispered Madame Culas to Denise. She wanted to add a little something to this dish. Denise chopped onions very finely and softened them in oil and butter, adding garlic and parsley at the last moment. This fragrant mixture went to line the enamelled individual *cocottes*. Meanwhile Madame peeled aubergines and took the pips out. Soon slices of the aubergine were sizzling in the pan. An egg was cracked into each *cocotte*, on top of the onions. A thin sliver of oil was run over the surface of each egg, and the dishes were popped into a fairly hot oven (mark 6; 400°F.) to cook for 5 minutes. (In this case the *oeufs sur le plat* are cooked in *cocottes*, and could be called *oeufs en cocotte*).

The family talked all the way through the meal but appreciated the succession of textures and flavours that passed over eager palates. The soft richness of eggs and aubergines gave way to the crisp salty potato cake and firm pink ham. The fresh, slightly sweet peas cleaned the palate for savoury cheese. On the wooden board, they had *caillades* from Correze, which is a creamy cheese set with rennet, small pyramids of goat cheese, and some *gruyère*, always the children's favourite. The *gâteau* was really ridiculous after such a meal, but it was a festive decoration and was swiftly washed down with champagne.

MENU

Now we come to the birthday dinner.

TRANCHES DE JAMBON	SLICED HAM
LOTTE À LA CRÉME	BURBOT *à la crème*
POMMES ANGLAISES	BOILED POTATOES
SALADE	SALAD
FROMAGES	CHEESE
PÊCHES MASQUÉES	PEACHES *masquées*

BURBOT À LA CRÈME. Monsieur Culas went off early in the morning to fetch the burbot, Many fishermen from other parts of the world are fooled by the appearance of this fish, with its three ugly barbels making a catfish-like snout. It is in fact a freshwater member of the cod family and may be prepared for the table in the same way. Joseph Culas liked it *à la crème*.

The fish is usually filleted, but may be cut into steaks. Toss the fillets gently in butter with a few sliced onions and bacon pieces. Remove from the pan and keep warm. Make a thickened sauce in the same pan. This is called a *roux* in the French kitchen, and is used again and again. The juices in the pan are absorbed by flour. White wine is mixed in and then milk and cream, or stock, is added until there is a rich, creamy sauce. Simmer the fish with the onions and bacon in this sauce. About 15 minutes should be enough.

When Henriette Culas looked back on the meal she found that all the dishes were very simple. The ham took time, and she could have bought some very good ham from the cooked meat shop. But it was worth doing it herself. She began the cooking of the fish and made the *roux* during the afternoon, then put them to cook at the beginning of the meal. The potatoes were peeled, shaped and put in salted water ready for boiling.

PEACHES MASQUÉES. After washing the salad, only the peaches remained to be prepared.

6 servings:

6 large peaches
4 eggs
2 pints (5 cups) milk

2 oz. (2 tablespoons) sugar
chopped nuts

Skin the peaches by gently boiling in water for 3 minutes. The skin will then pull away easily. Halve them, removing the stones, and place in a fairly deep dish. Cover with the eggs, beaten into the sweetened milk, and cook in a moderate oven (mark 4; 350°F.) until set. Sprinkle chopped nuts over the dish. Walnuts are good, but any nuts will do.

Madame Culas's two sons helped to lay the table and set in place the long dish of ham slices decorated with olives, sliced tomatoes, and thin wedges of melon. The fish was nearly cooked when they started the meal, and was left gently bubbling on the stove. The potatoes were boiled during the first course. The salad and cheese lay ready on a side table. Only one thing remained, the peaches had to go into the oven. So the Culas family had freshly cooked food and mother could enjoy the conversation.

Father had taken some pains and a lot of thought over the wine. He served a white wine from Cahors, then a Graves, *Château Couhins*, with the fish. For the cheese he had chosen with himself in mind, *Château Rausan Segla*. A champagne went very well with the peaches. On this occasion they all took coffee and tasted with it an Armagnac from the Mont de Marsan area in the Landes. After eating burbot at the meal the conversation quite naturally turned to the Culas' weekend trips to the Landes. Once on holiday Joseph Culas had sat up half the night extracting recipes of the Landes, from a friend of his who dealt in resin from the pine forest and knew the area like the back of his hand. Here are a few of the dishes.

WOODCOCK WITH GAME SAUCE

Game and game birds are much in evidence in this region. Even wild boar can still be found in the Hautes Landes. Woodcock is a small game bird that feeds on berries and herbs; it appears in France from September to February. It should be cooked uncleaned. The intestines are called 'trail' in such a gamebird. Roasting tends to toughen woodcock,

47

so it is tied with fat bacon and cooked, covered, in an ovenware dish. Now comes the part that makes the dish. Drain off the fat, and cut the bird into joints. If small, cut in half. If larger, cut into four – two legs and a breast cut in half. Cut away the bottom of the bird and the intestines. Separate the bones, and simmer them with water or stock, sliced onion and carrot and diced bacon. After half an hour remove the carcase, strain off the vegetables and make a *roux* (see page 47) with the liquid. When you have cooked out the flour taste, rub some of the intestines through a sieve into the sauce. This will add flavour and thicken it. Add a glass of red wine. Then heat the joints of meat gently in the sauce.

FOIE D'OIE, SAUCE À LA DACQUOISE (Goose liver. Sauce *à la Dacquoise*)

Again, here is a dish that is made by its sauce, which can be served with any kind of liver besides the goose liver of this recipe. Peas (petits pois) as cooked by Madame Culas, go well with this dish.

4 servings:

2 lb. goose liver	1 small onion chopped
4 oz. chopped ham	bouquet garni
2 oz. ($\frac{1}{4}$ cup) raisins	1 oz. (2 tablespoons) butter
2 oz. ($\frac{1}{4}$ cup) grapes	1 tablespoon ($1\frac{1}{4}$) Madeira
4 oz. ($\frac{1}{2}$ cup) white wine	stock

Cut the liver into thin slices, flour, and fry in oil and butter. Soften the onions in butter and add the grapes, raisins, ham, *bouquet garni*, and white wine. Cook until the liquid has reduced to half its volume, then add stock to make up to the original amount. Simmer for 15 minutes and add the Maderia. Pour the sauce over the liver before serving.

Just a word on this sauce and sauces in general. Reducing a sauce will increase the flavour, but make sure you have plenty of sauce to cover the dish. In most cases the sauce should be served separately. What a shame to spoil the appearance of a beautiful grilled steak with an ocean of liquid sauce! In this dish, the liver will absorb some of the sauce and its appearance is improved by this addition. Just think a moment and the answer to the problem will be a commonsense one. For example, why cover a fish cooked on the bone with creamy sauce, when you have to scrape the sauce aside to fillet the fish? It is quite understood that many cooks will not have ready-made stock. Have a supply of stock cubes always to hand.

BREZOLLES DE VEAU (Sliced veal cooked in the oven)

Chop onions, lean ham, spring onions and mushrooms. Season with pepper, salt and some garlic. Mix, and add some breadcrumbs. Line an oiled oven dish with a layer of this mixture, and cover with thin slices of veal (*escalopes*). Cover the veal with more of the mixture and top with *escalopes*. Dot with butter, cover and cook in a fairly hot oven, (mark 5; 375°F.) for 1 hour, or until the veal is cooked.

MENU

The family managed to talk Monsieur Culas into going into the hills for a short holiday. They took an old farmhouse near Millau for a few days and proceeded to enjoy the fresh air and quietness of the upland plateau, cut by the deep valleys of the Tarne, Joute and Dourbie, and pitted with caves and grottos.

Madame Pitou was an old friend of the Culas family. She had lived a life of want and hard work, but now that the valleys of the Tarn, the Joute and the Doubie were being developed as a kind of National Park, tourists were coming who needed country folk to cook, clean, and guide them round the wonderful natural sights. The shops would benefit, and local industries, particularly those connected with tanning, would have the impetus of an enlivened local market.

Marguerite Pitou was happy to cook meals for the Culas family because she felt like one of them. They all helped in the kitchen just as her grandchildren would have helped, if her son had survived the *wagons blindés* of a terrible journey east during the war. He was only fifteen when he died, so the grandchildren were never born.

She took her friends on a visit to the *cabanes* in the rock face where the Roquefort cheese was matured. The day was quite warm but the caves were chill, always 5° to 9°C. (41° to 48°F.). They learned that the cheese was always made of milk from ewes, and that 50 ewes milked twice would supply the milk for 2 kilos of cheese.

'Can you supply the world with Roquefort from this region?' asked M. Culas. It was no surprise to learn that the milk was supplemented from the Pyrenees, and, strange to relate, from Corsica.

MENU

This was the menu for their dinner. (Illustrated on page 66.)

CROUSTADE DE ROQUEFORT	ROCQUEFORT CHEESE TARTS
FILET DE MOUTON AUX LAITUES	FILLETS OF LAMB WITH LETTUCE
POMMES AU FOUR	ROAST POTATOES
SALADE	SALAD
MACARONS	MACAROONS

ROQUEFORT CHEESE TARTS. The first job in preparing that wonderful evening meal was to make up the pastry for the cheese tarts. Ordinary *pâte brisé* was used (see page 155) Marguerite liked to make individual tarts. She lined small oiled ovenware bowls, 4 inches across, with the rolled pastry a ¼-inch thick, pricked the pastry well, and poured a few beans into each bowl to weigh it down. These were baked for ten minutes in a moderate oven (mark 4; 350°F.), and left to cool. 1 oz. grated Roquefort cheese was sprinkled into each pastry case. These were filled with an egg and milk mixture; 4 eggs to 1 pint of milk. The *croustades* took 20 minutes to cook in a fairly hot oven (mark 5; 375°F.).

FILLETS OF LAMB WITH LETTUCE. Henriette was very interested in the method. From a saddle of lamb Madame Pitou cut the meat. This came away in two fillets which were then tied together with thin twine. The meat was larded (see page 32), and browned in melted butter. She lined a large braising dish with sliced carrots and onions, together with fat bacon pieces cut into little squares. A *bouquet garni* of parsley, bay leaf and thyme was pressed into the mound of vegetables. She placed the tied fillets of lamb on this aromatic bed, soaked in white wine and water; the dish was not quite covered with the liquid. The dish would take an hour to cook in a fairly hot oven (mark 5; 375°F.).

Lettuces, often cooked as a vegetable in France, were the garnish for this tasty dish. Small lettuces were washed well, trimmed but left whole. Marguerite then tied them in the middle and trimmed the tops. They were plunged into boiling water for 5 minutes then drained, ready to braise in the juice of the meat and vegetables for 20 minutes at the end of the preparation.

ROAST POTATOES. Medium-sized potatoes were peeled, cut into 4, and roasted in a hot oven (mark 7; 425°F.). The oven dish was coated with oil, and a trickle of oil added to the potatoes, with herbs, and salt to season.

MACAROONS. Marguerite had made the macaroons at home, but Madame Culas was eager to know the recipe. Here it is copied from the old lady's yellowing notebook.

8 oz. (2 cups) ground almonds   **1 teaspoon vanilla essence**
8 oz. ($\frac{1}{2}$ cup) sugar   **2 egg whites, beaten**

Mix the ground almonds and the sugar. Stir in the beaten egg whites and flavour with the vanilla. Make small balls of the mixture with oiled teaspoons, and drop them onto a baking sheet lined with plain white paper. Bake for 20 minutes in a moderate oven (mark 4; 350°F.). The macroons will appear to be soft, but will harden when cooled. Turn over the paper with macaroons attached, and moisten the paper with a clean sponge. The macaroons will slip off when the paper is soaked.

The gentle light of the oil lamps gave that evening meal an unreal fairylike glow. This was the sort of atmosphere that gave the family a real sense of being on holiday. It was all so different from the bright cheerful *salon* back home. Madame Pitou accompanied each dish with her cheerful country chatter, and Monsieur Culas had found an equally warming partner to the meal, the wine of Gaillac from the area of the Tarn. This was too soft for the lamb dish, but went wonderfully with the macaroons. One thing had worried M. Culas all evening but he couldn't remember. . . What was it? As they were helping with the washing up it came to him. 'How do the blue-green streaks form in Roquefort cheese, Madame?'

'It comes from mouldy bread!' The children burst into laughter. 'But Madame . . . .' The old lady was serious. 'Mouldy bread is very carefully dried and set with the ewes' milk'.

CONFIT D'OIE (Preserved goose).

Just as they were leaving the next day the old lady pressed a carefully folded sheet of paper into Henriette's hand. 'It's that most splendid dish, famous throughout Aquitaine, the *cassoulet*'. Henriette knew that the whole essence of the dish was to have well-prepared goose essence. This gives the full rich flavour to the dish. So on the first weekend home the whole family set to work to make the *confit*. M. Culas picked up a large goose, about 16 lb., from the butcher, making sure it was well-plucked and bled. It is better to clean the bird yourself to ensure that the liver is not damaged. They cut the bird into four pieces; two legs, and the body cut in two along the breast bone. The pieces were well salted and left in the refrigerator over-night. Next day the goose was wiped well and cooked in a moderate oven (mark 4; 350°F.) for three and a half hours.

Madame's recipe said: 'Cook with pure goose fat', but this was a little too extravagant, even for gourmets like the Culas family. Madame Culas added a few cloves, some roughly crushed peppercorns, and six cloves of garlic wrapped in a small muslin bag, and used plenty of good clear lard.

The goose was tested with a needle to see whether it was cooked. After cooling Madame took the flesh carefully from the bones and removed all sinew and skin. She drained some of the fat through a fine muslin bag into a lovely cylindrical earthenware dish that she had bought in Carcassonne one year. She allowed this to set hard and then carefully piled the meat up, nearly to the top, so that there was a gap between the meat and the sides of the dish. It only remained to pour in the liquid fat so that the receptacle was full, and the goose meat completely encased in a layer of fat. The *confit* was then left to set hard, and topped up with fat finally to seal the top.

CASSOULET. It was several weeks later that the Culas family prepared the *cassoulet*. The *confit* could be kept in the bottom of the fridge for a year, and used when needed. The preparations for this wonderful dish were long but is was worth all the effort.

12 servings:

1 lb. haricot beans	cloves
4 tablespoons (5) goose confit	2 large onions
pork dripping	2 tablespoons (2½) tomato pureé
10 small pieces pork fillet	4 lb. piece of bacon
12 chunky pieces neck of mutton	bouquet garni
½ lb. lean bacon	6 cloves of garlic
salt and pepper	1 cup breadcrumbs
6 large Toulouse sausages	

This is a dish for a willing team. The beans must be soaked for about 3 hours. (Do not soak beans too long or they begin to foment, and acquire an acrid flavour). Change the water, and simmer the beans for 10 minutes. Chop the pork, mutton and bacon, and brown them in pork dripping. Drain the beans and place in a large casserole. Mix the browned meat into the beans. Add salt and pepper. Add the onions (one stuck with cloves), and the tomato purée, and cover with water. Add the piece of boiling bacon, tied, and the *bouquet garni* and the garlic. Cook in a cool oven (mark 2; 300°F.) for 3½ hours. Towards the end, sprinkle the breadcrumbs over the dish after adding 4 table-spoons of the goose *confit*. This last touch makes a beautiful brown crust on top.

The guests assembled. Aperitifs were taken. Madame Culas drained the meat and put it on a large serving dish, surrounded with succulent beans. She then sliced the ham and added this to the *cassoulet*. The rich sauce finished off the dish. The silence while the *cassoulet* quickly disappeared was praise indeed! Salad, cheese and fruit completed a meal to remember.

Types of *cassoulet* are to be found all along the Pyrenees from Carcassonne to Bayonne.

The Western Pyrenees

The Pyrenees rear up, a great barrier between France and Spain; but this barrier is breached in many places. In this mountain range, passes appear and disappear among the peaks. Fresh green valleys wind between shear rocky faces, and nearly join hands below the snowy peaks. It is a land of secret places and hidden ways.

Through the centuries, people in need of a hiding place have come here because there are so many ways in and out. Protestants have hidden from the French king; Spanish left-wingers have hidden from the Spanish right wing; and, of course, the Basques have been here from time immemorial, trying to keep together as a people, struggling to avoid the great centralised powers that are all about them.

Let us consider the western area that is under the influence of the Atlantic; the Basque country, Béarn, and parts of Gascony. The main part of the plain, we have left behind in Aquitaine. This is the area of the river Adour and its tributaries. The rivers of this system are strong-flowing torrents with strong-swimming fish: trout and salmon.

The main towns are on the rivers; Pau, Tarbes, Lourdes, Oloron, and Lacq, with Bayonne and Biarritz on the coast. In the country the farmyard is important, with its flocks of geese, ducks, turkeys and chickens. On the higher slopes flocks of sheep wend their woolly way right into the foothills of the Pyrenees and up to the mountain pastures. As we shall find all over France, sheep have been cut back to make way for cattle, providing both milk and meat. Game is a useful addition to the table and, as the season starts, thousands of would-be hunters head for the hills to commit mayhem on the wild duck, teal and pigeon, and sometimes on themselves. Higher up, the chamois find sudden danger. The ubiquitous pig does not require hunting, and is a good standby if the chase fails.

Crops are grown as high as the lower mountain valleys. In the spring, vegetables make ground quickly under the influence of the ocean's warmth. Maize is much in evidence, mainly as cattle food. Fruit trees abound, and the sturdy vine clings to the hillsides. Indeed the harvest brings a blaze of glory in the wine of Jurançon – the wine of Henry IV.[1]

[1] The great Hugenot king of France and Navarre, AD 1553–1610.

Past and present seem to join hands in the people of this region of France. The Basques of the west with their special language, *Enskara*, their own customs, and even their own game, *Pelote*, give the impression of another place, another time. The Béarnais of Pau and the Bigourdins of Tarbes are only too ready to re-live the strife between Huguenot and Catholic. (In the interest of their tourist trade, however, they can reach an agreement about the new airport at Gardères, which will serve Lourdes).

The character of the area is reflected in its produce. Between Bayonne and St Jean de Luz fish abounds, with eel, squid, red mullet, octopus and lobster being perhaps the most characteristic. Inland, nearer to the mountains, winters are hard and work onerous, so dishes are rich and filling; luscious casseroles, tasty game dishes and warming soups. The mountain streams give trout and salmon; the mountain farms chickens and eggs. However rich the dish, however creamy the sauce, the rule of the kitchen states that the gourmet must be able to 'digest without remorse'. The menu must be balanced and not over-rich. Indeed many of the great dishes of the area need no accompaniment and are thus very useful to those of us who have limited time for cooking.

Anyone who can keep a few hens need never go hungry; the egg is available to make nutritious and tasty dishes. The Gascon kitchen has always been famed for the use of eggs. Here is a dish of fried eggs with a very tasty garnish.

OEUFS AUX AUBERGINES (Eggs with aubergines)

6 servings:

onion	**salt and papper**
tomato	**bacon** *or* **ham, chopped**
aubergines, sliced	**12 eggs**

To test for freshness, remember fresh eggs feel heavy and make no sound when shaken. Make a purée by softening a little chopped onion, then adding skinned and pipped tomatoes and simmering until a thick paste is formed. A little water can be added during the cooking. Add salt and pepper to taste. Put the purée aside and cook the aubergines in oil until soft. Salt well. Take out, and cook the chopped ham or bacon in the same pan. Empty the pan, and fry the eggs in the same oil. Line a warm serving dish with the aubergines, turn the eggs on top, cover with a sprinkling of bacon or ham, and pour tomato purée over the top.

No quantities are necessary for this dish as you can vary it as you like. Make sure you put plenty of flavouring into the aubergines, otherwise they tend to be rather tasteless. Garlic could be added. Fresh tomato purée made in this way will keep very well in the fridge and is a useful ingredient to have on hand, especially if you are concentrating on Basque dishes.

PIPERADE (Basque omelet)

The next dish is very special to the Basque country, and its success depends on a good tomato purée. Soften thinly sliced sweet peppers with onions. Add skinned and pipped tomatoes and make a purée. Beat eggs as for an omelet. Pour into a large omelet pan, containing a little hot oil, and as soon as the eggs start to set at the bottom pour in a good quantity of the purée. Pull a spoon through the mixture as for an ordinary omelet. The *piperade* is ready when set underneath but quite wet on top. Lay slices of cooked ham over the top, and cut it into portions. Bayonne ham is ideal, but use any ham that is available.

HAM OMELET

The typical omelet from the Pyrenees is made with Bayonne ham tossed in a little goose dripping. In the same fat, rounds of bread are fried golden brown and kept warm The omelet is started, the ham is added, and the whole is served on the slices of crisp. fried bread. (Very wet omelets are much tastier than the 'well-cooked' variety).

BROCHETTE   (Mussels with bacon)

Any of these dishes will make a simple meal. Let us now turn to something more ambitious. We are in a kitchen near St Jean de Luz. Fish in plenty comes from the hazy, moving Atlantic. Let's have a meal that smacks of the sea! Our kitchen is fresh and full of light. Earthenware pots jostle small iron cauldrons on the shelves. Dark jars full of mysterious *confits* crowd together in the large airy larder, ready to add their own special flavour to casseroles and soups. Bayonne was an old corsaire port and the dish we are going to try, *brochette*, is said to come from the pirate custom of skewering pieces of meat on a sabre and grilling them over the fire. We shall not use the sword but a kitchen skewer.

Open some mussels with a little white wine (see page 172). Pierce them on a skewer, alternated with pieces of streaky bacon, and cook under a grill or over a barbecue fire until the bacon is cooked. Serve with frizzy endive, sprinkled with a rich oily dressing and well salted. Cheese of course must follow. In this part of France the cheese might be made from ewes' milk, and come from the valley of Aspe.

The brochette admits to great variation. Pork, lamb or beef goes well on the skewer but always alternate with fatty bacon or ham; this will keep the brochette moist. As a sauce, try a fresh tomato purée as used for the *piperade*, heated up, with cayenne. The fish brochettes have a flavour of their own to be carefully savoured, and perhaps might be eaten without sauce.

You see. Suddenly we have a meal; for, with very little thought, complementary food groups itself round our dish. The meal has been simple, and the dry full Rosé from Béarn has brought it to life. A sweet dish would be just the thing to finish with.

CRÉME CHAUDE AUX PRUNEAUX (Prune cream)

$\frac{1}{2}$ lb. prunes	$\frac{1}{2}$ pint (1$\frac{1}{4}$ cups) milk
2 oz. (2 tablespoons) sugar	2$\frac{1}{2}$ oz. (5 tablespoons) butter
pinch of salt	vanilla
6 oz. (full cup) flour	tablespoon of rum
2 eggs	

Soak the prunes overnight in weak tea. Drain, and stone them. Mix the flour, salt and sugar in a bowl. Add the eggs and then the milk to make a thick batter. Melt the butter and whip it into the mixture. Add the vanilla and rum. Place the prunes in a greased tart dish and pour the mixture over them. Cook in a fairly hot oven (mark 6; 400°F.) for 35 minutes. Turn out while still warm. A glass of chilled white wine from Jurançon would go well with this dish.

MENU

SEICHES AUX TOMATES	SQUID WITH TOMATOES
NOISETTES DE MOUTON	NOISETTES OF LAMB
HARICOTS VERTS	FRENCH BEANS
POMMES AUX LARDONS	SAUTÉ POTATOES WITH BACON
SALADE	SALAD
FROMAGES	CHEESE
GÂTEAU AU CHOCOLAT	CHOCOLATE GÂTEAU

The Begou family often took a villa near Bayonne to escape from the hustle and bustle of Bordeaux. M. Begou felt that he could stretch his soul beside the fastnesses of the Atlantic. As he stood and watched the old *Sangsue* rattling out towards the *Barre de Bayonne* his insurance office seemed to be on another planet. With a jerk he remembered that he was cook for the weekend. There was shopping to do!

SQUID WITH TOMATOES. Squid is plentiful the world over, indeed in many places it is used only as bait. It is usually quite cheap, even the frozen variety. Hubert Begou always prepared some squid when the Martinez came to supper. He searched for fish of a good white colour that smelt fresh. 'No, not too large, Monsieur. The large ones are tough'. The beans were good in the market and there were crisp spears of chicory. They had potatoes. There was only the lamb to buy.

Alain hoped that his mother, who was also out shopping, would remember the chocolate for the *gâteau*! It was his sister Danielle's saint's day and the *gâteau* was her favourite. (Bayonne chocolate is excellent for cooking.)

At home, M. Begou got to work on the squid. It was satisfying to think that a tasty, handsome dish could be made from something so unprepossessing. He sliced off the tentacles, being careful to keep the ink sack intact. The dark liquid would be a welcome addition to the sauce. The transparent bony sheath was detached from the inside of the body sac and discarded. He ran water into the body and made sure that all the yellow spongy substance was washed away. Next the outside pinky skin was peeled off. A pure white tube was left and this he cut into circles, across the tube.

It was Alain's job gently to fry the circles of prepared squid and the tentacles. After 5 minutes cooking he added some dry white wine, covered the pan and left the squid to simmer until soft; about 15 minutes. Then M. Begou took out the cooked squid and made a sauce in the pan with fresh tomato purée, garlic, saffron, a glass of white wine, seasoning – and the ink. Extra wine was needed because the squid had absorbed nearly all the original cooking liquid. This dish could be prepared early because it was to be heated in the sauce.

NOISETTES OF LAMB. The *noisettes* of lamb in the market had been too good to resist. They were small, about 3 oz. in weight, and cut from the ribs. In fact they were pieces of the fillet. Hubert chose two for each guest. They could be cooked at the last moment, coated in beaten egg and sprinkled with breadcrumbs. Slim green beans, topped and tailed, gently simmered in salted water, and then tossed in clarified butter with a tinge of garlic, were the perfect garnish.

TO CLARIFY BUTTER. Clarifying makes all the difference to butter for cooking. The idea is to remove all the salt and water held in the butter. Heat gently without colouring until all the bubbling stops. Leave to stand in a bowl until any sediment has settled at the bottom. Pour off the molten butter into another bowl, leaving the sediment behind.

CHOCOLATE GÂTEAU. Madame Begou had made the *gâteau* the day before. It was a family recipe, passed on to her by her grandmother.

for the sponge:

5 eggs
8 oz. ($\frac{1}{2}$ cup) sugar
6 oz. (1 full cup) self-raising flour
vanilla essence

for the filling:
7 tablespoons (8$\frac{3}{4}$) water

12 oz. ($\frac{3}{4}$ cup) sugar
5 egg-yolks
8 oz. (1 cup) unsalted butter
4 oz. chocolate
2 oz. ($\frac{1}{3}$ cup) split almonds

Melt the chocolate and let it cool. Make sure the mixing bowl is very warm. Separate the eggs, and beat the yolks in the bowl, gradually adding the sugar. Add vanilla, and continue mixing until the mixture is very thick. (See if the whisk leaves its impression for a few moments). Fold in the flour, and then the egg whites, beaten solid. Pour the mixture into a deep round cake tin, well oiled, which should be only half filled. Bake in a moderate oven (mark 4; 350°F.) for about 1 hour. Test the sponge by inserting a clean dry knife. If the blade comes out clean, the sponge is ready. Turn out while still warm and leave to cool.

This sponge can be used as the base for many types of gâteau. Madame Begou used a chocolate filling but you can vary this to your own taste. She dissolved the sugar in water, and boiled until the solution was syrupy and fell from the spoon in a thread. She beat the egg yolks until frothy, and added the hot syrup gradually, whipping all the time. Then the butter, cut into pieces, was slowly whipped in. The chocolate, melted with a little water and a drop of oil, blended into the butter icing to make a rich creamy chocolate sauce. Madame cut the cooled sponge into three layers and spread the chocolate cream on each. She re-formed the cake, and covered it with the remaining chocolate. The nuts, roughly chopped, were pressed to the sides of the cake and a large ornamental D in piped chocolate completed this work of art, in honour of Danielle.

As you can see, once the sponge cake is made, and the butter icing, the flavour can be varied. Coffee boiled down to a very strong solution, or the grated zest of lemon or orange (or the juice of the fruit) could be added as a flavouring instead of chocolate. On the other hand we could forget the butter icing, and use fresh fruit, bound with a little syrup, as a filling, and pipe whipped cream on top.

Monsieur Martinez and his wife Colette came over at aperitif time; 6 o'clock. He was a customs official in the port of Bayonne and his wife had a part-time office job in a local school. *Pastis*[1] is a very popular aperitif in the region adjacent to the Pyrenees. Alain was old enough to sample this with the men, and then joined them to play a game of *boules* in the back yard. The ladies sipped chilled port, while Danielle washed down salted nuts with blackcurrant cordial, diluted with crushed ice and water.

SAUTÉ POTATOES WITH BACON. After the game the men adjourned to the kitchen to assemble the meal. This putting together of food which has been prepared beforehand is the secret of the French way of enjoying a meal with guests. M. Begou and Alain had ready: the squid and its sauce; the pieces of lamb already covered with egg and bread-crumbs; green beans cooked and drained; chicory washed and separated for salad; cheeses on a plate, and the gleaming chocolate gâteau. Only the potatoes and the vinaigrette dressing were left to prepare. Alain made the vinaigrette (see page 82) while M. Begou peeled potatoes, dried them, cut them into small cubes and tossed them in a frying pan with plenty of steaming oil. When the potatoes were beginning to brown he added chopped bacon, tossed the mixture a few times, and slid it into an ovenproof dish. A hot oven (mark 7; 425°F.) finished the job for him in about 15 minutes.

For this great occasion, Begou had made up a small wine list, and by the time his mother and father arrived the table had been laid and the bottles arrayed. There was a rosé from Béarn for the squid, a red from the Landes, and a rich white of Jurançon for the gâteau.

The squid was ready in the oven, heated in its rich sauce. The beans were gently tossed in hot butter with a little garlic, and placed in the oven as the fish dish was taken out. Just as Alain was serving the first dish M. Begou laid the *noisettes* of lamb in a sizzling pan and left them gently cooking.

The sharp, highly acid, rosé wine was a great success with the unctuous sauce of the squid. The crisp, crackling bread swiftly passed round the table to an increasing volume of conversation. Grandfather asked about the dredging of the port. Martinez discussed Rugby. The ladies spoke of the shopping in Bayonne. M. Begou had time to turn the *noisettes* under cover of the talk.

ESTOUFFADE (Pork and turkey casserole)

Grandfather was very enthusiastic about the red wine from the Landes and thought it to be a good partner for an *estouffade*, which is a casserole dish famous in the region. 'You've never written down your recipe, Grandmère', interposed Madame Begou. Madame Martinez wanted to know the recipe as well, so after the gâteau, while Danielle was serving the coffee, paper and pens were procured and the dish discussed.

'Of course, on the farm when I was quite young we made the dish from goose as well as turkey. It depended on which were lucky that week, the geese or the turkeys', Grandmère stated.

---

[1] *Pastis, Ricard, pernod* and *anisette* are examples of this drink, which is flavoured with aniseed.

turkey *or* goose pieces

turkey dripping *or* oil

pork cutlets

sliced onions

garlic

tomatoes

bay leaf

thyme

parsley

salt and pepper

white wine

Brown the cutlets in the dripping, then add the turkey, and fry it to colour. Stir in the sliced onions and cook until they are just brown. Add garlic, bay leaf, thyme, parsley, salt and pepper. Moisten with white wine and simmer for 2 to 3 hours.

Grandmère remembered that her mother always had to add more wine or stock during the cooking. 'On ordinary days we added potatoes in the last half hour of cooking, but on special occasions boiled and skinned chestnuts were the favourite garnish', (see page 34). 'If the *estouffade* meant that the turkeys were unlucky, mother always added some *confits de dindon* from a stone jar in the pantry'.

The two wives eagerly wrote down the method of making the *confit* which was similar to that used by the Coulas family in Aquitaine when they made goose *confit* (see page 50). The *confit* is mainly used for adding to soups and casseroles, though enthusiasts do eat it as a dish. Why not make some confit at Christmas and keep it as a flavouring for the whole year? You can use turkey or goose.

GÂTEAU BASQUE

Grandmère and Grandpère came from Pau, where there is a great deal of Basque influence. Although they did not speak *Enskara* they used many Basque words. 'The *confit* is called *lou trebouk*. There is a special *basque-gâteau* for days such as this. Perhaps you'd like to try it for Alain's saint's day?'

pastry:

½ lb. (1½ cups) flour

4 oz. (½ cup) butter

2 eggs

5 oz. (5 tablespoons) sugar

1 oz. (3 tablespoons) yeast

filling:

4 oz. (4 tablespoons) sugar

2 egg-yolks

1 tablespoon (1¼) flour

1 oz. (3 tablespoons) arrowroot

pinch of salt

milk

Dissolve the yeast in warm water. Make the pastry, kneading for 5 minutes to distribute the yeast. Mix together the ingredients for the cream filling, and add the boiling milk, stirring all the time, to make a thick paste. Cook for a few minutes and add more milk if necessary. Pour into a bowl and leave to cool. Line a tart tin with half the pastry, rolled out thin; cover with the cream and top with the other half of the pastry. Decorate with a Basque cross.[1] Cook in a moderate oven (mark 4; 350°F.) for 20 minutes; glaze with gooseberry jam and cook for a further 5 minutes.

---

[1] This cross is typical of Basque decoration. It is called the 'cross of four commas'.

WOOD PIGEON

Grandfather used to go hunting high up in the mountains. He was never a very dedicated hunter, for his eyes would keep straying to the beauties of the mountains. 'Gavarnie must be the most beautiful place in the world. Never have I seen such rich greens, never such gracious flowers, with the light yellow of the narcissus contrasting with the deep blue of the gentian'.

He gave them his method of cooking wood pigeon. Clean the birds and make sure that the gullet is clean. Tie some fat bacon loosely over the bird, and roast in a fairly hot oven (mark 6; 400°F.) for about 20 minutes, or longer, depending on the size of the birds. Drive a sharp knife through the thigh of one of them; if the blade comes away clean the bird is cooked. While the pigeons are in the oven, brown chopped onion, carrot and garlic in a little oil. Thicken with flour and moisten with water and a little white wine if available. Add the juice from the pigeons and pour the sauce over the birds. Put in a warm oven for 5 minutes.

SOUPE DU BERGER (Shepherd's soup)

As an afterthought he remembered that he drank a red wine, Madiran, very full-bodied, with many a dish of pigeon, and that his favourite soup in those days was *Soupe du Berger*. Soften onions and leeks in oil. Add skinned tomatoes, and moisten the resulting thick sauce with water. Season well, and add grated cheese. Grandfather remembered eating this soup with fresh black bread or *miches noires*.

They were all invited to visit the Grandparents in Pau. 'Come in the spring and you'll see how beautiful our country is'. The visit was much discussed in the Begou household, and they arranged with the Martinez to meet one weekend in April, in Pau.

MENU

M. Begou managed to get off early that Friday and they drove straight to Pau. The sound of the *Gave de Pau* could be heard as soon as they approached the town and the air smelt fresh and fragrant. The road seemed to climb steadily, a wonderful view showing the Pyrenees in the far distance.

The Martinez were arriving for aperitifs on Saturday, and Grandmère wanted to get on with the cooking, so she packed them off to see the grottos of Betherram near Lourdes. This is her menu:

SOUPE DE POTIRON (*elzekaria* IN BASQUE)	CREAM OF PUMPKIN SOUP
SAUMON, MAYONNAISE VERTS	SALMON WITH GREEN MAYONNAISE
POULET RÔTI, SAUCE AUX POIVRONS	ROAST CHICKEN, SWEET PEPPER SAUCE
POMMES NOUVELLES	NEW POTATOES
SALADE DE HARICOTS VERTS	FRENCH BEAN SALAD
TOURONS	TOURONS

The first job was to make the *tourons*. When tackling a menu it is most important to decide on the order of cooking. Grandmère decided this order: tourons, salmon and mayonnaise, green beans for salad, dressing, chicken into the oven, soup, sweet pepper sauce, potatoes.

TOURONS.   Tourons are a type of *petits fours*.

almond paste:	**1 egg white**
½ lb. (4 cups) ground almonds	**3 oz. pistachio nuts**
2 egg-whites	
6 oz. (¾ cup) caster sugar	*filling:*
icing:	**2 egg whites**
½ lb. (1 cup) icing sugar	**grated zest of 1 orange**

Almond paste.   Mix the almonds with the egg whites, and knead with the sugar. Roll out the paste to a ½-inch thickness.

Icing.   Beat sugar and egg-whites together in a bowl and cover with a damp cloth.

Filling.   Chop the nuts and mix with the egg whites and 6 oz. (¾ cup) sugar. Grate in the orange zest. Mix the filling with the icing in the bowl. Cut the almond paste into circles and spread the mixture on them. Dry out in a low oven (mark 1; 300°F.), on a floured baking sheet. Cool and ice.

POACHED SALMON.   Grandfather had bought the salmon ready cut into steaks. Grandmère covered the fish with water and wine, very well seasoned, then added finely sliced onions and carrots. (A large spoonful of these mixed vegetables is enough). Into the stock went a tied *bouquet garni*. The steaks took about 10 minutes to simmer. They were removed from the stock and drained.

GREEN MAYONNAISE.   Chopped chervil and chives were gently whipped into some mayonnaise (see page 85). Grandmère decided to make this sauce for the fish when she realised how many egg yolks would be left from the *tourons*. It's a very good idea to have this in mind when you make up a menu: the ideal is not to waste anything.

FRENCH BEAN SALAD.   Grandmère cooked French beans until just crisp, cooled them, and tossed them with a very little chopped shallot, olive oil, lemon juice and plenty of salt and pepper to make a delicious salad.

ROAST CHICKEN.   There would be eight for dinner, so 2 chickens of about 3½ lb. each went into a fairly hot roasting oven (mark 6; 400°F.), lightly trussed, with a rasher of bacon on top, and stuffed with sprigs of fresh thyme. They cooked in 50 minutes.

CREAM OF PUMPKIN SOUP.   This soup is very easy to prepare. Skin a pumpkin, cut it into chunks, and cook in salted water. The cooked vegetable is then forced through a *moulin légumes* to make a purée. (You could use an electric mixer for this). To this purée is added hot milk, butter, pepper and salt. Grandmère re-heated the soup and served it with *croûtons*.

SWEET PEPPER SAUCE. Soften sliced onions and peppers in oil. Add fresh tomato purée and cook for a moment. Thin the sauce with water, and season it.

While the sauce was being made the family arrived back and a little later Monsieur and Madame Martinez came, with the baby. Little François was scarcely a baby any longer. At two years old he really sat up and took notice. 'But what will he eat?' 'He eats anything Madame'. As the rest of the family settled down to aperitifs, Grandmère and Madame Martinez fed François on sliced chicken, and potatoes that had been hastily cooked and skinned. With a crisp apple to follow he was well content.

While the baby was being put to bed Grandmère heated the soup carefully, stirring all the time; she cut the cooked, warm chicken into portions and covered it with the rich sauce. This dish could stay in a warm oven with the potatoes, cooked, skinned, and coated with a little butter. The salmon was set out on a dish with the attendant bowl of mayonnaise. 'To the table'.

Grandfather had been describing an exciting game of *pelote*. He felt as hungry as if he'd been playing himself. His daughter-in-law saw to the bread while he drew the corks of the wine. He had already chilled a surprisingly dry white from Vic-Bilh and some fruity Jurançon. The red was *Irouléguy* from Tannat. 'They can have some of the dry white with the chicken, or choose some of the red. In that way everyone can be pleased'. He himself nearly always drank red, irrespective of the dish to be consumed. 'White goes too much to the head', he explained.

MENU

Next day, Sunday, was bright and sunny – just the day for a picnic! The ladies helped Grandmère with the food, and packed the dishes and cutlery. If truth be told, the French picnic is usually quite a grand affair – impossible to eat in a car, sitting on a stone wall, or even just sitting on the ground. A table and chairs are usual equipment for a French meal in the open air. This was the 'menu des montagnes', illustrated on p. 83.

OMELETTE FROIDE	COLD OMELET
RÔTI DE BOEUF, SAUCE BÉARNAISE	COLD ROAST BEEF, SAUCE BÉARNAISE
SALADE	SALAD
FROMAGES	CHEESE
GALETTE SUCRÉE	SUGARED GALETTE

COLD OMELET. The cold omelet was a strange new dish to Madame Begou; but any well-flavoured omelet eats well on a picnic. Grandmère thought that the advent of metal foil and plastic for wrapping had brought this type of cold dish to the fore. She made two omelets with plenty of grated cheese, rolled them tighter than usual and slipped them onto foil. Chopped parsley carried in a small pot would add the colour.

ROAST BEEF. A 4 lb. piece of topside of beef had been put into the oven the night before. For roasting, make sure that there is some fat in the meat, this shows up as a 'marbling' effect. If the cut does not have its own sliver of fat, ask the butcher to cut you a piece and loosely tie it to the top. The time for roasting any meat is very variable, depending on its quality, and the thickness of the cut. Grandmère cooked this piece for 1¼ hours in a hot oven (mark 7; 425°F.) and it was still very red inside. She tested it after an hour by pressing the sides, but did not stick in a knife as this releases the juice and makes the meat shrink and go tough. Remember, a whole piece of meat, with a complete brown cooked layer round the outside, can be removed from the oven and, if still warm, can be replaced at any time without spoiling. Once the cooked layer is broken the meat is heated again at peril.

SAUCE BÉARNAISE. Madame Martinez made the sauce, which originated in the region and is good with hot meat as well as cold.

1 teaspoon chopped shallot　　　**4 egg yolks**
1 teaspoon tarragon　　　**¼ lb. (½ cup) butter**
¼ pint vinegar and water

Simmer the tarragon and the shallot in a solution of vinegar and water in a saucepan. Mix the egg yolks in a bowl. Melt the butter in a double boiler, and slowly add this to the yolks, whipping all the time. The eggs will begin to cook and thicken. Pour this thickened mixture back into the double boiler and keep stirring. Add the vinegar flavoured with tarragon and shallot, pouring it through a sieve. Keep the double boiler on a very low gas, and stir all the time. When you have a thick, creamy sauce, remove the pan and let it cool. If the sauce becomes dry and begins to 'scramble', add a little more of the tarragon vinegar, then an egg-yolk. If the sauce is too thin add an egg-yolk.

SUGARED GALETTE. The galette was simplicity itself. Grandmère rolled a piece of flaky pastry (see page 72) into a large circle ½ an inch thick, brushed the top with beaten egg and baked it on a metal tray in a fairly hot oven (mark 6; 400°F.) for about 15 minutes. While still hot, she sprinkled plenty of icing sugar on top. A little apricot jam was a luxurious addition to the *galette*.

Fortunately the day was warm and they could take the planned drive through Pierre-fitte up the gorge to Luz and then higher to Gèdre and Gavarnie. The snowy peaks stood clear against the bright green of the valley with its yellow clumps of narcissus. Here, at the foot of the mountains, with appetites honed by the sharp air, they had a royal feast. Grandfather had brought one or two bottles of the red from Madiran to grace the camping table.

RECIPES

'What a wonderful weekend'. The Martinez were speeding back to Bayonne. 'We must invite them all to our house, perhaps for our wedding anniversary'. 'I'd better look out some fish recipes for Begou', laughingly replied the customs officer. 'He'll grow gills one day'. The next evening they looked up a few recipes.

HOMARD GRILLÉ (Grilled lobster). A live lobster weighing about a pound will do for two. This is plunged in boiling water for only 4–5 minutes. When cooled, split it in half along the length. Run some melted butter over the flesh and cook under a medium grill until the flesh is tender. Use a small sharp knife to test the meat. When they are cooked, break off the claws and crack them with a hammer.

THON À LA BASQUE (Tunny-fish *à la Basque*). Heat pieces of tunny in the same tomato sauce that M. Begou used for the squid (see page 55) and serve in scallop shells or small ovenproof dishes. The fish is protected by the sauce, so this is a good dish to keep in the oven until required.

TTORO (Fish soup). Another great fish dish of France, this time a Basque speciality. It can be complicated, with a great number of fish; or simple, with two or three fish that are available.

In a large flameproof pot, make an aromatic bed of sliced onions, sliced fennel, *bouquet garni*, sliced and skinned tomatoes, and chopped garlic. Add oil, and cook gently for 10 minutes. Place on top one or two cod heads and tails, a few pieces of conger eel and a crab cut in pieces. Cover well with water, add salt and pepper, and simmer for an hour. Skim, and check the seasoning. Open some cleaned mussels with a little white wine in another pan, and strain in the fish stock. You can strip off any fish from the pieces and add to the finished soup.

Fish that can be added if available are angler, hake, gurnet, and hog fish. In fact any edible fish will make a good fish soup. Remember to take out the eyes from the fish heads, as these give an unpleasantly sharp taste to the soup. Other fresh fish can be cooked in the soup and served separately. Serve fresh *croûtons* at the table.

Madame Martinez was not keen on fish so she put forward one or two ideas of her own.

GARBURE   (Bacon and vegetable soup)

This rich soup with a piece of meat cooked in it can constitute a whole meal. Soak haricot beans in fresh water for 3–4 hours. Drain, wash, and simmer in salted water until tender. Chop carrots, French beans, potatoes and onions, and put them into a large flameproof pan, with thyme, marjoram, garlic, salt and pepper. Place a piece of boiling-bacon in this bed of vegetables, and cover with water. Add the haricot beans, and simmer until the meat is tender. Slice a green cabbage finely. Remove the meat, keep warm, and cook the cabbage in the soup for 30 minutes. Strain off some of the vegetables to serve with the meat. Serve the soup poured onto slices of stale bread. Cut the meat into slices and cover with the vegetables and a little soup. A spoonful of the *confit* of goose mentioned before will do wonders for this soup.

POULE AU POT   (Stuffed boiled fowl)

One of the great family dishes of this part of France. Again you have a soup and a meat dish in one.

Make a stuffing of sausage meat, chopped ham, breadcrumbs, thyme and parsley. Mix well and bind with an egg. Stuff a boiling fowl with this, making sure that the opening in the bird is well secured by tying or sewing with fine thread. Place it in a large pan, with sliced carrot, celery, and onion. Add a *bouquet garni*. Cover with water and simmer until the bird is cooked. Cook a little *pasta* into the soup, and serve the chicken separately, garnished with new potatoes and carrots. Experiment with the garnish yourself; it could be rice and sliced mushrooms.

A cotriade (p. 18) from Brittany, the true fisherman's meal. The mackerel is cooked in the creamy sauce but served separately.

Languedoc and Roussillon

The Pyrenees continue as a great barrier until they reach the Mediterranean. The same peaks, the same mountain pastures, the same streams and rivers roaring down towards the plain are to be seen. The trout and the salmon are the same as their cousins further west – and yet, as soon as you turn your back on the mountains, there is such a difference! It is of course the presence of that great sea of classical times that changes everything.

We can consider as an area, the coast from the Pyrenees to the Rhône, and its great hinterland that climbs in the north towards the Cevennes mountains; in the centre to the Causses of the Massif Central; and in the south to the land near the Spanish border that we have already spoken of.

In this part of France the line between France and Spain is more clearly defined; here is no Basque race. A small triangular area, Catalan France, bounded by the towns of Perpignan, Cerbère and the mountain state of Andorra, does intervene, but as far as the kitchen is concerned the French soon hold sway as the frontier is crossed from Spain.

The influence of the Mediterranean is all important to the people of Languedoc and Roussillon. It moulds their character. It influences their style of living. It invades the kitchen with sun, warmth, and with all its products. The hill slopes over the whole of the region are covered with vines. The basins and valleys are nursed through the arid heat of summer by irrigation, and have become vast garden plots that pour forth tons of fruit and vegetables. The farms profit from the climate to produce early crops that are exported to less fortunate regions in the north. Near Spain, the potatoes are new in winter and strawberries are ripe, uncovered, in May.

North of the River Aude, which cuts the area into two, things are not so good. The poor land that is an extension of the limestone plateau of the Causses in the centre, and the foothills of the Cevennes in the north, is difficult to work. But stock-rearing, particularly for veal in the Cevennes region, and the growing of vines further up the slopes, in the Midi, has raised the standard of living in these areas.

Filet de mouton aux laitues (*p. 49*) *as cooked in Aquitaine; and Roquefort cheese tarts.*

The river system of the region is simple. The Tech, the Tet and the Aude pour forth from the Pyrenees. Of these, only the Aude is of any great length; it flows north and is deflected to the sea at Carcassonne. It has become part of the great canal system linking the Atlantic and the Mediterranean. From the Cevennes flow the Orb, important to Béziers, and the Hérault. Other rivers are part of the Rhône system and only skirt the region.

Like the rivers, the towns show a simple pattern. Only Carcassonne, because of its position on the Aude, is inland. The other important towns cling to the coast: Perpignon, Narbonne, Béziers, Montpellier, and Nîmes. In all these cases the sea has retreated and these great sea-towns of the past are left dry.

Above all, this is the region of France where the greatest quantity of wine is produced. Its very weakness in the past has been this quantity, for reliance on one crop is dangerous. The crop may fail (although in such a diverse area this is highly improbable), or, and this did in fact happen, the crop can be too abundant. Over-production of wine has been the curse of the area in the past. One political fact has helped; cheap wine no longer flows from Algeria. Also, horticulture and stock-rearing are on the increase, while the wine producers aim at quality rather than quantity.

The dishes of Languedoc and Roussillon have great variety, but because certain produce is very special to the region the dishes are characteristic. The olive is much eaten and olive oil is universally used as a cooking agent, and as a dressing for salad and cold dishes. The kitchens are fragrant with thyme, fennel and garlic. Mediterranean fish glisten deep in well-cooled, dull-brown baskets.

Although this part of France knows shimmering heat, brilliant light, and dry fragrance, it is also acquainted with winds of great force and persistance, the *tramontane* in the south and the *mistral* to the north. As a result, the dwellings of the countryside have massive stone walls behind protective screens of reeds, rushes and trees. The kitchens seem hidden, secret places; Ali Baba's caves full of rich treasures.

Olive trees shimmer like silver from nearly every slope. The oil extracted from the fruit offers its protective blanket against the heat of pan and oven, and adds its own distinctive flavour to many a dish. If you don't like the flavour use one of the other oils on the market. But remember, you lose the flavour of the region – and it may only be that the taste is new to you, and not that it is really unpleasant. Also make sure that the oil is steaming, so that the food you cook is seared on contact, and will not absorb the oil. In the end you may find that it is oily food you don't like (and who can blame you), and not the subtle flavour of the olive.

During the year, the olives turn from green, through yellow and violet, to black. The crop is harvested throughout the year, and this is why we find green and black olives in shops all over the world. In general, the young green olives, picked from October onwards, are eaten as a snack outside the meal, while black olives, picked in the summer, are eaten either separately or in dishes.

TAPENADE   (Olive, anchovy and tunny)

In this region there is a special preparation called a *tapenade* made from black olives. Chop finely 8 oz. (2 cups) of stoned olives with 4 oz. (⅓ cup) anchovy fillets and 4 oz (½ cup) tunny. Add a little English mustard and 6 oz. (1 cup) of capers. Either pound down very finely with pestle and mortar or pass through a food mixer. The paste can be spread on toast, as an hors d'oeuvre; it can be mixed with the yolks, to stuff hard-boiled eggs, or added to a casserole of beef to give a really southern flavour.

SARDINES

There is one fish perhaps above all others that sums up the flavours that come from the Mediterranean: the sardine. Poor mortals brought up to recognise these fish only from the tin, and covered in salt or oil, can have no idea of the delicious flavour of fresh sardines. It has one drawback, for the smell of cooking sardines tends to take over the kitchen, the house and the whole street, if not the neighbourhood. If you doubt your friends' capacity to accept this smell, do not grill the fish with a little fennel – which is surely the simplest and the best way – but shut the odours up in an oven.

In an ovenware dish, lay a bed of sliced tomato, onion, thyme and parsley. (Remember that tomatoes are always better skinned first in this type of dish. Just plunge them into boiling water for a few seconds and the skin will lift away easily). Take off the heads, bone the fish, and cover the layer of vegetables in the dish with them. Top with tomatoes and onions. Lay on slices of lemon, sprinkle with breadcrumbs and a little oil. Cook in a moderate oven (mark 4; 350°F.) for 1 hour. Of course you can use several layers of fish, depending on the number you have to cook for. This is also a good method of cooking fresh herring. Experiment with the fish!

How could we fit this dish into a menu? It is the type of dish that has such a definite flavour, and is so filling, that it would be a mistake to serve it with other main dishes. Why not start with cold, finely sliced cooked potatoes, tossed in a little oil, vinegar and garlic? Salt this hors d'oeuvre well and garnish with olives and fresh parsley. Enjoy the sardine (or herring) dish with a tangy red wine; a wine from the Costières area would do well. Serve with a bowl of frizzy lettuce, known as endive to the Anglo-Saxons. Finish with fresh fruit; peaches or apricots would be ideal.

SARDINE BOUILLABAISSE

A rich bouillabaisse can also be made from fresh sardines.

4 servings:

2 lb. sardines	thyme
1 lb. potatoes	bay leaf
½ lb. tomatoes	fennel
2 medium onions	sliver of orange rind
garlic	saffron
salt	chopped parsley
pepper	

Clean and scale the sardines. In a large pot make a fragrant bed with the onions, chopped finely, tomatoes, peeled and chopped, and the herbs. Season well, and place the potatoes, cut into pieces, on top. Cover generously with water and cook briskly for ten minutes. Add the sardines and continue boiling for 5 minutes, or until the potatoes are cooked.

Drain off the stock, and remove the sardines and potatoes to a dish. Serve the liquid and remaining vegetables with garlic croûtons. Serve the sardines and potatoes sprinkled with chopped parsley.

This dish is enough on its own. Perhaps a slice of melon to follow, and you will have had enough to eat.

To show how varied are the dishes of this area perhaps it might be a good idea to imagine a journey from the Pyrenees in the south, through the undulating plain, to the flat shimmering coast, and north to the lower Rhône valley. Although the dishes may change as we make our journey we will notice the aspects of the kitchen that unify Languedoc-Roussillon.

The Pyrenees not far from Andorra hide fine salmon and trout in their lakes. It is not unknown to find ice on these waters in June, but I don't think that we shall choose such a day to fish for our supper.

TROUT *AU BLEU*

Without doubt the best way to get the real taste of trout is to cook them *au bleu.* The fish must be freshly caught, knocked on the head, cleaned quickly, and plunged into a simmering stock. This is made of white wine, water, finely sliced onion, carrot and a *bouquet garni*, cooked together for 15 minutes. The trout are cooked in the stock for about five minutes and acquire a distinctive blue tinge. Don't wash the fish before cooking, because they must be cooked with their natural oil, which is constantly exuded from the body.

CLEANING FISH. Cleaning fish causes some people all sorts of trouble. Try to make as small an incision as possible, and scrape round the gills to detach the guts from the inside. The slit for cleaning is made from the tiny hole towards the tail that is the natural outlet from the body. Again, if the fish is freshly caught do not wash it. You can gently swill the inside, to wash away parts of the gut that can give a bitter taste to the fish, but don't plunge the fish in water.

MENU

At the end of a day in the mountains you can feel pretty hungry so a full menu is the order of the day.

TRUITE AU BLEU	TROUT AU BLEU
ENTRECÔTE AUX ANCHOIS	ENTRECÔTE WITH ANCHOVIES
CÉLERI BRAISÉ	BRAISED CELERY
SALADE	SALAD
FRAISES	STRAWBERRIES

ENTRECÔTE WITH ANCHOVIES. Tender steak, no matter what the cut, is at its best grilled or fried. Remember to seal the outside first. Any sauce or garnish should be added at the last moment or, better still in most cases, served separately. We shall place slim anchovy fillets across the steak in a criss-cross pattern with stoned olives in the squares.

BRAISED CELERY. Celery is a delicious cooked vegetable. You must trim it, wash it well, and pare the stems carefully to take out the tough strings. Cut into pieces and blanch for five minutes in boiling salted water. Drain well, and place in a buttered saucepan. Add a little water, and cook gently over a low flame until tender; about 20 minutes.

SALAD. You must have noticed that in the regions the French nearly always have salad after the main course, and take every opportunity to escape the usual lettuce. In this part of France, leaves of wild angelica are used. The leaves are much smaller than the cultivated variety, whose crystillised stems are used in confectionery. As with lettuce, the leaves are broken, not cut, and dressed with olive oil and a little wine vinegar. The bowl is caressed with garlic.

STRAWBERRIES. Strawberries should be handled very carefully and not washed. They may be sprinkled with lemon juice and powdered sugar. Even cream spoils the flavour for the real amateur.

We might have some cheese after the salad, and we really need something strong after the aromatic angelica leaves. Perhaps a tasty piece of goat cheese, or a Roquefort.

CHERRY FLAN. Ceret is famed for its cherries, so we might vary our sweet course and bake a cherry flan. Using shortcrust pastry (see page 24) line a tin, brush the rim with egg yolk, and prick the bottom well with a fork. Stone the cherries. This is a tedious job without the proper tool which is easily obtained and not expensive. Line the pastry case with a single layer of cherries, sprinkle with sugar and bake in a fairly hot oven (mark 6; 400°F.) for about 30 minutes. Allow to cool, and pour over some red currant jelly. (In the last 15 minutes of cooking you could top with an egg and milk custard, 2 eggs to a pint (2½ cups) of milk).

The trout has such a delicate flavour that dry white wine could interfere with it, so let's leave the wine for this course. A good lusty local red wine goes well with the steak and the cheese. We might try a wine from the valley of the River Tet. Before every good meal, particularly in this region, there are nuts and olives, washed down with *pastis* or, more often, a chilled sweet wine from Banyuls.

MENU

Carcassonne, in the very heart of our region, is perched on a hill, looking out over the plain from behind medieval walls and fairy-tale pointed towers. It is in a farmhouse nearby that we are to share a feast with the Jeyrac family. It is Grandmère's eightieth birthday so it had better be good!

Grandmère Jeyrac could not stop working. Her son had done well; the 604[1] often sped off with attendant caravan for weekends and long holidays; but Madame liked to stay at home, to clean and dust, to cook and wash up. Her daughter-in-law liked to cook but Grandmère was in charge. Especially for her own birthday.

FIGUES, ARTICHAUX, OLIVES, PÂTÉS D'ANCHOIS	FIGS, GLOBE ARTICHOKES, OLIVES AND ANCHOVY PASTRIES
MOULES FARCIES	STUFFED MUSSELS
PERDRIX	PARTRIDGES
ASPERGES	ASPARAGUS
POMMES SAUTEÉS	SAUTÉ POTATOES
SALADE	SALAD
FROMAGES	CHEESE
MELON FARCI	STUFFED MELON
CÉRISES À L'EAU DE VIE	CHERRIES IN BRANDY

Madame Jeyrac started preparations the day before. The fresh figs were selected, washed and laid out in a cool place. The grocer, Durand, had a good selection of olives and she chose some black, green, and red. The artichokes and the anchovy pastries remained to be cooked.

ANCHOVY PASTRIES. The anchovies were to be cooked in flaky or puff pastry, and Chantal, Madame's daughter-in-law, wanted to watch the method.

1 lb. plain flour **5 oz. (full $\frac{1}{4}$ cup) butter**
5 oz. (full $\frac{1}{4}$ cup) margarine **salt**

Grandmère never used butter alone for pastry, always a mixture of half margarine and half butter. She creamed the fat, and divided it into four, mixing a basic pastry with one of the portions, with the flour and a little water. The pastry was left to rest for two hours. She then rolled it out into a large oblong about $\frac{1}{2}$ an inch thick. The short side of the pastry oblong was facing her on the table. Starting from the top she dotted another portion of the fat evenly over $\frac{2}{3}$ of the surface, and sprinkled on a little flour. She folded up the bottom $\frac{1}{3}$ of her dough and folded down the top $\frac{1}{3}$, then turned the thick oblong of pastry so that the short side was facing her again. This was then rolled out to about $\frac{1}{2}$ an inch thickness. The dotting of fat was repeated in the same way as before. The folds were made again and the turn so that the short side was always facing her. The last $\frac{1}{4}$ of the fat was used in the same way, the turn and the rolling out repeated. There was some fat over so she made a fourth turn. Finally she rolled out the pastry and turned it over in half to keep it in the fridge for two hours.

---

[1] A *Peugeot* car; sign of a certain affluence.

The margarine and butter must be creamed very well, and must be cool. Before folding, sift over it a very little flour. Do not roll too hard or you will press the fat through the pastry. The secret is to keep the fat and the pastry in separate layers.

When the pastry had rested long enough, Grandmère asked Chantal to cut it into four and roll it out to a $\frac{1}{4}$-inch thickness. 'The only way to learn something in the kitchen is to help to prepare it'. The flaky pastry was cut into long strips as wide as an anchovy fillet, usually about 3″. An anchovy fillet was placed near the top. The pastry was folded down over it, crimped down, and cut. This process was repeated until Chantal had made over thirty small rolls of pastry, each containing a fillet. The rolls were baked in a hot oven (mark 7; 425°F.) until well risen and golden brown.

GLOBE ARTICHOKES. Grandmère decided to cook the artichokes that evening to leave the important day comparatively free. The small plump vegetables were first soaked in a mixture of olive oil, lemon juice, chopped garlic, celery, parsley, fennel, and thyme. This was well salted, and finished with one or two twists of black pepper. When they were well soaked, Grandmère covered the artichokes with water, checked the seasoning and simmered them for 20 minutes, trying the underside with a sharp knife to see if they were soft. Small, tender artichokes should never take over 30 minutes. The artichokes were drained, and the liquid reduced to make a sauce.

Young Madame Chantal Jeyrac and her daughter Marie Christine were in the kitchen early to help, but not early enough to beat Grandmère. 'Alain has taken Joel with him to the *Co-operative*'. The wine co-operative is the life centre of the *communes* of the region. All over France the main products of an area are marketed through the co-operatives. Alain Jeyrac's father had known the terrible difficulties before the war. His son thanked his lucky stars for their co-operative.

STUFFED MELON. Marie Christine was set the job of stuffing the melons. These had been chilled overnight and her fingers were soon frozen as she cut a slice from the top of each melon and scooped out the soft middle with its glittering seeds. This completed, she made up a fruit salad of apples, peaches, grapes and some chopped walnuts. Well sugared, and flavoured with mixed spice, the luscious mixture was spooned into the hollow centre of the melons, Grandmère added a glass of armagnac to each, and the tops were replaced.[1] 'Into the fridge! Let's start the mussels'.

STUFFED MUSSELS. Alain had driven into Sète to pick up the mussels. The kitchen team was soon hard at work, scraping the weed away and plucking from between the shells the strand by which the mussel had been attached for feeding when it was harvested. 'Pull along the shell towards the thin end, Marie Christine. Like that!' Soon a mountain of gleaming blue-blackness was ready to be toppled into a giant pan. Grandmère added wine, parsley, and garlic, to open the mussels, while Chantal Jeyrac made the stuffing for the dish.

1 lb. (2 cups) butter	**parsley, chopped**
1 lb. (4 cups) dried breadcrumbs	**pepper and salt**
1 large lemon	**garlic, well crushed**

---

[1] This is extravagant, it is true. Even a teaspoon of Armagnac will make a difference to the melons, with perhaps an extra sprinkle just before serving.

She creamed the butter and mixed it well with the breadcrumbs. She then added the juice of the lemon, parsley, pepper and salt. Well crushed garlic was mixed in to taste.

The mussels were taken from the pan in which they had been opened and laid out in two large oven dishes, each mussel resting in one half of its shell. Marie Christine had the job of spreading a little of the savoury butter onto each mussel. Just before the start of the meal the dishes would be put into a moderate oven (mark 4; 350°F.) until the breadcrumbs were brown.

MUSSEL RISOTTO. 'I nearly cooked a risotto of mussels, but with all the food we have . . . . ' Grandmère's expressive shoulders finished the sentence better than any words. 'It's a good dish for supper. So try to remember it. Start the rice cooking with chopped onion and saffron in a little oil. Cook slowly. Mix in some of the mussels, add water and the juice of the rest of the mussels already opened. When the rice has cooked in the oven, add in the rest of the mussels detached from the shells, mix well and serve hot or cold. Grandfather loved that dish cold, with a bowl of *aioli*.'(garlic mayonnaise).

PARTRIDGES. M. Jeyrac and Joel had done their duty the evening before and had cleaned and plucked the partridges. They would be sixteen at table, so they prepared four plump birds, two hens and two cocks. Grandmère covered each bird with a large slice of streaky bacon. They would cook on top of the stove in a large iron pan called a *cocotte*, slowly sizzling in a mixture of oil and butter. In a saucepan, pieces of garlic were boiled up with slices of lemon. Madame Jeyrac would drain the oil from the birds when cooked and replace it with the garlic and juice. This makes a delicious sauce!

SAUTÉ POTATOES. The potatoes were fried in oil after being cooked in water and cut into slices. They were browned on top of the stove, sprinkled with salt and thyme, and finished off in the oven. Grandmère wanted to cut down the time spent in the kitchen once the meal had started, so she cooked the potatoes first, browned them and kept them on one side ready to re-heat.

'Now what do we have ready and what will we have to do? The hors d'oeuvres can be set out on the table. The salad and cheese can be put on the sideboard – by the way, I've made the dressing with walnut oil. The melon can be taken straight from the fridge. Marie Christine, you look after the bread. I shall start the mussels in the oven, and the partridges, when the hors d'oeuvres are being tackled. There is only one main thing to do – carve the birds and arrange them on a plate'. 'Alain will do that, Grandmère, you sit down and enjoy yourself'. Grudgingly the old lady let herself be persuaded.

The table, with the first dishes arranged between little bowls of flowers, looked splendid, and sighs of contentment arose as the food and the wine, chosen carefully by Alain Jeyrac, blended into a harmony of taste, smell and sight. Choosing the wines was something Alain really enjoyed.

WINE LIST

Rosé from the Aude, dry and light, with the hors d'oeuvre.
White from the Pyrenees, dry, full bodied, with the mussels.
Red from Carcassonne, light, dry wine, with the partridge.
Full dry red from Corbières, 5 years old, with the cheese.
Blanquette de Limoux, soft sparkling wine, with the melon.

CHERRIES IN BRANDY. Grandmère had, of course, saved a treat for the end of the meal; cherries in brandy, that she had preserved herself. Here is the recipe she used.

Place well-grown cherries, quite firm, with half the stalk still attached, in a large glass jar. Cover with sugared brandy, $\frac{1}{2}$ lb. ($\frac{1}{2}$ cup) of sugar to a quart (5 cups) of liquid. Seal the jar and leave. In this area there is a crop of cherries in April; and these are full of alcohol, and therefore ready, by Christmas time.

This was not the end of the treat for she produced some old *eau-de-vie* that had been bricked up in a cellar at the time of the German occupation. The strong black coffee defeated drowsiness and allowed the conversation to flow.

PASTY

'Maman, Monsieur Sellier wants to know what he can take to eat on fishing trips'. Alphonse Sellier was very large, and was always hungry. Grandmère thought a pasty would be a good idea. 'An aunt from Béziers gave me the recipe'.

the pastry:

2 eggs
1 lb. (3 cups) flour
$\frac{1}{2}$ lb. (1 cup) margarine
water
the filling:
$\frac{1}{2}$ lb. ($1\frac{1}{2}$ cups) chopped cooked veal
$\frac{1}{2}$ lb. calf's kidney

1 small onion, chopped
butter
salt and pepper
$\frac{1}{2}$ lb. ($\frac{1}{2}$ cup) brown cane sugar
grated peel and juice of 1 lemon
1 egg
1 tablespoon ($1\frac{1}{4}$) water

Chop and cook the kidney. Next make the pastry. Rub the fat into the flour. Mix in the eggs and make up a pliable pastry with a little water. Chop the veal finely and mix it with the chopped kidney. Soften the onion in butter in a pan, and add the meats. Stir well, season, and cook gently. Add the sugar and the lemon. (The sugar binds the mixture). Line a flat oven dish with a layer of pastry. Spread the filling over and cover with pastry. Whip the egg with the water. Coat the pastry with this mixture and bake in a hot oven (mark 7; 425°F.) until golden brown; about 20 minutes.

BRANDADE DE MORUE (Brandade of Cod)

'Brandade de Morue is a special luxury to take on a picnic. Would you like the recipe Monsieur?' The thought of that wonderful creamy, tangy, garlicky preparation piled on crisp toast, and devoured on some sunny bank of the Garonne, filled Monsieur Sellier with indescribable pleasure.

1 lb. salt cod	1 pint (2½ cups) of milk
½ cup of olive oil	2 tablespoons (2½) of plain flour
juice of 1 lemon	salt, pepper and garlic

Soak the fish overnight. Drain, place in a pan, cover with fresh water, and simmer gently until soft. Drain, cool and carefully take off all the skin and bones. Break the fish into tiny pieces and heat in a saucepan with a little oil. Stir with a wooden spoon until the fish is broken down into a purée. Stir in the rest of the oil. Sprinkle in the flour and cook for a few minutes. Slowly add the milk, warmed slightly, stirring all the time. Add salt, pepper and garlic to taste. Serve chilled.

SPINACH OMELET

The fishing trip went splendidly. Monsieur Sellier always went with the same 'team', his sister, her husband and their son Claude. On this occasion he decided to cook them a spinach omelet.

He washed the spinach carefully, cooked it with very little water, drained it and chopped it finely. He mixed the eggs for the omelet and added a good helping of spinach. The omelet was then cooked in the usual way. Before folding the omelet, he added a light sprinkle of chopped anchovy fillet. The fishing 'team' had the omelet cold for supper, at the start of the meal.

MENU

OMELETTE AUX ÉPINARDS FROIDE	COLD SPINACH OMELET
DAUBE	MEAT AND WINE CASSEROLE
SALADE DE CHOU-FLEURS	CAULIFLOWER SALAD
FROMAGES	CHEESE
PÊCHES À L'ARMAGNAC	PEACHES IN BRANDY

It was their first supper and Jeanne, Monsieur Sellier's sister had cooked the *daube* at home, sealing it in the casserole and placing it carefully in the boot of the car. When reheating it in the oven she added some potatoes.

DAUBE (Meat and wine casserole)

2 lb. stewing steak	½ bottle dry white wine
4 onions	salt, pepper
¼ lb. chopped lean bacon	1 glass of Armagnac (as a luxury)
1 clove	

Skirt of beef is very suitable for this dish. Cut the meat into small pieces. Toss lightly in oil, with the bacon, to colour. Put in a casserole with the onions, one stuck with the clove, the wine, crushed garlic, pepper and salt. Cook in a cool oven (mark 2; 300°F) for 4 hours. Add the Armagnac just before serving.

CAULIFLOWER SALAD. Cauliflower is often eaten cold as a salad in France. Cook the vegetable, leaving some of the young green leaves round the heart, in plenty of salted water, so that there is some crispness left in it. Drain at once and leave to cool. Use a vinaigrette dressing with plenty of salt and chopped parsley.

PEACHES IN BRANDY. Robert, Monsieur Sellier's brother-in-law, particularly enjoyed the peaches, which he had grown himself. Here was one thing that he could cook. (Robert was not the world's worst cook, but he must have been a close runner-up!). He stoned the peaches and halved them. They were then simmered gently in butter, with plenty of sugar added. The sugar, butter and fruit juices made a tasty caramel for the peaches. When all was sizzling and beginning to colour he added a good glass of Armagnac. The effect was heightened, for everything burst into flame and Robert nearly dropped the lot. 'Hurrah for the chef!'

STUFFED TROUT

Jeanne had two ways of serving trout that she was proud of. One hot and one cold. This is the hot dish.

For the stuffing, chop a large onion finely, and cook it in a little oil until tender. Add chopped mushrooms and a little chopped garlic. Remove from the pan, and add equal quantities of finely grated breadcrumbs, chopped chives, and chopped parsley. Moisten and bind with a little milk. Add salt and pepper to taste.

Clean the trout, and stuff with the mixture. Place the fish in an oven dish on a bed of lightly fried, chopped onions. Add a *bouquet garni*, and a glass of dry white wine. Dot with butter and cook in a fairly hot oven (mark 5; 375°F.) until tender, basting frequently with the juice. This will take about 15 minutes for trout weighing 6 oz. Drain and serve, reducing the liquid to make a sauce.

COLD TROUT

The trout is cooked gently in a *court bouillon* stock (see page 30), then skinned and filleted.

BUTTER SAUCE. Simmer in a little water some chopped parsley, tarragon, chervil, and chives. Crush in a morter (or mix in a blender) the cooked herbs, with 3 egg yolks from hard boiled eggs; 2 gherkins; 3 capers; a little garlic; and several anchovy fillets. Add 4 oz. (½ cup) of softened butter, and a little wine vinegar flavoured with tarragon. Mix well, and slowly add two tablespoons (2½) of olive oil. This will give the sauce a good creamy texture.

Arrange the trout on a bed of salad, and garnish with thin rounds of cucumber. Serve the sauce separately.

APPLE CHARLOTTE

In the warm atmosphere of the plain of Languedoc cooked sweets are not very popular. Fresh fruit is usually taken after the cheese. However, one cooked sweet, served chilled, can be very successful after a meal fragrant with the tastes and scents of the south.

½ lb. apples	2 oz. (2 tablespoons) sugar
6 oz. (3 cups) breadcrumbs	2 oz. (4 tablespoons) butter
3 oz. (½ cup) grated suet	cinnamon
grated peel and juice of 1 lemon	melted apricot jam

Peel, core and slice the apples. Cook them gently with a little butter and cinnamon. Don't mash the apples; let them retain their sliced form. Mix the breadcrumbs, suet, lemon peel and sugar. Put a layer of apples in a buttered pie dish. Cover with the breadcrumb mixture. Repeat the apple layer then the breadcrumbs. Continue until you have used up all the ingredients. Finish off with breadcrumbs. Dot with butter. Cook in a moderate oven (mark 4; 350°F.) for about 1 hour. Chill – serve. Bon appetit!

MENU

An old school friend of Monsieur Sellier, Monsieur Oddos, was at the *Faculté* of Montpellier. The two were to hold a reading of Occitan poetry for a few friends. This, with Provençal, was the language used by the great *trouveurs* of the south, in the Middle Ages. Alas, it is gradually disappearing.

This is the menu for their dinner:

L'AIGO BOULIDO	SAGE AND GARLIC SOUP
BALLOTTINES D'AGNEAU	BALLOTTINES OF LAMB
CARDE EN SAUCE BLANCHE	CHARD IN WHITE SAUCE
SALADE	SALAD
FROMAGES	CHEESE
POIRES AU VIN ROUGE	PEARS IN RED WINE

L'AIGO BOULIDO. The soup is heavily flavoured with sage. It is very easy to make, as you can see from the recipe.

Boil in salted water plenty of crushed garlic. Add a bunch of sage with ½ a bay leaf and a piece of thyme. Leave to stand, then thicken with an egg yolk. Careful with the thickening! Separate the yolk into a bowl and add some of the hot liquid. Whip until the egg begins to cook and thicken. You may then add this to the rest of the soup. This soup may also be thickened with mayonnaise (see page 85), but its strength is in the natural flavour of the sage. Don't spoil this with the thickening. Serve on bread sprinkled with olive oil. Offer grated cheese.

Fish may be poached in this soup, particularly angler-fish (*baudroie*) which is a speciality of the area. In this case fennel is added, and sometimes a little fresh tomato purée is added to a cup of the soup to make a sauce. Try a fish that needs flavouring. Whiting would be good. The dish is called *Baudroie à l'aigo sau*.

BALLOTTINES OF LAMB. Ballottines make a good, reasonably priced, dish.

6 servings:

1 lb. minced lamb	**1 teaspoon (1¼) thyme**
1 medium onion, finely sliced	**2 eggs**
1 tablespoon (1½) parsley	**2 oz. (1 cup) breadcrumbs**
garlic to taste	**oil**

Mix the meat with the finely chopped onions, and the herbs. Separate the eggs, and use the yolks to bind the mixture. Dry off with a little flour. Beat the egg whites stiff. Coat balls of the mixture with the whites and breadcrumbs. Gently fry in sizzling oil.

CHARD IN WHITE SAUCE. Chard can be a delicious vegetable and is much used in this region. Cut into pieces and cook in salted water until tender – not soft! Madame Oddos served it with a white sauce (see page 95).

PEARS IN RED WINE. The pears were peeled and cleared of pips and hard skin. Madame poached them in wine, well sugared, with a flavour of spices. She chilled them, and reduced the sauce, serving this separately in a bowl. A bowl of whipped cream stood ready.

The meal was prefaced by a good dry Rancio wine, continued with a red St. Saturnin and finished with some chilled Frontignon. Needless to say one or two Occitan poems accompanied the meal. A perfect evening in the Languedoc!

CHICKEN WITH RICE AND AUBERGINE. As usual in France, this region has chickens everywhere. The habit of keeping chickens and a few rabbits, ready to slaughter for a meal, has died out as apartment blocks get higher and the housewife, understandably, becomes more squeamish as her country roots weaken. Chicken dishes are usually simple and full of flavour, a quality that many a chicken bought in a city butcher's is likely to lack. What more simple chicken dish than this one?

Cut up a chicken and cook it in sizzling oil. Peel tomatoes and cook them with a little finely sliced onion and garlic. Moisten with white wine, and cover the chicken with this sauce. Serve with rice cooked in the oven with saffron (see page 74) and rounds of aubergine tossed in oil.

Have you noticed, by the way, how little kitchen equipment we need in order to cook as they do in the regions of France? Let's take an inventory as we go along, and make a list at the end of our visit to the kitchens of French families. Even though Monsieur Sellier is a batchelor he is always careful to clean and sharpen his knives and look to his pots and pans. All cooks should take advantage of this lesson.

Provence

The Provençal expatriate notices one thing above all else on returning to his native land; the smell of herbs and trees in the sun. This wonderful aroma pervades the Provençal kitchen and is aided by another characteristic fragrance, that of olive oil. Oil is the cooking agent for the whole of the south of France. Butter, being a comparatively late import from far off 'barbarian' lands, is only proper to the regions of the north.

True Provençal cooking is of the sea and the hills. The *mas*, the upland farmhouse, is a treasure-store of simple aromatic dishes, noted for the sparing use of meat. The fishing ports of the indented coast are redolent with the very essence of fish over the grill. The farmer or the fisherman, as everywhere in France, talks about food, cooks and eats with passion.

The hills of this aromatic region are typified by the hills of the Maures and the Esterel. Here, the very few people have very little produce, but eat surprisingly well. Game of all sorts is much pursued. In autumn the wild boars lie stretched out in the market square to be weighed, measured and discussed. The 'one that got away' is always, of course, larger and more dangerous than the one that did not. In little towns, hugging the curves of the hillside – Draguignan, Brignolles, Grasse – herbs hang in bunches from the kitchen ceiling: thyme, rosemary, fennel, bay, garlic, parsley, sage, savory, origan – the list could go on and on. The basil sits green and lush in its pot. The street markets offer olives by the barrel-load straight from the trees on the slopes, and sweet peppers, tomatoes, courgettes, aubergines, and small blue artichokes from the valley. The potato is not much in evidence, but rice stands in most nobly; if such a thing as a starchy vegetable is needed when the bread is so good.

The tourist industry that thrives among the rocky coves, the pine trees and the islands, has had a marked effect on life by the sea. But the Provençal kitchen has stood firm against the invasion from the north; and anyway from September to May things are back to normal. On the coast there is an abundance of all produce except meat, but this does not matter, for the fish is king. Fish, crisp on the grill or steaming in the pot, are massaged with oil and caressed with herbs. They are enjoyed free of vegetables, as much serious trencher work has gone on before the main dish. Saffron lends its golden hue. Garlic murmurs mysteriously in soup and sauce. The *bouillabaisse* is one dish among many, but it is the dish that exploits to the full the harvest of the sea. A good *bouilla-baisse* is a festival of the Mediterranean.

Let our kitchen enjoy both the faces of Provence. It is on a hillside near the sea, and well stocked with things that conjure up the smells and tastes of this lovely region. Let us not forget that wherever possible the vines crouch low in the sun and give their fruit for the white, rosé and red wines of the Côtes de Provence.

It is traditional in Provence to have the important meal of the day at midday, and then to take a siesta. The warm stillness of the south lies about us, but the kitchen is shady and cool with tiled floor, slatted shutters, and beaded door screen. A light mistral is rising. Time to get to work.

CIVET DE LAPIN (Rabbit cooked in red wine)

Most cooking in Provence is done on top of the stove, and the dish we are going to try is no exception. It can be prepared long before the meal and is perhaps even better re-heated.

6 servings:

onions, chopped	thyme
1 handful of streaky bacon and ham, chopped	salt and pepper
nut oil	1 large tablespoon ($1\frac{1}{2}$) of flour
1 rabbit cut in pieces	red wine
parsley	mushrooms

We have the rabbit but no blood. With the blood of the animal we would thicken and flavour the sauce. But even without this important ingredient we can still make the dish. Olive oil is too expensive for a weekday, so we'll use nut oil instead. Better chop that parsley a bit finer!

Using enough oil to cover the bottom of the pan, gently fry the onions and some of the chopped bacon. Now add the rabbit pieces and cook until golden brown. Add the rest of the chopped bacon and ham, and the parsley. Season with salt, pepper and thyme. Mix in the flour, and cover with wine and water. Cook on a gentle heat until the rabbit is tender. Then add the mushrooms finely chopped. Happy is the cook who has a small glass of brandy to pour in! If we had the blood, we would wait until the cooking was completed and gently stir it in. But be careful not to bring the sauce to the boil once the blood is added.

We have not been particular about amounts in this dish. Let's hope that it will be repeated many times, and that you will arrive at the quantities that please you. However, don't swamp the dish with onions, and let the flavour of the bacon and ham come through. If you think that the rabbit has the muscles that come with much exercise let it soak in wine overnight, and drain it off to brown in the oil. This juice will of course be used to cook the dish, with the addition of water.

MENU

Our dish is now ready. Let us add something to make up a meal.

CIVET DE LAPIN	RABBIT IN RED WINE
SALADE	SALAD
FROMAGES	CHEESE
FRUIT	FRUIT

SALAD DRESSING.   Here's a dressing noted in Le Lavandou:

mustard	**salt**
oil	**pepper**
vinegar	

Start with mustard in the bowl. Sprinkle in the vinegar. Season well. Mix with the amount of oil you like. With a little practice you'll find that you can make a good even mixture. Add more salt and pepper to taste.

PAIN BAGNA

Tante Mathilde is coming from Draguignan on Saturday. She will probably bring some thrush pâté. We'll prepare a special lunch, and keep a place on the menu for the pâté. Lets make *pain bagna* for lunch on Friday, and then begin our preparations for Saturday. *Pain bagna*? On half a thick, round, bread roll put: sliced hard boiled egg, onions, tomatoes, olives, anchovies and a sprinkling of olive oil.

MENU

There will be room for the pâté among a selection of hors d'oeuvre which are the most distinctive part of the Provençal cuisine. Our menu will be:

HORS D'OEUVRE	HORS D'OEUVRE
POISSON GRILLÉ	GRILLED FISH
SALADE DE CÉLERI	CELERY SALAD
FROMAGES	CHEESE
TARTE AUX FRUITS	FRUIT TART

The hors d'oeuvre will be: pâté de grive; pissaladière; oeufs mimosa; tomates farcies. For grilled fish, we will wait and see what is in the fish shop. Celery makes the typical salad of the region. For the tarte aux fruits, peaches are a good idea.

A picnic in the Basque country (p. 61). Cold roast beef and salad is preceded by cold omelets and followed by a galette sucrée.

PISSALADIÈRE

shortcrust pastry (see page 24) **anchovy fillets**
3 large onions **grated cheese**
12 olives

This is simply a flat circle of pastry, baked with a covering of cooked onions, anchovy fillets, and olives. It is often made with a bread pastry, but more often cooked at home using an ordinary shortcrust pastry. Use your own pastry recipe, and remember to make enough pastry for our fruit tart as well. Two parts of flour and one part fat, rubbed together with a pinch of salt, and blended with water? Agreed! Slice the onions finely and cook them in a little oil until soft. Roll out the pastry and line a 12-inch oven tray. Top with the cooked onions, and decorate with anchovies and olives. Perhaps someone dislikes anchovies, so leave a space and sprinkle instead with grated cheese. If we like, now is the time to add garlic. Finish off the rest of the cheese over the whole tart. Cook in a hot oven (mark 7; 425°F.) until the pastry is ready. (Illustrated p. 84.)

TOMATES FARCIES

1 large tomato for each person **1 onion, chopped**
sausage meat **bread crumbs**
minced meat scraps **1 egg**

These can be served hot or cold. Large, firm tomatoes must be used. Cut off about a third of each tomato. Take out some of the pips and leave the cut side down, to drain off some of the juice. Start cooking the onion in a little oil. Add the sausage meat and minced scraps. Cook for a few minutes, and then mix in the breadcrumbs. You should have a good, dry, mixture. Take from the heat and blend together with an egg. Scoop out a little of each tomato, and stuff with the forcemeat. Sprinkle with salt, pepper and parsley. Replace the tomato tops and cook in a fairly hot oven (mark 5; 375°F.) until soft; about ½ an hour. We all like garlic, so add a little, chopped, to the oven tray. (Illustrated p. 84.)

MAYONNAISE.   We are going to start on the *oeufs mimosa*, but first we will make the mayonnaise enough for 6–8 people.

6 egg-yolks **pepper**
1 pint (2½) cups olive oil **mustard**
salt **vinegar**

Get the wire whisk from the drawer. Put salt, pepper, olive oil, vinegar and Dijon mustard on the table beside a large mixing bowl. Put the egg yolks in the bowl with two tablespoonfuls (2½) of mustard. Sprinkle in pepper, salt and a little vinegar. Mix all together but don't whisk. Take a cup of the oil, and use this to start with. Whisk the eggs and add the oil by the teaspoon, making sure that the eggs and the oil are well blended. Carry on until the cup of oil is all blended in. Now a pleasant surprise, for your mayonnaise is virtually finished. Keep whisking and add the rest of the oil in four large dollops. The mixture will thicken rapidly; thin with a little warm vinegar.

Provençal hors d'oeuvre (p. 82): pissaladière, oeufs mimosa, and stuffed tomatoes, with stuffed mussels (p. 73).

OEUFS MIMOSA. Stuffed eggs are a useful addition to a menu; you can vary the stuffing as you like.

1 hard boiled egg per person	**mustard**
chopped parsley	**salt**
mayonnaise (see above)	**pepper**
oil	**egg yolks**
vinegar	

Split the hard boiled eggs, and take out the yolks. Mix these with an equal amount of mayonnaise, and sprinkle in the parsley. If you can sieve the stuffing into the whites through a vegetable mill, the mimosa effect is striking. If not, just spoon the stuffing in. Just before the meal, we can finish off with some chopped parsley. (Illustrated p. 84.)

FRUIT TART. You made up enough pastry for the tart when you made the pissaladière. Line a tin with it, and sprinkle on some sugar. We bought peaches in the market but any fruit would do (apples, plums, apricots). Slice the fruit finely, and lay it in the pastry case, piece by piece, circling the tart from the outside. A squeeze of lemon to bring out the flavour and plenty of sugar dusted over the top. Bake in a fairly hot oven (mark 6; 400°F.) until the pastry is ready; about $\frac{1}{2}$ an hour.

FRENCH CHEESES. That's nearly everything ready for Saturday. We only have the fish to grill, the salad to prepare and the cheese to lay out. Perhaps there is time to talk about cheese. Most of the cheeses of France are available all over the country, so we always have a great choice. Goat cheeses and *brousse* are the specialities of Provence. Better to have a few good sized pieces on the cheese board than a dozen miserable scraps. We'll have a ripe camembert. Keep it in the warm kitchen overnight. It should be slightly runny, and soft to the touch. You can try a goat cheese. Pick a hard one. There's a large piece of gruyère left from yesterday; that will be enough.

PÂTÉ DE GRIVE (Thrush pâté). Saturday had started badly for Tante Mathilde. And the *mistral* had worked itself up to a crescendo. It was good to leave the burning tang of the wind in Draguignan and descend to the comparative shelter of the coast. The whole family was waiting for her at the bus stop in the square and this gave her the pleasant sensation of importance.

They say that the *mistral* tightens the nerves and sharpens the appetite. Whatever the reason, our plates were cleared with amazing celerity. Naturally the wine, rosé from the Côtes de Maures, and an amazing red from a domaine between St Raphael and Hyères called Tibourin, played its part. Tante Mathilde was so happy at the reception given to her pâté that she gave us the recipe. One may ask, would anyone outside France be passionate enough about food to sacrifice thrushes for a pâté. One never knows, so here is the recipe.

12 servings:

2 dozen thrushes	**1 egg**
streaky bacon	**1½ tablespoons (2) salt**
juniper berries	**2 oz. (4 tablespoons) lard**
4 oz. ham, chopped	**ground black pepper**
4 oz. breadcrumbs	**chicken fat**

86

In Provence the birds feed from the juniper bushes, so this is the herb used. The birds are plucked, cleaned, covered with bacon and roasted lightly in the oven with juniper berries, until the flesh may be stripped off easily. About 20 minutes in a hot oven (mark 7; 425°F.). Mince the flesh finely and mix with the chopped ham, breadcrumbs, and the whole egg. Add salt. Put in a bacon-lined casserole. Mix the thrush meat with the juices from the pan, slice the lard and place on top of the meat. Cover with the bacon rinds trimmed from the casserole lining. Cook in a moderate oven (mark 4; 350°F.) for 2 hours. When the pâté is cool, turn out and serve with croûtons.

GRILLED SEA-BREAM. The fish course was particularly well received. Luckily the early morning was calm, or the boats would not have put out. There were sea-bream glistening in the baskets by the quay, and these are always excellent fish for the grill. The fish were cleaned and stuffed with fennel twigs. Smoothed over with some oil, they were soon sizzling under the grill.

CELERY SALAD. A good idea with the softness of the fish. Perhaps the celery stalks could have been split along their length a shade more finely; but then one should never prepare a dish after the *pastis* aperitif. The vinagrette dressing was the one used often before.

BOUILLABAISSE

The local firemen have invited us to share their annual *bouillabaisse*. The recipe should be a good one. The *mistral* has stopped blowing and the signs are good. Monsieur Bettini, one of the firemen, comes round to borrow our largest black iron pot, and to invite us for the *bouillabaisse*. 'My friends the fishmongers are making sure we get the best of the catch'.

The fish that give flavour to a *bouillabaisse* are caught close inshore, and are called 'the fish from the rocks'. Away from the Mediterranean you might find it difficult to obtain some of them. These are the fish that went into this particular dish:

fish: for 10 servings, about 5 lb.
rascasse (hog fish)
congre (conger eel)
lotte (angler fish)
Saint Pierre (John Dory)
vive (weaver)
moules (mussels)
merlan (whiting)—soft fish
rouget (red mullet)—soft fish
crabbes (small crabs)

other ingredients:
onions

tomatoes
garlic
fennel
bay leaf
thyme
parsley
rind of orange
savory
saffron
salt and pepper
olive oil
potatoes

Clean the fish and shellfish, and scale the fish if necessary. Make a bed of sliced onions in a large flame-proof pot and gently cook them with oil. When they start to colour, add peeled and chopped tomatoes, the herbs, salt and pepper. On this aromatic bed place the firm-fleshed fish and a good handful of mussels. Add a glass of olive oil. Stir, and cover well with water. Add some potatoes. Check the seasoning, and boil fast. After ten minutes add the soft fish: whiting and red mullet. Continue cooking very fast. Add a few small crabs. When the potatoes are cooked, the dish is ready. Enough of the liquor is taken off to make a soup, and the fish are drained and kept warm.

A simpler *bouillabaisse* can be made. A one-fish dish could be made, perhaps with mussels; the method of cooking and the herbs are the same. Sardines, red mullet or mackerel could be tried.

Serving a *bouillabaisse* is like some votive ceremony. Small jars of olive oil, bright bowls of grated cheese, golden crunchy rounds of bread roasted in the oven with oil, salt and garlic, these were the instruments of ceremony for the high priests. One or two of the guests dipped toast in the bowls of *rouille*.

ROUILLE. This is a luxury – a sauce accompaniment to the *bouillabaisse*. To fresh mayonnaise add crushed garlic, tomato purée, and cayenne pepper. The sauce should be blood red, hot with pepper and garlic. The firemen spread chunks of bread with the *rouille* and ate it with the soup. We hoped there would be enough of this sauce left to eat with the bowl of steaming fish.

SALADE NIÇOISE. The meal had started with a *salade niçoise*. This hors d'oeuvre consisted of sliced tomatoes, green peppers sliced fine, hard boiled eggs halved and decorated with anchovy fillets, black olives, and a sprinkling of tunny in oil. The dressing was olive oil, lemon juice and garlic. The plates were wiped clean with slices of bread and then the serious work started.

BOURRIDE

Monsieur Bettini told us that the original dish from which *bouillabaisse* evolved, was perhaps the *bourride*. This is made with slices of white fish, and whole white fish. Take steaks of cod and whole whiting. Cook the fish in a *court bouillon* (see page 30), for about 10 minutes. Add some of the liquid to mayonnaise (see page 85) well laced with crushed garlic. Add one egg yolk for each person, to thicken the sauce (see page 43). Put slices of stale bread on a dish and pour the sauce over them. This tasty dish of bread is served at the table. Fillet the whiting after cooking. Drain the fish, lay out on a dish, and serve with a good tablespoon of the garlic-flavoured mayonnaise, called *ailloli*, for each helping. The bread, sauce-laden, is eaten with the fish.

PROVENÇAL RECIPES

On a return visit to Tante Mathilde we were allowed to see her mother's old book of recipes. 'See how well people used to write'. Indeed the clear script looked beautiful on the page. Tante Mathilde pointed out a starting dish, a main dish, a vegetable, and a sweet dish.

GNOCCHI NIÇOISE

4 oz. (½ cup) butter	**4 eggs**
½ pint (1¼ cups) water	**1 lb. potatoes**
6 oz. (1 full cup) plain flour	**salt and pepper**

Melt the butter in boiling water, and when the mixture bubbles up add all the flour, taking off the heat to stir in the flour. You should end up with one solid lump that does not stick to the pan. Add a little more flour to dry out, if necessary. Mix in the beaten eggs. Add an equal quantity of cooked and finely mashed potatoes. Allow to cool. Shape the mixture into about the length and thickness of a little finger, and poach in simmering salted water. The fingers of mixture will rise to the surface, but allow them to simmer a few minutes longer. Make a white sauce (see page 95). Pour this into a casserole, add the *gnocchi* and cook in the hot sauce for five minutes in a hot oven (mark 7; 425°F.). Sprinkle with grated cheese and brown under the grill.

The pastry made of water, butter, flour, and eggs is the same as choux pastry, and is very useful for other dishes.

POULET SAUTÉ (Fried chicken)

Cut up a chicken, and cook the pieces in oil in a frying pan. Take them out and keep them warm. Add a little oil to the juices in the pan, and cook 2 or 3 chopped onions, crushed garlic, a bay leaf, some grated nutmeg and pieces of bacon. Put back the chicken pieces, and add a glass of white wine. Boil to reduce the sauce, and turn out onto a hot dish.

RATATOUILLE

In a pan, soften sliced onions in olive oil. Add skinned, cleaned and cubed aubergines, then sliced green peppers, and chopped courgettes. Lastly skinned sliced tomatoes and garlic, pepper, and salt. Cook until the vegetables are soft.

TOURTE À LA FRANGIPANE

At the Christmas table the people of Provence offer 13 sweets. This tart made with almond paste is one of them.

6 oz. ground almonds	**finely grated orange peel**
6 oz. caster sugar	**½ wine glass of milk**
1 egg	**flaky pastry** (see page 72).

You need enough flaky pastry for a tart and its cover. In a saucepan mix the ground almonds, sugar, egg and grated orange peel. Add the milk so that you have a thick, creamy consistency. Cook gently until the first bubbles rise. Line a tart tin with the pastry and cover with the almond paste. Cover with a rolled out circle of pastry, crimp the edges and coat with beaten egg and milk mixture. Bake in a fairly hot oven (mark 6; 400°F.) until the pastry is cooked: about 25 minutes.

SOUPE AU PISTOU

6 servings:

$\frac{1}{2}$ lb. French beans	$\frac{1}{4}$ lb. kidney beans
1 large onion	$\frac{1}{2}$ lb. small noodles
$\frac{1}{2}$ lb. carrots	2 cloves garlic
$\frac{1}{2}$ lb. courgettes	1 tablespoon ($1\frac{1}{4}$) fresh basil
$\frac{1}{2}$ lb. tomatoes	$1\frac{1}{2}$ tablespoons (2) olive oil
$\frac{1}{4}$ lb. dried haricot beans	salt

Of all the dishes of Provence, perhaps the most popular with the people of the region is Soupe au Pistou. This soup, highly flavoured with sweet basil, was supposed to be a stimulant, hence perhaps its popularity. There are many ingredients, but the method is simple. Chop green beans, onions, carrots, courgettes, and skinned tomatoes. Boil the vegetables in plenty of salted water, with the white beans and red beans that have been soaked for 2–3 hours. Simmer for $1\frac{1}{2}$ hours. At the end of the cooking time throw in two handfuls of small noodles or broken spaghetti. While the soup has been cooking, you have crushed the garlic in a mortar with plenty of green basil leaves. Add olive oil and mix to a paste. When the vegetables are cooked mix a scoop of the hot soup into the garlic, basil, and oil paste. Add the highly flavoured sauce to the soup. Bring to the boil and serve. On the table must go a jar of olive oil, and some grated cheese.

BASIL. Fresh basil may only be had in the summer. The plant is grown in a pot and it would do well in a greenhouse in colder climes. Dried basil is readily obtainable but needs the treatment that all dried herbs need. Put the amount necessary for the dish into a saucepan, and simmer gently for 5 minutes in a little water. Use the water and the herb to flavour the dish.

A great friend of the family, Pierre Martinon was going to visit his family in the region to the north of Provence, the Dauphiné. 'I'll send you back the recipe for the *saucisson* you like so much. My friends make it themselves. Better still, why not come with me?' What a good idea!

Dauphiné and Savoy

The long summer of Provence attracts holiday-makers from the north, and drives the inhabitants of the region to seek fresh air in the mountains of the Dauphiné and the Savoy. Monsieur Martinon thought of cool, fresh nights in the Chartreuse, of seeking the flashing trout in mountain streams, and savouring that wonderful heady mixture of wood smoke and pine trees that seems to rinse the palate and prepare it for the *cuisine* of the region.

A large part of this region comes under the influence of the south. It is the only region of truly high alps in France, and yet the southern section, with Castellane on one side and Gap on the other, is short of water. There are fewer valleys in this part, so the great gap in the mountains cut by the river Durance is of great importance. Here the juniper trees and dry bushes show black against blue Provençal skies. Small stone built settlements are more and more deserted. Fewer herds of sheep are to be seen. The only thing that grows well is the spiky lavender, feeding eager swarms of bees that provide fragrant honey.

In the north and west life is easier. Ventoux and Vercours have good arable soils, and benefit from the irrigation system developed on the Rhône side of the Dauphiné. The vine clings to valley slopes, while lower down cereals are grown. Wherever there is space, cattle are reared.

Round Grenoble, the capital of the region, the air is keener and more often filled with rain, or snow in winter. Thick forests clothe the mountain slopes. Oaks, elms and pines tower above rushing streams and lonely paths. Everywhere you can hear the rush and bustle of water. Mount Belledonne is a peak of virtually perpetual snow, but the valleys are deep and protected. In the valley of Gresivaudan spring seems to last for ever. In this region of mountain and deep valley the animals and birds have kept their natural habitat. Chamois leap the crags in summer and the wild boar and deer root through the thickets. Game-birds of all sorts are in plentiful supply: quail, woodcock, brown thrush, partridge, hazel-grouse. There is no need to go hungry in the hunting season! Rivers abound with trout, salmon, and a fish special to the region, char. In deeper water the great pike hunts along the depths and is hunted for its tasty flesh.

The flowers too play their part in sustaining man, and add flavours to liqueurs made in the Chartreuse, particularly by the monks of the great monastery. Green or gold, their secret formula adds aromatic tastes that are unforgettable. The flowers of the alpine gardens also look wonderful. Carnations, lilies, anemones, narcissi add their glowing colours to the wild plants of the upper slopes.

A large part of mountainous Dauphiné is protected as a natural reserve. But the needs of the tourist are beginning to submerge natural life. The town dweller needs areas such as this in which to breathe and to be with nature again. Unfortunately there are so many town dwellers, and nature is not enough for them. They need, or the organisers of holiday centres think they need, glass and stainless steel centres, chair lifts, golf courses, boating, theatres, cinemas. These facilities can crowd out the tiny hamlets with their life-giving pastures. The people of the villages prefer their life as it is.

Dauphiné does not only consist of mountains. The region spreads right to the Rhône, from Orange to Vienne. Here the life and customs of Provence surge along the great Rhône valley, as though the powerful river boats were trying to join Marseille to Lyon.

SAUCISSON (Sausage)

Monsieur Martinon was to spend several days in the Drôme, not far from Orange. His old friend Dalmas had come back from Indo-China many years ago to settle among vineyards on the rolling plain between the hills and the great river.

The Dalmas property was on the edge of a village that squatted under a château and had done so since the time of Guillaume d'Orange.[1] A lot of the building was very old, much of it built out of the walls of the château, but here and there new shops and houses were to be seen, bright, clean and somewhat out of place.

Pierre Dalmas had bought an old silk workshop and the land that went with it. Now he had a new villa on the old site and Madame Dalmas had a brand new kitchen that looked on to the château. The old work-shop housed chickens, and a half a dozen dogs and cats. We had telephoned before leaving, so the whole family was assembled to greet us in the yard.

The promised *saucisson* was just as delicious as Pierre had described. The pig provides many of the meat dishes of this area, and the *saucisson* and *boudin*, a black pudding, are two of the tastiest; and two that are good to keep for some time. Indeed Madame made sausage at the end of the summer which was eaten at Christmas. Most butchers could supply the intestine needed for the skins.

leg of pork, *or* fillet (2 lb. without the bone)	1 glass red wine
1 oz. (1 tablespoon) salt	½ oz. (1 tablespoon) caster sugar
½ teaspoon freshly ground pepper, mixed white and black	1 glass rum
3 cloves garlic	½ oz. (2½ tablespoons) mixed peppercorns
	pigs' intestine, for skins

[1] Also Guillaume de Poitiers et d'Aquitaine; the first of the Troubadours. His daughter Alienor (Eleanor) became the wife of Henry II of England.

Bone the leg of pork, and take off nearly all the fat. If you use fillet, trim it well. Cut the meat into pieces and mince it finely. Weigh the mince. To each 2 lb. add 1 oz. (1 scant tablespoon) of salt and ½ teaspoon of fresh ground pepper from black and white peppercorns. In a large bowl, crush plenty of garlic and leave it to soak in wine for one hour. Take out any pieces of garlic, and mix the meat in the bowl with the wine. The mixture should be damp, with no excess liquid. Add the caster sugar, a glass of rum and the mixed peppercorns, whole. Knead the meat to mix well, and leave for two hours.

Cut the intestines into the lengths you require. Tie one end of each piece with strong fine thread, and stuff with the meat preparation. Make sure you do not trap air in the skin. Push down firmly and tie off. The skin should be packed very tightly. Keep the *saucissons* in a cool place and leave to dry for at least two months. They must hang in a well-ventilated place – not in the fridge.

BOUDIN (Black pudding)

The boudin is much simpler to make but it does need fresh blood from the pig, and perhaps some ox blood to supplement this.

1 lb. onions	**salt**
1 pint (2½ cups) blood	**pepper**
6 fluid ounces (¾ cup) cream	**mixed spice**
½ lb. suet	**pigs' intestine, for skins**

Chop the onion very finely. Cook in pork dripping until soft. Mix in the shredded suet, the blood, and the cream. Season with plenty of salt and pepper, nutmeg and spices. You can dry off the mixture, if it seems too wet, with a handful of oatmeal. Tie the intestines as for the *saucisson* and stuff with the mixture. Simmer in a large pan of water for twenty minutes. The *boudins* can be kept for some time before use, and are delicious lightly grilled.

MENU

Somehow Madame Dalmas had managed to make her brand-new kitchen very French indeed. The preserves on the shelves, the black pans, the *saucissons* gently swinging from the ceiling, the bunch of herbs and garlic, all spelt good home-made food. She told us that much of her cooking was done in a hurry, as she was very busy with the chickens, the vines and the vegetable garden. The supper that night showed how simple a good meal can be.

SAUCISSON	HOME-MADE SAUSAGE
RADIS	RADISHES
TOMATES	TOMATOES
OEUFS AU FROMAGE	EGGS BAKED WITH CHEESE
PICODON	PICODON CHEESE
PÊCHES AU GRATIN	BAKED PEACHES

93

The *saucisson* was sliced as thin as paper and laid out on a large dish with a garnish of radishes and tomatoes. Madame sprinkled some vinaigrette dressing over the tomatoes, but the radishes were just eaten with plenty of salt. 'What do you think of that rosé wine?' In fact M. Dalmas's grapes went to the co-operative that made the wine, so he was very proud to serve it to us.

EGGS BAKED WITH CHEESE.   The egg dish, none of us had tasted before. Madame soaked thick slices of bread in warm salted milk and placed them on an oiled dish. She made a depression in each slice of bread and sprinkled with grated cheese. An egg was cracked into each depression. Cheese, salt, and pepper were sprinkled over to finish off and the dish was placed in a hot oven. When the whites had turned opaque, the dish was cooked.

PICODON CHEESE.   Salad was served after the egg dish to make a bed for the picodon. This is a special goat cheese that is always sold in two varieties in the markets; strong, and very strong. The cheeses are in small rounds, and should be kept cool and hard.

BAKED PEACHES.   Monsieur Dalmas laughed when the *pêches gratinées* were served. 'My wife thinks that every Dauphiné meal should have one *gratinée* dish in it'. It is true that there are many such dishes in the region. '*Au gratin*' means that the dish has been subjected to intense heat, and has acquired a crusty brown surface. Often the ingredients are blended with a white sauce and the top sprinkled with cheese or butter. Breadcrumbs may also be used to assist the formation of a crust.

In this peach dish none of the usual things could be used to form the crisp appetising surface. Madame split the peaches, taking out the stones, and poached them in a little butter and white wine. She separated the eggs, beat the whites until firm, and made a sauce with the yolks and apricot jam. The half peaches were placed on an oven tray and the juice blended into the sauce which was poured over the cooked peaches. Beaten whites were carefully spooned over the top. A sprinkle of sugar, and the dish was put into a hot oven (mark 7; 425°F.) to cook and crisp the egg whites.

Here is a good chance to experiment. The beaten whites protect the peaches and should protect ice cream. Try a small scoop of ice cream into the hole in a peach and finish off with the beaten whites in the same way. You will then have hot peach and hot meringue surrounding cold ice cream.

GRATIN DAUPHINOIS

Making a dish *au gratin* adds extra flavour and makes it look good. The dish itself can be very simple. The *Gratin Dauphinois* is a good example. There are only potatoes, and a few extra flavours, in this fragrant preparation.

potatoes	**1 egg**
milk	**nutmeg**
grated cheese	**pepper and salt**

Slice the potatoes finely. Rub a deep earthenware oven dish with a clove of garlic and a little butter. Line the bottom with a layer of potatoes. Add salt and a sprinkling of cheese.

Repeat the layers, potatoes, salt and cheese. Pour in milk until the potatoes are nearly covered. Finish with grated nutmeg, cheese and dots of butter. Cook in a moderate oven (mark 4; 350°F.) for about 1 hour until the potatoes are cooked. Serve before the main dish.

COOKING AU GRATIN

What could be more simple! And how easy to vary the process adding more dishes to our repertoire. Most vegetables would lend themselves to the *gratinée* process.

COURGETTES.   Simmer in salted water until soft. Drain, and slice if large. Lay in a dish. Pour over a thin béchamel sauce (see below). Sprinkle with cheese and dot with butter. Brown under the grill or in a hot oven.

CARROTS.   Cooked *à l'etuvée* (see page 24). Cover with béchamel. Topped with cheese and butter. Brown under the grill.

MUSHROOMS.   Slice if large and flat. Leave whole if small (button). Toss lightly in a little oil. Tip into an oven dish and proceed as for the other vegetables.

TURNIPS.   Cut into thick round slices. Simmer in salted water until just soft. Cover with béchamel and top with grated cheese and a little butter. Brown under the grill or in the oven. The list could go on. . . .

BÉCHAMEL SAUCE.   Melt 2 oz. (4 tablespoons) of butter in the pan. Add 2 oz. (6 tablespoons of flour and cook for a moment, stirring. Add 1 pint (2½ cups) of milk gradually, gently beating all the time. Add salt and pepper to taste.

Meat and fowl dishes can be finished in the same way. Slices of cooked breast of chicken are particularly successful with béchamel sauce. Meat, on the other hand, is usually cooked, and then browned under the grill, with a coating of breadcrumbs and a little butter. Here are two examples.

COTELETTES D'AGNEAU AU GRATIN.   Grill the cutlets until pink in the middle. Arrange in a fire-proof dish. Coat the top with some melted butter and sprinkle over breadcrumbs. Brown under the grill and garnish with tomatoes provençale (baked with onions and anchovy) and sprigs of parsley.

BOEUF SAUTÉ AU GRATIN.   Cut frying steak into cubes and toss in a pan with steaming oil. Add a little chopped onion, thyme, and parsley, just before the meat is cooked, then salt, pepper and a little wine. Shake for a few seconds and turn out into a dish. Sprinkle with breadcrumbs and, if you are so inclined, some crushed garlic. Put under the grill. The juice in the dish, which is heavily charged with oil, will absorb some of the breadcrumbs and go to make the crust. You may have to brush with a little oil just before putting under the grill.

MENU

What about a menu from the gratinée dishes?

GRATIN DAUPHINOIS	GRATIN DAUPHINOIS
COTELETTES D'AGNEAU AU GRATIN	LAMB CHOPS AU GRATIN
COURGETTES ET CAROTTES AU GRATIN	COURGETTES AND CARROTS AU GRATIN
POMMES AU GRATIN	APPLES AU GRATIN

Cook the small courgettes for 10 minutes in boiling water, and the carrots as for *carottes à l'etuvée* (see page 24). Lay the cooked courgettes and carrots side by side in the same dish, ready for the addition of béchamel and grated cheese. Peel the apples (use large eating apples), cut into thick slices, arrange in a buttered dish and sprinkle with sugar, cinnamon and melted butter. Cook under the grill for about 3 minutes or for about 6 minutes in a moderate oven (mark 4; 350°F.). Be careful not to overcook or the fruit will be too soft.

MENU

Monsieur Dalmas wanted to take his guests on a little tour of the region. 'When we first arrived, coming from the other end of the world, we wanted to get to know the whole area'. He and Madame were soon aware of the mixture of cultures, even of civilisations, in this part of France; it is full of history. The stone shields and emblems round the courtyard of a château had been defaced during the Revolution. Their tour took in a Romanesque church with an altar-stone made from a pagan sacrificial stone, and a lonely Roman temple, with its bath in front still intact, and the statues of the gods replaced by those of the Virgin Mary.

They had all helped with the preparations for the picnic. These were the dishes they took with them.

AUBERGINES AUX TOMATOES	AUBERGINES WITH TOMATOES
LAPIN FROID	COLD RABBIT
SALADE	SALAD
FROMAGES	CHEESE
POGNES AUX CONFITURES	SWEET BUNS WITH JAM

AUBERGINES AUX TOMATES. The most interesting dish, Madame Dalmas had made the day before. She skinned, pipped and cubed some aubergines and cooked them gently in a little oil with a light sprinkle of finely chopped onion. Tomatoes, skinned and chopped, were added to the pan. The mixture was quite liquid and needed lots of salt and pepper and a little garlic. It was then allowed to cool and chill in the fridge. (The dish should be quite red from the tomatoes).

If you use a very little tomato and crush the preparation with a wooden spoon until it is a rough paste, you have another dish, *bohemienne*. This is served piping hot, covered with béchamel and browned under the grill, with a sprinkle of grated cheese and some chopped anchovy fillet as flavouring.

RABBIT. Rabbit, especially the domestic variety usually bought in butchers shops, tends to be very short of flavour. Madame Dalmas added the flavour of bacon, bay-leaf and garlic. Remember, if you cannot get used to the taste of garlic, omit it from the dish. Try other herbs.

She cut up the rabbit, cutting off the front and back legs, and cracking through the body under the rib cage, cutting the lower trunk, the saddle, into two. Thus she had 6 portions. (The rib cage could not be used for this dish). She made an incision in each piece of rabbit and pushed in a clove of garlic. Then each piece was wrapped round with a bay leaf and a rasher of streaky bacon, and tied with a length of fine twine. These 'packets' were browned in oil in a heavy iron pot and then left to cook slowly over a low heat. She finished with a sprinkle of white wine.

POGNES AUX CONFITURES. The guests helped to pack the bread, butter, several bottles of red wine, a *Côte Rôtie*, salad and cheeses. Madame packed some odd china plates and thick glasses. The food was put into plastic containers and the *pognes* carefully enveloped in a fine white cloth. Here is the recipe for these sweet buns:

1 lb. plain flour	6 oz. (6 tablespoons) caster sugar
scant 1 oz. of yeast	teaspoon of salt
$\frac{1}{2}$ lb. (1 cup) softened butter	1 tablespoon ($1\frac{1}{4}$) orange extract
6 eggs	

Dissolve the yeast in $\frac{1}{2}$ a cup of warm water, and add a teaspoon of sugar. The yeast mixture should froth slightly. Rub the butter into the flour. Add the salt and orange extract. Make a dough with four of the eggs (beaten), the flour and butter mixture, and the yeast solution. The dough should double in size. Knead again, and make balls from the dough. Half the balls should be about $\frac{1}{2}$ an inch in diameter, the other half twice the size. On oiled trays make up brioche shapes: make a hole with your finger in a large ball, elongate a smaller ball, make a point at one end and push it into the hole. Allow the brioche shapes to rise again, and bake in a fairly hot oven (mark 5; 375°F.) for about 35 minutes, until golden brown.

BLACKCURRANT JAM

On the picnic, the *Pognes* disappeared rapidly with their accompanying fresh black-currant jam. Everyone in the country districts of France seems to make jam at home, and the Drôme is no exception. Blackcurrant is one of the easiest jams to make for it needs no extra acid. Fruit like strawberries need lemon juice to obtain a good set. Each pound of fruit needs a pound of sugar. The clearest test for a good set is to pour a little of the jam onto a saucer and let it cool. Touch the surface, which should wrinkle like a skin. Here is the recipe for the jam eaten with the Pognes.

4 lb. blackcurrants	2 pints water
4 lb. sugar	

Remove the blackcurrant stalks and wash the fruit well. Simmer in the water until tender, about $\frac{1}{2}$ an hour. Take the fruit from the heat and dissolve the sugar in it. Heat very slowly until the sugar is quite dissolved. Boil until you get a good set. Test as described above, from time to time.

Fill the jars, that have been left to sterilize in the oven for 20 minutes[1]. Put a wax paper disc on the top of the jam. Leave to cool and cover with transparent sealing paper. Attach with a rubber band.

MENU

They lunched among the vines by the side of a road, near the wine *caves* that they had just visited. The air was very still. They talked of the great oak casks that held the wine for four years, the coolness of the *caves* and the high alcohol content of the wines of the area. Pierre Martinon dreamed of dinner that night.

PÂTÉ DE CAILLES	QUAIL PÂTÉ
SOUPE DAUPHINOISE	SOUP DAUPHINOISE
DAUBE DE MOUTON	MUTTON CASSEROLE
POMMES DAUPHINES	DAUPHINE POTATOES
POIVRES FARCIS	STUFFED PEPPERS
SALADE	SALAD
FROMAGES	CHEESE
MOUSSE D'ABRICOTS	APRICOT MOUSSE

QUAIL PÂTÉ. Quails arrive in France in the spring. Many are caught and fattened in cages during the summer. The connoisseur will only use quail killed in the wild for the kitchen, but the quails used by Madame Dalmas were bought in the market, and had lived probably most of their lives in captivity.

6 quails	**2 lb. pastry**
2 lb. stuffing	*bouquet garni*
streaky bacon	**aspic jelly**

Pluck and clean the quails. If you bone them yourself, start cutting along the backbone and work down the body. This is not difficult, so long as your knife is sharp. Take off the legs, bone them, mince the meat and add to the stuffing.

To make the stuffing, take any cooked meat, some sausage meat, breadcrumbs, finely chopped onion, and a little thyme. Plenty of salt and pepper. Mix all the ingredients in a bowl with your hands and bind with 2 eggs.

Stuff the boned quail bodies with this preparation and wrap each bird in a piece of bacon. Make 2 lb. shortcrust pastry. Oil a pie dish and line with half the pastry. Line the pastry case with pieces of streaky bacon. Put a layer of birds on the bacon. Madame's dish could take three birds to a layer. Sprinkle some of the stuffing around the birds. Put the rest of the birds on top, and then the rest of the stuffing. Top with bacon pieces, and cover with the rest of the pastry, rolled out thinly. Brush with egg, and decorate with pieces of pastry. Make a hole in the top about 1 inch in diameter. Bake in a moderate oven (mark 4; 350°F.) for 1½ hours. When cooked pour some aspic jelly through the hole and allow to cool. Serve cold.

---

[1] Jam jars will be sterilized if held at boiling point, 212°F, for 20 minutes. This temperature is reached at very cool, mark ¼, in a gas oven. Allow an extra 10 minutes for the oven to heat.

ASPIC JELLY.   Just a word about the jelly. Gelatine and aspic preparations in packets are very good for making jelly, but should not be used diluted only with water. Why not try boiling some bones, beef and veal, with a few carrots, onions and celery. Any large pot three-quarters filled with good thick bones particularly marrow bones, covered with water, should make good jelly. You should cook for about three hours, strain off the liquid and pass it through a muslin. Allow to set in the fridge. If it does not set well enough, then add some dissolved gelatine.

SOUPE DAUPHINOISE.   Soups in the Dauphiné are usually white and creamy. For this soup we need: onions, leeks, carrots, cooked white beans (see page 111) skinned tomatoes, sorrel, fresh cream and butter. No extra thickening; this is provided by the cream and the beans.

Chop the onions, carrots and leeks, and cook gently in butter for about 20 minutes. Add a handful of cooked white beans. Cover with water or light stock. Add salt and pepper. Cook some sorrel leaves in butter, and add a half cup of cream. Take from the heat and stir well. Put the sorrel into a hot soup-tureen and pour on the hot vegetable soup. Use salt and the pepper mill to flavour. Serve with toasted bread. Sorrel is easy to grow – but not in the middle of a city. You can use dried sorrel; but remember to simmer the dry leaves in a little salt water for 3 minutes before using.

MUTTON CASSEROLE.   This can be made from chops, or slices of leg of lamb. Into the casserole put a little pork dripping. Brown the pieces of lamb in a frying pan, and add them to the casserole. Add onions, carrots, and *bouquet garni*. Just cover with wine and water. Season with salt and pepper. Put two small rashers of bacon on top. Cover, and cook in a warm oven (mark 3; 325°F.) for 1½ hours, or until the lamb is cooked. If you really do use large mutton the cooking may take longer!

POMMES DAUPHINES.   These are potatoes cooked in a most impressive way. Boil potatoes until soft, and mash. Make sure that the potatoes are quite dry. Salt well, and mix when cool with an equal quantity of *pâté à choux* (see page 37). Make balls of the mixture, about the size of a walnut, and drop into steaming deep fat or oil. (Use the same fat that you use for frying chips). The potato balls will sizzle in the oil and gradually rise to the surface. Wait until they are golden brown before you scoop them out and drain them. These potatoes will keep quite well in the oven for ten minutes.

STUFFED PEPPERS.   Very often the vegetables are eaten separately from the meat in France. As a result the vegetable, so humble and subservient in the Anglo-Saxon kitchen, comes into its own in France. Here Madame served stuffed peppers after the lamb. She split the peppers in two, carefully cleaned out the seeds and pith, and stuffed them with a mixture of cooked rice, cooked chopped meat, breadcrumbs and egg yolks. The peppers stuffed in this way take about 20 minutes to cook in a moderate oven (mark 4; 350°F.). Large tomatoes can be scooped out and prepared in the same way.

The salad this time was made of sorrel leaves and young spinach dressed with vinaigrette (see page 82). The cheeses were Picodon (praised before), a blue speckled cheese from Sassenage, and a large piece of beautifully flavoured Gruyère. 'This cheese did not come from a factory! I have a cousin who is in charge of a *fruitière* in the Jura. He sent me the cheese from his own store'.

APRICOT MOUSSE

¾ lb. ripe apricots
6 oz. (6 tablespoons) icing sugar
juice of ½ lemon

1 oz. (3 envelopes) gelatine
½ pint (1¼ cups) whipped cream

Plunge the apricots into boiling water. Drain, and remove the skins. Take out the stones and put the fruit through a sieve, or purée in an electric blender. Weigh the fruit, and add the required sugar. Melt the gelatine with some water in a pan and stir the fruit into it. Mix well. Add whipped cream. Allow to set in individual dishes.

BOEUF EN DAUBE (Beef casserole)

Pierre at last had to say goodbye and continue his vacation in the Alps. He had a chalet near Laffrey, not far from Grenoble. There was plenty of fishing in the region and, if he felt lonely, Grenoble and friends were not far away.

Before leaving the Drôme he had been given the secret of the special taste of the Boeuf en Daube of the Dauphiné.

6 servings:

2 lb. stewing beef
1 tablespoon (1¼) flour
1 large onion
5 small carrots
bouquet garni

½ pint red wine
1 tablespoon (1¼) anchovy fillets,
  crushed
½ tablespoon olive oil
½ tablespoon wine vinegar

Cut the beef into chunks. Brown the pieces in a little steaming oil. Place in the casserole. Sprinkle a tablespoon of flour over them and mix well. Lightly cook some onion rings clean a handful of small carrots, and make a *bouquet garni*; mix these in with the meat. Just cover with a mixture of wine and water. Add salt and pepper from the mill to season.

Now for that special flavour. Crush some anchovy fillets; blend with oil and wine vinegar. Add this to the casserole. Cook for 2 to 3 hours, depending on the cut of meat, in a moderate oven (mark 4; 350°F.).

This was a useful addition to Pierre's notebook. It is a good idea to note all recipes that interest you in your own way. Much better than collecting hundreds of magazines and torn out pages. Here are a few of the dishes that Pierre noted.

TRUITE AUX AMANDES

6 servings:

6 trout
3 tablespoons (4) flour
oil

3 tablespoons (4) butter
½ lb. almonds

Roll the fish in flour, lightly frizzle in hot oil. Add a nob of butter near the end of the cooking. This will add flavour to the crisp skin. To check if the trout is cooked, look inside the cut where the fish was cleaned. When all the redness has gone, it is cooked. Keep the cooked trout warm. Fry skinned almonds, split in two, in the trout pan. Arrange the nuts over the fish, melt a little extra butter and pour over them.

SAUCES FOR COLD FISH

For the successful fisherman, these sauces are invaluable. Salmon, trout and char – which has the wonderful name *omble chevalier* in French – make very successful cold dishes. Clean the fish and cook in a *court bouillon* (see page 30). Leave to cool in the liquid. Serve with a piquant sauce. When you serve a fish with sauce it is better to fillet the fish. Serve the sauce in a bowl separately.

SAUCE RAVIGOTE.   Chop and mix capers, onions, chives, parsley, chervil, and tarragon. Add oil, vinegar, pepper and salt.

SAUCE REMOULADE.   Prepare a mayonnaise (see page 85). Add mustard, and chopped gherkins, capers, parsley, and chervil, with pepper from the mill and a little salt.

PIEDS DE COCHON (Pigs' trotters)

Wipe over the pigs' trotters with a clean, damp cloth. (You should buy trotters from a good butcher already prepared). Simmer in plenty of water with carrot, onion, and a *bouquet garni*. This may take as long as four hours, but they must be really tender. If you use a pressure cooker, cooking trotters until tender will take you only about 40 minutes and even the bones will be soft. Drain and carefully dry the trotters, and coat with melted butter and breadcrumbs. Crisp under the grill.

SAUTÉ DE VEAU À L'ESTRAGON (Sautéd veal with tarragon)

Use any of the tender cuts; leg, fillet or rib, and cut into small cubes. Cook the meat in a frying pan with a little oil. Add finely chopped onion, and bacon pieces moistened with white wine and fresh tomato purée. Add fresh tarragon, and simmer for a few minutes. Pork can be prepared in the same way.

RATATOUILLE DE NAVETS

Turnips are a strangely neglected vegetable. Boiled in water they are really pretty uninteresting. This way they are not. Slice onions and cook them gently in oil in a large thick pot for a few minutes. Slice the turnips and mix with the onions. Skin tomatoes, chop and add to the *ratatouille*. Use pepper, salt and crushed garlic to flavour. Cook slowly in the oil until soft. Serve with a sprinkle of cheese.

NOUGAT BLANC

½ lb. (½ cup) caster sugar
½ lb. (½ cup) honey
peel of ½ orange, grated

white of 1 egg, beaten
1 lb. (1¾ cups) chopped almonds
2 sheets of rice paper

Cook the sugar with the honey. Add the grated orange peel and the beaten white of an egg. Heat until the syrup will set on the back of a spoon. Remove from the heat and add 1 lb. (1¾ cups) of roughly chopped almonds that have been gently heated. Line a baking sheet with rice paper. Cover with the mixture, and top with rice paper. Press, with a weight on a flat piece of wood. Leave until lukewarm, then cut into squares.

MENU

The Monticelli family were always pleased to see their old friend Pierre Martinon. 'After two weeks in that chalet he probably needs a square meal'. Gabrielle Monticelli went to an office every day, but still managed to cook sumptuous meals at night.

SOUP AU FROMAGE	CHEESE SOUP
COURGETTES FARCIES	STUFFED COURGETTES
CANARD AUX PÊCHES	DUCK WITH PEACHES
POMMES DAUPHINES	DAUPHINE POTATOES
CARDON À LA MOELLE	CARDOONS IN WHITE SAUCE
SALADE	SALAD
FROMAGES	CHEESE
CROISSANTS AU PIGNONS	PINE-KERNEL CROISSANTS

CHEESE SOUP. The soup is very quick to make and needs very few ingredients. Make some béchamel (see page 95). Dilute with milk and water. Add salt and pepper to taste. As this is gently simmering, sift in finely grated cheese, stirring all the time. (Gruyère with some Cheddar will give a very good flavour).

STUFFED COURGETTES. Gabrielle had no meat scraps to make up the stuffing for the courgettes. She bought ½ lb. of minced beef and cooked it slowly in a pan, with oil and a little chopped onion. Using no liquid, she flavoured with thyme, pepper and salt and waited until the meat was cooked. Then she added ½ a cup of water and a good teaspoon of fresh tomato purée. This was reduced until it had a thick runny consistency. She simmered the courgettes in salted water until soft, split them in two, laid them in a dish and covered them with the stuffing. Just before serving, breadcrumbs were sprinkled over and the dish was put under a hot grill.

DUCK WITH PEACHES. Duck was one of Madame's specialities. A 4 lb. duck would be enough to feed four. The bird was lightly smeared with butter and stuffed with half a large peach, then roasted in a hot oven (mark 7; 425°F.) for 1¼ hours. Half way through the roasting Gabrielle poured off most of the fat that had collected in the roasting dish; the remainder would be poured off when the duck was cooked. She tossed peach halves in hot butter and sugar and used them as a garnish for the dish.

To serve, a duck of this size can be cut into quarters, which is an easier process than carving in slices. Drain all the juices from the duck, and put it on a wooden board. Cut in two along the breast bone. A sturdy knife will do this. Divide the halves in two at the hip joint. If you cut behind the leg into the groin you only have to sever cartilage, not bone.

CARDOONS IN WHITE SAUCE. *Cardon*, in English cardoon, is a little known vegetable of the artichoke family. Only the stems are used. Trim the stems and cut into slices. Simmer until tender in salted water, with sliced carrot and onion to flavour, and a *bouquet garni*. Pour a thin béchamel over the top, dot with butter, and glaze in the oven or cook marrow slices in salted water, and in an oven dish put alternate layers of cardoon and marrow.

CROISSANTS AUX PIGNONS. After the salad and cheese (there was a cheese new to Pierre, Tommes de St Marcellin), Gabrielle served crunchy, nutty biscuits flavoured with pine kernels. Of course Pierre asked for the recipe. Here it is:

pine kernels	**½ lb. (½ cup) sugar**
½ lb. (2 cups) ground almonds	**whites of 5 eggs**

Mix the almonds, sugar and egg whites together. Make into balls the size of a walnut. Roll each ball in pine kernels. On an oiled oven sheet form the balls into a crescent shape. Bake in a moderate oven (mark 4; 350°F.) for about 20 minutes. They will still be quite soft when taken from the oven but will set hard on a wire rack.

The wines for the dinner were all from the region: rosé from Suze-la-Rousse in the Drôme with the courgettes, red *Tain l'Hermitage* with the duck. There was another bottle of the *Hermitage* for the cheese, and some sparkling *Clairette de Die* to accompany the croissants. And both yellow and green Chartreuse to aid digestion afterwards.

CHAMOIS

Seated in the cool on the balcony his friend asked: 'Did you see a chamois in the mountains, Pierre?' 'No, they are usually much higher up, near the Italian border'. Madame Monticelli felt that she could not possibly eat meat from such a graceful creature. 'But all creatures are full of beauty, and we kill thousands of them to eat', the hunter defended his sport. But Pierre could not stand the wholesale slaughter of game and was pleased to see hunting strictly controlled.

He had eaten young chamois and found it delicious. It is cooked like lamb, but the older animals need marinating overnight in red wine with a few roughly crushed black peppercorns. Most large game is improved by this treatment. You do not have to cover the meat completely; the effect of the soaking in wine seems to seep through it.

This discussion of the nature reserve versus the needs of man goes on over the length and breadth of France. The argument is easily extended to the value of food products in their wild state and in an unnatural environment. All the dishes of Dauphiné, and any other region, taste better if prepared from natural products. The quail taken on the hillside tastes of the herbs of the countryside. Fresh herbs give a better flavour than the dried variety.

Perhaps the advent of battery fowls for the table will encourage cooks at home to try sauces and garnishes that add flavour to food. The tasty sauces and herbs of French cooking will then really come into their own. But do not let us forget natural flavours. Pierre Martinon felt that the savoury chicken of the farmyard, cut up and gently fried in oil and butter on top of the stove, was infinitely superior to old battery hens cooked to pieces and smothered in a tomato and pepper sauce.

He planned to take some of his holiday to the North of the Alps, in Savoy. Here are the great rain forests that reach up darkly from the valley rim towards the alpine pastures. This is the great winter-spots area that is dominated by Mont Blanc.

Pierre was going on a specially arranged tour for taking photographs; an idea that has been growing for some time. The first thing he noticed in the Vannois was the lushness of the valleys and the amount of stock feeding there. The abundance of dairy produce is reflected in the first dish that Pierre sampled.

FONDUE DES MONTAGNES

You will need a thick pan or fondue dish to keep hot over a spirit lamp.

¼ bottle dry white wine	cubes of bread
1½ lb. Gruyère cheese, sliced	salt
small glass of kirsch	white pepper
clove of garlic	

Rub the pan with garlic. Heat the pan; or you may find it easier to start the dish on the stove. Pour in the white wine, add salt and pepper. When the wine is simmering add the cheese a little at a time so that it gradually melts. Add the kirsch, (brandy could be used). Put the dish over a spirit lamp to keep the cheese melted. Each guest has a fork and a pile of bread cubes. Charge the bread cubes with the molten cheese.

Anyone who drops bread in the fondue must supply an extra bottle of wine! As you can see this is a most convivial dish.

Just a word about the cheese. Try to get true Gruyère for the dish. This is quite a hard cheese and has virtually no holes in it. The cheese we usually know as Gruyère is in fact Emmental. Any dry white wine is good with this dish, but Pierre enjoyed a Seyssel from the region. (Illustrated on p. 133.)

GRATIN DE POMMES AUX CHAMPIGNONS

A full day's tramping round the mountains sharpened Pierre's good appetite. He appreciated many regional dishes and noticed how economical they were, and how filling. Also simple. 'Just the dishes to add to the repertoire of a poor bachelor', he thought to himself.

Potatoes were much in evidence. He noticed that the Savoyarde *gratinée* was made in the same way as the Dauphiné variety, but stock or water was used, not milk. On the other hand a local gratin dish with potatoes and mushrooms was very creamy.

Slice the potatoes thinly. Chop the onion and parsley. Slice the mushrooms. Rub an oven dish with garlic and butter. Cover with a layer of potatoes, and sprinkle with onions, parsley, salt and pepper. Top with a layer of sliced mushrooms. Start again with potatoes and continue the layers until the dish is full. Cover with milk. Add pepper and salt, and dot with butter and cheese to finish. Cook in a moderate oven (mark 4; 350°F.) until the potatoes are soft and all the milk has cooked away; about 1 hour.

POTÉE

1 **large firm cabbage**	**garlic**
2 **lb. potatoes**	**pepper**
1 **lb. carrots**	**salt**
large onion, chopped	**bayleaf**
boiling sausage	**thyme**
$\frac{1}{2}$ **lb. pork belly**	**wine** (optional)
1 **lb. salt pork**	

Cut the cabbage into large chunks. Cut the peeled potatoes into pieces. Slice the carrots.

Soften the onions in a large pot with oil and butter. Add the meat and sausage, cut into pieces. (Use any variety of sausage intended for boiling). Put in the carrots and potatoes. Turn the ingredients and let them sizzle for 5 minutes. Add salt, pepper and the herbs, then the chunks of cabbage. Pour in water, and white wine if you have any. Cover tightly. Braise until the meat is tender; about $1\frac{1}{2}$ hours on top of the stove or in a moderate oven (mark 4; 350°F.).

CANAPÉ DE LA REGION

This dish delighted Pierre by its simplicity. Make puff pastry (see page 72). Roll out to about $\frac{1}{4}$-inch thickness. Cut into oblongs about 3 × 2 inches. Bake in the oven. Cover each pastry with a slice of ham, a spoonful of béchamel (see page 95) and grated Gruyère cheese. Toast under the grill. You could use lightly toasted bread as the base. It's nowhere near the Savoyard dish, but makes a very tasty savoury dish.

OMBLE CHEVALIER AU FOUR

The char is a fish that Pierre ate quite often in Dauphiné. Any fish about $\frac{1}{2}$ lb. in weight could be prepared in a similar way.

Clean the fish. Lay in an oven dish. Season well and surround with sliced mushrooms. Sprinkle with lemon juice, dot with butter and add a good dry white wine. Cook in a moderate oven (mark 4; 350°F.) for 15 to 20 minutes, depending on the weight of the fish. Remove the fish, when cooked, and arrange on a dish with the mushrooms. Heat the juices on top of the stove and add a tablespoon of fresh tomato purée and a cup of thick cream. Stir well while heating. Check the seasoning and pour over the fish.

FRIED FISH

The meal that Pierre enjoyed most of all was a fish fry-up on the shores of Lake Geneva. He gave a hand himself with the frying, and found himself working with a girl called Agnes who explained the technique to him.

The fish was *fera*, a kind of lake trout, and this particular catch was of small fish. They were cooked *à la meunière*, which means dusted with flour and fried in butter.

Clean the fish, and scale if necessary. These young fish scarcely needed scaling; but to be sure Pierre ran his knife, with its blade at right angles, across the fish, working from tail to head. He scraped a small area at a time, making sure the scales were off.

The fish were then laid in flour, and turned so that they were covered completely. Then the *fera* were fried in smoking oil and butter, and cooked quickly. It is important not to burn the coating of flour. The skin should not be broken. When cooked and golden brown all over the fish were arranged on a serving dish. Butter was added to the pan and, when it melted, lemon juice was added. The fish were salted well and the melted butter poured over the top.

MENU

FERA À LA MEUNIÈRE	LAKE TROUT MEUNIÈRE
SALADE FRISÉE	SALAD OF ENDIVE
REBLOCHON	REBLOCHON CHEESE
FRUITS	FRUIT
VIN CHAUD	MULLED WINE

Reblochon is the finest cheese of the region. The fruit consisted of bowls of apples, pears and cherries. The *vin chaud* revived and warmed.

MULLED WINE.   Heat red wine with mixed spices and bay leaf. Prepare the glasses, with sugar in each. When the wine boils, you may ignite the top for effect. Pour into the glasses and stir. The red wine for this drink came from Annecy. With the fish there was a good supply of white Crepy.

Pierre was rested by his holiday and full of ideas for his kitchen. Perhaps more important, he had met Agnes who shared his enthusiasm for the mountains and for country fare. Ah well! It's good to have a partner to wash up the dishes.

The *Massif Central*

To the west of the Rhone Valley lies another mountain area very different from the alps of Dauphiné and Savoy. This is the *Massif Central*, a great block of old granite with much evidence of volcanic activity. In this block rise many of the major rivers of France: the Loire, the Allier, the Gironde and the Lot.

At the real heart of the *Massif* are the headstreams of the rivers Loire and Allier. At Le Puy we can see the remnants of ancient volcanoes. The plain of the Allier, the Limagne, has fertile soil and an abundance of crops. This rich heart of the mountain block is surrounded by rocky peaks where thin soil clothes the upland slopes where sheep-rearing still resists the encroachment of increasing milk and beef herds.

The eastern edge of the *Massif* looks out, from steep rocky heights, over the Rhône to the Alps. No wonder the Protestants of the sixteenth century managed to hold out here against Catholic forces. In winter violent streams crash down wooded slopes of pine, birch and sweet chestnut; in the heat of summer, nothing remains but dry stream-beds. Crops are virtually non-existent.

The western slopes are gentle and grassy. Here the sheep of Auvergne and Cantal have given place to cattle. Calves are fattened on milk for the markets of Lyon and Paris. Great *fourmes* of cheese are made in Cantal, and also smaller mysterious blue-veined delicacies. Rye and potatoes nestle into the hillsides, and everywhere man tries to replace the trees that he has cut down through the centuries.

Water flows everywhere, and in the streams are trout and salmon. From the upper Loire and the Allier this water supply, carefully controlled, now waters the crops of the plains. All the market vegetables are grown, and wheat and green lentils. The Allier valley grows abundant fruit: cherries, apples, peaches, plums and nuts. Walnut oil gives a special flavour to salads.

Water does not only flow, but springs from the ground and the whole area is known for medicinal thermal springs. The kitchens are now well supplied, but inherit the skills of a frugal past. Much of the high land was depopulated in the past, its people supplying the tinkers, beggars, chimney sweeps and shoemakers that roamed over France. A famous figure, in legend and fact, was the *bougnat*, the itinerant coal merchant, who took his wares from the coal seams about Clermont-Ferrand and then roamed far and wide in search of customers.

Above all, perhaps, the characteristic of the region is a sense of the religious past. The route to Compostella[1] passed through here in the Middle Ages. Earlier, the Celts worshipped in hill groves and beside foaming streams. Roman shrines gave place to Christian churches. Magical rocks cured fevers and bad luck. The famous natural bridges, or *ponts*, excavated by fast-flowing streams, seem to be the entrances to a dim paradise or a dimmer Hades.

In the kitchens of valley or mountain-slope mystery ends and wholesome common sense prevails. Herbs do not hang in profusion, but perhaps lie in a box in the corner. Sage, thyme and bay leaf come into their own. The onion and the shallot give flavour and body. South of the Loire garlic is used, but this flavour gradually disappears as we go north.

MEAT PIES

But perhaps mystery does lurk under the golden crusts of *tourte*, *chausson*, and *pâté*. In this region meat, fish and fruit are gently protected from the heat of the oven by crusts. Under those crusts, what lies in store for humans made hungry in the clear air of the *Massif Central*? Winter in the area can be rugged, and for most of the year there is a freshness in the air. Pies are hot and full of nourishment. Let us also look at the making of the pastry, so important to this type of dish.

The technique is the same as for shortcrust pastry (see page 24). Use two parts of flour to one part of fat. For example 1 lb. (3 cups) plain flour would need ½ lb. (1 cup) of butter or margarine. Salt the mixture well and use water very sparingly to mix. Roll into a ball and cover with a cloth. Pastry does improve if left to rest for an hour.

Now for the filling. However tender the cut of meat on your kitchen table, it will take some time to cook. Beef fillet for example will take about an hour. Pie pastry takes about ½ an hour in a hot oven. Hence the difficulty.

Why not take the short cut that many French cooks take? Cook the meat separately then cover with the crust.

BEEF STEAK PIE

4–5 servings:

1½ **lb. stewing steak**	*bouquet garni*
1 **cup red wine**	1 **tablespoon (1¼) flour**
8 **small onions**	**stock**
½ **lb. carrots**	**salt and pepper**

The simplest *pâté de viande* is perhaps one filled with beef. Trim the meat carefully, leaving no fat or sinew. Chuck steak is a good cut for this but any stewing steak will do. Cut the meat into small chunks and sear all over in dripping. Put into a large pot. Mix the juices from the frying pan with a little red wine and pour over the meat. Add small whole onions, sliced carrot, and a *bouquet garni* of celery, bay leaf, thyme and parsley.

[1] One of the most famous pilgrimages of the Middle Ages was made to the tomb of Sant Iago (St. James, patron saint of Spain) at the Spanish city of Compostela (English Compostella).

Heat together in the pot, and sprinkle over them a tablespoon (1¼) of flour. Cook for a few minutes. Add stock or water to cover, and salt and pepper to taste. Cover, and simmer until the meat is cooked. Try with a fork. The time of cooking will vary tremendously from just under an hour for fillet to, perhaps, three hours for skirt.

Divide the pastry in two, and roll one part into a long wide strip. Smear butter round a pie dish and line the sides and the rim with the pastry. The bottom of the dish is left uncovered.

After the beef has cooled, remove the *bouquet garni* and pour the stew into the dish. Roll out the rest of the pastry and cover the pie. The rim should be moistened to get a good join. Score the edge with the back of a knife. Brush the top with beaten egg yolk and milk, and bake in a moderately hot oven (mark 6; 400°F.) until the pastry is golden brown. After ten minutes you will find that the air trapped in the tart has expanded and blown up the pastry top. Stab the top several times with a sharp knife to let the air escape (or if you prefer, make a hole in the pastry before cooking).

TOURTE FROM THE ARDÈCHE

The traditional pie of the Ardèche or the Cantal is called a *tourte* and has a pork, veal and ham filling.

4–5 servings:

½ lb. pork	nutmeg
½ lb. veal	mixed spice
¼ lb. ham	sage
1 shallot	parsley
1 clove of garlic, crushed	knob of butter
1 glass white wine	1 lb. puff pastry (see page 72)

Mince the meats together, making sure they are well mixed. Chop the shallot finely and soften in the butter. Add the wine and herbs to the shallots. Simmer gently for 5 minutes. Mix them into the minced meat. Add salt and pepper to taste. Divide the pastry. Roll half into a round and cover with meat, leaving the edge free. Roll out the other half and cover the meat. Trim, and press the edges together. Bake in a hot oven (mark 7; 425°F.). The meat will take at least 40 minutes to cook. After ½ an hour, cover the pastry with a circle of foil. Leave for 15 minutes to allow the meat to cook. Remove the foil and brown the top of the pastry.

This type of pie may be eaten hot or cold and will fit very nicely into a simple menu, as you would not need a starchy vegetable with the thick pastry.

MENU

TOURTE DE VIANDES CHAUDE	HOT MEAT PASTY
CHOU-FLEURS AU GRATIN	CAULIFLOWER AU GRATIN
SALADE	SALAD
FROMAGES	CHEESE
PURÉE DE POMMES	APPLE PURÉE

CAULIFLOWER AU GRATIN. Trim the cauliflower, leaving an edge of green leaves. Divide into portions, and cook in salt water until tender. Leave a certain crispness in the vegetable. Cover with béchamel sauce thinned with some of the cauliflower stock. Dot with butter and brown in the oven.

SALAD. Crisp lettuce or frizzy endive could make the salad. But remember to try tender young leaves of vegetables such as spinach, beet, or broccoli. Olive oil is normally used for dressing, but experiment with other oils. Walnut oil is much used in the Cantal. Rich solid Cantal cheese, and fragrant blue cheese from the Auvergne, could be on the cheese board.

APPLE PURÉE. A purée made from apples is the easiest of sweets to make. Well presented it can rise from the prosaic to the special. Peal and trim the apples. Cut into slices. Cook gently with sugar, a slice of lemon, and very little water – a quarter of the volume of the apples in the pan will be ample. When soft, mash roughly in the pan. Turn out and leave to cool in a dish. Powder with cinnamon and serve with whipped cream.

Such a meal could be enjoyed with a dry white wine from the Allier, *Saint-Pourçain* There are no great wines in this area, but there are good honest table wines. The Puy-de-Dôme, the Allier and the Haute-Loire are the main areas of production. Anywhere that the vine can grow, country people grow it and enjoy wine from the grapes.

MENU

Madame Dupont had not prepared a special dinner for some time. The fact that her son, Paul, was coming home on leave from the naval air base at Hyères, in the Var, and bringing a friend with him, was a sufficient excuse. She did not like Serge very much; 'But he certainly knows how to eat', laughingly remarked her husband, Guy.

So the dinner was arranged. Cècile, the Duponts' daughter, and her husband lived in Le Puy, which was only a few kilometres away, and Francis loved Madame's food.

6 servings:

SOUPE À L'ONION	ONION SOUP
MOUSSE DE SAUMON	SALMON MOUSSE
CARRÉ D'AGNEAU, FLAGEOLETS VERTS	LOIN OF LAMB WITH KIDNEY BEANS
SALADE	SALAD
FROMAGES	CHEESE
PÂTE DE FRUITS	FRUIT PIE

ONION SOUP. Every region of France has its own type of onion soup. This variety is very easy to make. Madame sliced onions finely, and gently cooked them in beef dripping, stirring in a sprinkling of flour when they were transparent. She salted them well, and added crushed garlic and freshly ground white pepper. She stirred in some water as the flour cooked and thickened, added more water, checked the salt, and left the soup to simmer for 20 minutes. It was then poured onto bread dried in the oven and sprinkled with grated Cantal cheese, a few minutes before serving.

SALMON MOUSSE.   Marianne Dupont used the next dish a lot because she could buy odd pieces and heads of salmon. Even in this region where salmon is fished, the great fish is expensive.

1 lb. of salmon	**salt, pepper**
whites of 2 eggs	**juice of ½ lemon**
½ pint (1¼ cups) thick (heavy) cream	**mixed spice**

Fillet the fish, chop and pound it down finely. Add the egg whites a little at a time. Add the spice, lemon juice, and seasoning. Fill a mould three-quarters full of the mixture and poach, standing in water, in a moderate oven (mark 4; 350°F.) for 30 minutes. Turn out while still warm, and chill. Serve with lemon slices and sprigs of fresh parsley.

KIDNEY BEANS.   The soup and mousse were made long before the dinner. Madame's first job then was to take the beans that had been soaking for an hour and simmer them in salted water, with sliced carrot, and a large onion studded with cloves. When cooked, after three hours, she decided to mash them and make a purée with butter and cream.

LOIN OF LAMB.   The carré is best end of lamb. The job of sawing through the ribs belonged to M. Dupont. He laid the fat side of the meat on the board, and trimmed off the ends of the ribs, leaving compact chops. The chops are not separated for this dish. He cut pouches in the fat and pressed in cloves of garlic. The joint was then sprinkled with thyme and parsley, well salted, and roasted in the oven. They had half a small loin of lamb for six people, and it took 1¼ hours to roast in a hot oven (mark 7; 425°F.). To serve, M. Dupont chopped the roast loin into small joints of about three chops each person.

FRUIT PIE.   The fruit pie was put into the oven just as they sat down to the soup. Cécile, the Duponts' daughter, enjoyed preparing the fruit and making the pastry. She always made an ordinary tart pastry (see page 24). Her father enjoyed her pastry very much, but refrained from telling her mother so.

½ lb. shortcrust pastry	**slices of lemon**
3 lb. stoned plums	*for coating:*
sugar	**beaten egg**

She took a small piece from the pastry and rolled out a strip for the top of the pie dish. The plums were placed in the dish, with plenty of sugar, and the slices of lemon. ½ cup of water was added to start the fruit cooking. She rolled out the rest of the pastry and used it to cover the pie. The beaten egg coating made a beautiful golden top surface. She cooked the pie in a fairly hot oven (mark 6; 400°F.) for ½ an hour.

It is difficult to lay down the weight of fruit needed. The important thing is to fill the pie dish. Remember to prick the top crust several times to let out trapped air. Any quick cooking fruit – apples, plums, damsons, pears – can be used. Small fruit, strawberries, blackcurrants and loganberries, are best presented in an open tart.

Serge Coutet was spoilt by his mother in Paris. She had someone to cook for her, and they ate as one would in a fine restaurant. But he had to admit that he enjoyed the country dishes prepared by Madame Dupont better than anything he had ever tried before. The fresh wines of the region helped, a white from Saint Pourçain and a red from Brioude, remarkably like Beaujolais, served at cellar temperature, about 14°C (57°F.). The friendly conversation, with a *marc*[1] from the country and strong black coffee, rounded off a perfect evening.

SALMON PIE

Later Cécile asked about fish pies. Paul suggested that the fish should be cooked in a boat on Lake Issarles. Serge wanted to set forth there and then. This was the more practical method suggested by Madame.

$\frac{1}{2}$ **lb. salmon**	**pepper and salt**
$\frac{1}{4}$ **pint ($\frac{3}{4}$ cup) cream**	**lemon juice**
whites of 2 eggs	**1 lb. shortcrust pastry** (see page 24)

Bone the salmon. Chop and mash it with the cream, egg-whites, pepper, salt and lemon juice. Line a tart tin with the pastry and fill it with the fish paste. Lay slices of freshly sliced salmon on top, and thinly sliced mushrooms tossed in a little hot oil. Cover with pastry, and press down the edges. Coat with beaten egg and prick the top with a sharp knife. Bake in a hot oven (mark 7; 425°F.) until the pastry is brown; about half an hour.

POACHED SALMON. 'Seems a waste of good salmon to me', remarked M. Dupont. As far as he was concerned salmon should be simmered in a *court bouillon* (see page 30) for ten minutes to the pound. Then it should be drained, dried with a soft cloth, and eaten at once. By the way, always start with *bouillon* cold and heat it up slowly. Give a slice from the thick end and a slice from the tail end for each portion.

MENU

The two boys on leave made a bet that they were to rue the following day. 'Men are the best cooks so we'll cook the lunch tomorrow'. This was greeted with the howl of derision that it deserved.

Madame Dupont decided that she would be the chef, while they did the work. All her brothers (there were five of them) had had to give a hand with the cooking at home, and they all ended up by enjoying it. This was the menu she thought out for them, remembering that neither had ever cooked before.

6 servings:

OEUFS AU FROMAGE	EGGS IN CHEESE
STEAK, SAUCE AU VIN ROUGE	STEAK WITH RED WINE
TRUFFADE	HOT POT
SALADE	SALAD
FROMAGES	CHEESE
FRUITS	FRUIT

[1] Spirit made from the skins left in the press after the wine has been extracted.

Lunch was at twelve and the 'chef' started them at 11.15 with the *truffade*. Whatever they were to cook Madame made them put everything on the table to start with.

TRUFFADE (Hot Pot)

potatoes	**pepper**
onions	**salt**
bacon	**tomatoes**
oil	

They peeled the potatoes, sliced the onions, chopped the bacon and skinned the tomatoes. The potatoes were kept in salted water until needed. Serge heated some oil in the pan while Paul cut up the potatoes, making about ¼-inch cubes. These were slid into the hot fat and left to sizzle. 'Turn them now and again to brown all sides'. When the potato cubes were brown, they added the slices of onion, then the bacon. Salt and pepper came next, and then the tomatoes, roughly chopped, were added to the pan. The oven dish had been heated, with a little oil, in the fairly hot oven (mark 5; 375°F.) and the potato mixture was poured into this. At 11.45 they closed the oven door on the *truffade*, which would cook for 30 minutes.

The pan was cleared by pouring a little wine into it, swilling round and emptying into a bowl. 'We can use that for the steaks'. Serge meanwhile was washing and drying the lettuce. He made a vinaigrette dressing and tossed the lettuce. 'You should leave that till the last moment, but the lettuce is very crisp so it does not matter too much'. He laid the cheeses on a plate: Cantal, and cream cheese mixed with parsley and garlic. Cécile kindly laid the table for them while they prepared the first dish.

OEUFS AU FROMAGE

12 eggs	**six tablespoons (full ⅓ cup) of cream**
¼ lb. Cantal cheese, grated	**pepper and salt**

They separated the eggs by juggling the yolk and white back and forth between the two halves of the shell. Each shell was left with its yolk inside, and placed in one of the depressions of an egg carton. So they had the whites in the mixing bowl and twelve half shells containing yolks in the egg carton. Serge whipped the whites until solid with a rotary whisk, adding some salt at the same time. These beaten whites were put into an oiled oven dish. Paul was shown how to make 12 depressions in this thick white preparation with the back of the spoon. Into each depression was placed the yolk of an egg. The grated cheese went over the top of the dish, and then the cream, a spoonful at a time. Into the fairly hot oven (mark 5; 375°F.) went the eggs, to join the potatoes, and the kitchen team was ready.

STEAKS WITH RED WINE. The eggs took ten minutes and the dish was put on the table at 12.10 – not bad for beginners. The steaks could not be cooked until the first dish was eaten. They were cut from a sirloin of Charollais beef. This area of excellent beef is to the north of our region. Paul had trimmed them and laid the six portions on a plate. To cook the steaks he used very little oil in a large frying pan. The pan was steaming when the steaks went in and one surface was immediately seared. Three minutes on one side, then three minutes on the other, and the steaks were still red inside. Paul set them to keep warm. He added a small glass of red wine to the pan, a large knob of butter and a sprinkle of fresh thyme. His mother reminded him of the juice they had collected from the potatoes. He served the steaks on a large warm serving dish with some of the potatoes along one edge.

They all admitted that it was a good meal and the boys were both given the rank of 'chef-assistant'. Serge, who had never lifted a hand to help his mother, felt very proud of the meal and was eager to learn other kitchen secrets. 'We can entertain our friends in Hyères', he suggested to Paul. Madame Dupont presented him with a notebook and they wrote down a few recipes.

Cécile suggested that they began with a starter, a main dish, and a following dish.

OMELETTE DE LA RÉGION

3 servings:

4 whole eggs
2 yolks of egg
2 tablespoons (2½) cooked bacon, chopped

2 tablespoons (2½) cold potato, sliced
1 tablespoon (1¼) cream cheese
1 tablespoon (1¼) thick (heavy) cream

Start to make an omelet (see page 23). To improve its texture, try Madame Dupont's trick. Put aside the whites from a third of the eggs. For example, a six egg omelet will have 4 whole eggs and two yolks. Draw the omelet up in the pan so that it is thick, and sprinkle over it chopped cooked bacon, finely sliced cold potato, cream cheese and thick cream. Remember you must have at least two eggs per person. A wedge of this filling omelet will do as a starter, or a large piece as a main course.

COQUELET

6 servings:

3 small cockerels or 6 spring chickens
½ lb. cold meat, minced, or pork sausage meat
1 medium onion, finely chopped
½ tablespoon chopped mixed herbs
salt and pepper

1 cup breadcrumbs
yolks of 2 eggs
butter and oil
1 glass wine
3 tablespoons (4) cream

Small cockerels, or spring chickens, like most poultry cooked whole, are generally stuffed. Any minced cold meat will do (or pork sausage meat) mixed with finely chopped onions, herbs, pepper and salt, breadcrumbs and the yolk of an egg. The stuffing for four individual chickens can be bound by one egg. Stuff the birds, and truss the legs together to keep the stuffing in the body. Use an iron cocotte or a thick pan and gently fry the birds in butter and oil. After 20 minutes add small whole onions to the pan. Cook until the birds are tender. Serve with the onions and some peas. Put the chickens on a hot serving dish and add a glass of wine to the pan. When this foams up, add butter, cook for one minute, and add cream. Allow the cream to thicken, and pour over the vegetables.

CROÛTES AUX MORILLES

2 servings:

½ lb. morels	¼ pint (¾ cup) milk or cream
2 tablespoons (2½) butter	salt and pepper
1 tablespoon (1¼) flour	2 slices of bread

Morels are like black pointed mushrooms, with a honeycomb cap. They grow in mountainous country. (You can use mushrooms for this dish). Simmer the morels in butter. When just cooked, remove them from the pan. Sprinkle flour on the melted butter and mushroom juices and stir so that it absorbs the juice. Thin with milk or cream. Add pepper and salt and the yolk of an egg. Fry slices of bread in butter. Place the morels on the fried bread and pour the sauce on top. This dish could be used as a starter, or eaten as a separate vegetable, particularly after pork or veal.

CHAUSSON

This is simply a pastry turnover, for which you can use shortcrust pastry. Apple turnovers make a wholesome sweet. Cook the fruit as for the *purée de pommes* (see page 110). Roll the pastry thinly and cut into circles about 5 inches across. Damp the edges of the pastry and put a large spoonful of apple on half the circle. Fold over the pastry to cover the filling and crimp the edges. Brush with beaten egg, and bake in a hot oven (mark 7; 425°F.) until the pastry is golden. Serve with a red jam.

FRIANDS (Savory meat rolls)

This makes a good snack for a picnic. Make puff pastry (see page 72), roll out, and cut into strips about three inches wide. Mash sausage meat with chopped parsley and sage, pepper and salt. Place a spoonful of this stuffing on the end of one strip of pastry, roll over once, and cut out the edge of the roll. Damp the edges before crimping together and brush with beaten egg. Continue up the strip of pastry. Bake these savoury meat rolls in a fairly hot oven (mark 5; 375°F.) for 20 minutes.

Paul and Serge went back from leave vowing to try these dishes on their friends. 'I wonder how long the kitchen craze will last', said M. Dupont. It did last. After a year, the two friends had increased their repertoire and were seriously thinking of opening a restaurant when their National Service was at an end. 'Why don't you visit your godmother in Lyon? She is a wonderful cook. Her father was a chef, and M. Bentley is in the wine trade. You might learn something about wine as well'.

They took Madame's advice and during their last leave before demobilisation borrowed Francis' old Renault and chugged off from Le Puy to Lyon. Serge had never seen Vivarais, so they went south to Monastier and over the ridge of the mountains. The descent to Lamastre was incredibly beautiful, and hair-raising, as someone seemed to have forgotten to put walls to the roads.

Louise Bentley, like all godmothers and godfathers in France, took her responsibilities very seriously indeed. She took it for granted that Paul should ask her advice about his future, and had many a serious discussion with her husband Emile on this subject.

'Restaurant indeed! With his *baccalauriat* he should go to the *Faculté*'. 'To study what?' replied her husband good-naturedly. 'There are far too many students in the Arts Section. He could teach, but he must have the vocation'. Emile Bentley's experiences during the war as a prisoner had given him a respect for his fellow men and a disrespect for outward show. He always claimed that he inherited this from his English forbears.

To greet her godson and his friend, Louise prepared a feast. Emile Bentley saw to the wine. 'Lyon means Beaujolais, so Beaujolais we shall drink!'

MENU

HORS D'OEUVRE	HORS D'OEUVRE
QUENELLES DE BROCHET	PIKE QUENELLES
BRAYAUDE DE MOUTON	BOILED LEG OF MUTTON
POMMES LYONNAISE	LYONNAISE POTATOES
CARDON AU GRATIN	GRILLED CARDOONS
SALADE	SALAD
FROMAGES	CHEESE
MILLIARD DE CÉRISES	CHERRIES FRIED IN BATTER

This was a very special feast, with many dishes, but even so Madame Bentley was only occupied in the kitchen for any time at all with the *quenelles* and the *milliards*. The hors d'oeuvre were cooked the day before, and by themselves would have made a very respectable cold table for a lunch or a supper; or a birthday party or anniversary. They consisted of: a *pâté en croûte*; *saucisson et cervelas*; *oeufs durs mayonnaise rouge*; *coeurs d'artichaux farcis*; and *tomates en salade*. A regal table.

PÂTÉ EN CROÛTE (Pâté pie)

2 lb. chicken livers	**garlic**
¾ lb. steaky bacon	**black pepper**
½ lb. sausage meat	**1 lb. shortcrust pastry**

Line the casserole with bacon, well trimmed and with all the rind removed. Fill with the livers. Spread the top with the sausage meat, the rest of the bacon, and the rinds. Press a large piece of garlic into the pâté. Grind plenty of black pepper over it. Cover with the lid of the casserole and cook in a warm oven (mark 3; 325°F.) for 3 hours. When cooked, remove the bacon rinds and mash the pâté finely; then cool. Make up the pastry (see page 24) but mix with hot water. Roll into a ball and leave for one hour. Roll out to about ¼-inch thickness, and line a large, oblong metal cake tin. Press down well into the corners and trim at the rim. Leave an overhang of pastry on each side. Fill the pastry crust with the cool pâté. Roll out some pastry for the top. Cover the pâté, trim, and pinch the edges. Brush with egg and use the trims of pastry to make a leaf design on top. Bake in a fairly hot oven (mark 6; 400°F.) until the pastry is golden. Leave to cool, and turn out. If you have any of the liver mixture left, press it into a bowl and serve as a terrine. You could mix a few chopped gherkins into the terrine.

SAUCISSON ET CERVELAS. Lyon dry *saucisson* is made in a similar way to the *saucisson* of the Dauphiné (see page 92). Cervelas was originally made of brains, but is now made of pork. It is bought for the home. Only the most adept cook would attempt to make it. Very often red pimento is added for colour and the *saucisson* is dried quickly over the stove to redden the skin. Madame Bentley took the skin from the *cervelas*, sliced it finely and mixed it with chopped gherkins. She then added a few spoonfulls of vinaigrette. The dry *saucisson* was sliced wafter thin.

OEUFS DURS, MAYONNAISE ROUGE. Hard boiled eggs with mayonnaise (see page 85) but with a little variation. Make the mayonnaise, and redden it with tomato purée. Add a little cayenne pepper. Cover the halved eggs with the sauce, and sprinkle paprika over them.

COEURS D'ARTICHAUX FARCIS (Stuffed artichoke hearts). Cook artichokes (see page 73) and cut out the hearts. Cook some rice, drain it, and mix with some mayonnaise and chopped parsley. Stuff the hearts with this mixture and sprinkle some chopped anchovy fillets on top.

TOMATES EN SALADE. (Tomato salad). Slice tomatoes with a sharp knife. Serve sprinkled with fine chopped onions, parsley and vinaigrette.

PIKE QUENELLES. For this dish use a whole pike, or a large piece of pike according to the size of the fish. Simmer in a *court bouillon*. Take out when cooked, skin, and remove the bones. Mash finely with a fork or pass through an electric blender. Weigh the minced fish. Make a pâte à choux (see page 37), and mix equal quantities of the pâte and the fish. Add salt, pepper and grated nutmeg. (This mixture will cook well in boiling salted water, but may be lightened by adding two whole eggs and two egg whites). Form the mixture, when cool, into cylinders about 2 inches long, and roll these in flour on a plate. Drop them into boiling salted water, or the stock from the fish, and simmer.

When the quenelles rise to the surface, leave them for a further three minutes, then drain, and keep them warm. Coat with a thin white sauce made with the fish stock, and sprinkle with grated cheese.

BOILED LEG OF MUTTON. This was in honour of Paul's parents because it is a dish of the *Massif Central*.

Take a large leg of lamb and cut out the bone at the top, the pelvis bone. This will enable you to carve more easily when the joint is cooked. Tie the leg round firmly with twine. Stud with garlic pieces to your own taste. Six cloves will flavour the meat well. Pour oil into a large pot, heat to steaming, and brown the leg in it. Lower the heat and add plenty of chopped carrot, onion, pepper and salt. Stir so that the vegetables absorb the oil. Add a *bouquet garni*. Cover with cold water. Check the salt. Simmer for two hours, or until the joint is cooked. Serve with red beans cooked like the *flageolets* of the *Massif* (see page 111).

LYONNAISE POTATOES. Peel potatoes and cut them into cubes. Sauté in hot oil, and when nearly cooked add plenty of sliced onion. Keep in the oven until needed. Do not add the onions until the last possible minute, otherwise they will colour and burn.

GRILLED CARDOONS. Cook cardoon until tender (see page 103). Lay in a heat-proof dish, cover with a thin béchamel, sprinkle with grated cheese, and brown in the oven or under the grill.

SALAD. For the salad Madame Bentley took firm lettuces, trimmed them and cut them into quarters. She washed them well, and drained by swinging the quarters round in a cloth. They were laid in a flat dish undressed. (The dressing was served separately).

CHEESES. Picodon cream cheese mixed with softened butter and chives, cervelle de Canut (a white, mild cheese from Lyon), and a ripe Camembert.

CHERRIES FRIED IN BATTER. This is a very simple sweet but most impressive. Serge was bursting to know the recipe. Again, it is to be found to the west of Lyon.

4 oz. (¾ cup) flour　　　　　　　　**1 egg**
1 oz. (2 tablespoons) butter　　　**about ½ pint (1¼ cups) of milk**
pinch of salt　　　　　　　　　　**large, ripe cherries**

To make a frying batter rub the butter, softened, into the flour and add the salt. Beat the egg into the mixture and add milk a little at a time, until the batter is thick enough to coat the back of a spoon. Leave to rest for an hour.

Carefully stone large ripe cherries. Coat with the batter and drop into deep, steaming oil. They soon rise to the surface. Madame turned them with a spoon to make sure they were brown all over. She drained them and arranged them on white kitchen paper. Sifted with sugar, they melted in the mouth.

M. Bentley chose white and red Beaujolais for the feast. For the cheese he was tempted, and succombed to a Fleury. This is one of the finer of the Beaujolais wines, he informed them. The fresh keen white wine underlined the softness and rich fishiness of the *quenelles*. The red served quite cool – the cool of the cellar not of ice – bit deep into the tender lamb. The Fleury? Paul could not describe the effect; but noticed that while drinking the wine he seemed to get the full flavour of the cheeses.

Conversation after the dinner naturally turned to the boys' plans for a restaurant. The Bentleys had invited two friends who had been in the restaurant business in Burgundy; Monsieur Grasset had trained in a great hotel in Vichy and there met his wife, Marianne, who was in service.

The two had bid farewell to the 'great palace', and had taken a small farmhouse restaurant not far from Macon. The money was good, but the worry and hard work proved too much for them. Hercule Grasset now worked with M. Bentley as a transport manager for the wine company. 'What a relief to say goodbye to all that worry and let someone else do the worrying for me'.

Paul and Serge recognised Madame Bentley's tactics and steered the conversation away from taxes, credit and loans, to kitchens, sauces and soufflés. Madame Grasset had lots of ideas about cooking. Here are some of them.

BETTERAVE

Cold beetroot, sliced and dressed with vinaigrette, makes a good addition to the hors d'oeuvre. Bake the beetroots in a hot oven (mark 7; 425°F.) until they give to the touch. Skin them, and cook in salted water until tender.

RAMEQUIN (Cheese soufflé)

Make a béchamel sauce (see page 95). Enrich this with 1 egg-yolk for every two people. Add grated cheese – Gruyère is a good cheese for this – until the mixture tastes very cheesy. Beat the egg-whites solid and fold into the cheese sauce. Bake in a moderate oven (mark 4: 350°F.) for 15 minutes in individual dishes. Serve hot.

RAVIOLI

This is usually easily obtainable, but why not make up your own? Make shortcrust pastry with 8 oz. (1½ cups) flour (see page 24). Halve the pastry and roll both halves out as thinly as possible. Use chopped, cooked, chicken, pork or veal as a filling. Make a little thickening in a saucepan; 1 oz. (3 tablespoons) flour to 1 oz. (2 tablespoons) butter, thinned with milk and/or stock. To this thickening add the meat, with chopped parsley, pepper and salt. Place spoonfuls of the mixture on to one layer of pastry. Moisten with milk the spaces between the meat, and the edges. Cover with the second layer of pastry and press the edges, and the spaces between the meat. Cut with a sharp knife into the squares so made.

Drop each piece of ravioli into boiling salted water, and simmer for 15 minutes. Serve with grated cheese and a sauce. Fresh tomato sauce would do very well, but Madame Grasset had a very good idea for ravioli with a chicken filling. She used a shrimp sauce and this is her recipe:

SHRIMP SAUCE. Make white sauce with a fish stock made from fish heads and tails simmered for 15 minutes in salted water, with sliced carrot, onion and a *bouquet garni* with fennel. Crush 2 oz. shelled shrimps with 2 cooked egg-yolks. Flavour with cayenne pepper. Mix into the white sauce.

POISSON EN PAPILLOTTES (Fish cooked in foil)

Again Madame Grasset had a new idea. 'I have always found making paper containers for the fish too difficult. Why not make them with kitchen foil? Oil a piece of foil large enough to envelop the fish. Lay the fish on it. Loosely fold over the foil, and turn the edges to seal. Cook in a hot oven. Leave the guests to remove the foil, which will have blown up in the oven. Trout is excellent cooked in this way. Remember to clean the fish carefully and to season well. A 6 oz. trout would take 20 minutes to cook by this method, in a hot oven (mark 7; 425°F.).

COQ, OR POULET, AU VIN (Chicken in red wine)

8 servings:

3½ lb. chicken	1 glass brandy (optional)
butter and oil	thyme, bayleaf, parsley and garlic
2 medium carrots	2 tablespoons (2½) flour
1 onion *or* 4 shallots	1 glass red wine
¾ lb. mushrooms	

They had wonderful young cockerels to make this dish in Lyon, but you might use any chicken.

Cut the chicken into pieces. A 3½ lb. bird would make 8 portions. Cut the leg from each side. If you cut down the groins you will sever cartilage and not bone. Sever the legs from the thighs. Cut along the breast-bone and divide the breast into two, then cut each part in half. Brown the pieces in a frying pan, using a mixture of butter and oil. While the chicken is frying, add finely chopped carrot, shallot or onion, and ½ lb. mushrooms, also some diced bacon. Transfer to a casserole and cook gently until the chicken is nearly done. If you are lucky enough to have some, pour in a glass of brandy, ignite and immediately blow the flame out. Add chopped thyme, bayleaf, parsley and garlic. Sprinkle with flour, and cook for five minutes. Add red wine, and cook until the chicken is tender.

Toss ¼ lb. whole button mushrooms in hot oil. Take the tender chicken pieces from the vegetables and sauce. Place in a dish, with the vegetables and mushrooms round. Check the seasoning of the sauce, and thicken with the blood of the chicken if you have it. Pour the sauce over the chicken and vegetables.

GRAS DOUBLE (Tripe and onions)

2 lb. tripe	pepper
2 large onions, sliced	salt
oil	wine vinegar
butter	chopped parsley

Tripe is usually very well prepared by the butcher. *Triperies* in France often have it on display in tanks washed by running water. Soak the tripe for an hour in salted water, drain, and dry with a cloth. Cut into strips about 1 inch wide and boil in salted water until tender, about 1¼ hours. Drain, and fry in the oil and butter, until brown.

Cook the onion slices in a separate pan until transparent. Add the cooked tripe. Sprinkle with wine vinegar and mix thoroughly. Sprinkle with parsley before serving.

CAPILOTADE

This is a very good way of using up cold meat left-overs. Soften chopped onion, shallot and mushrooms in oil and butter. When cooked, sprinkle over 1 tablespoon ($1\frac{1}{4}$) of flour. Cook for a minute. Add white wine and water, pepper, salt and fresh tomato paste (see page 53). Sprinkle into this mixture the cold meat, chopped up; stir and heat. Serve in a circle of rice.

MARRONS (Chestnuts)

Take two pounds of sweet chestnuts. Make a cross cut at the end of each nut with a small knife. Put on a baking tray in a hot oven (mark 7; 425°F.) until the skins crack. Cool, and remove the shells and the husks, and trim well. Boil in water until soft. Crush and then mash. Work in 4 oz. ($\frac{1}{2}$ cup) butter, one egg yolk, and a glass of rum. Oil small moulds and fill with the mixture. Cool, and turn out before serving.

'Just think! With these dishes, and only a few more alternatives, you could start your small restaurant'. Madame Gresset, much to Louise's horror, actually seemed to be supporting the boys' crazy idea! Champagne kept them going marvellously. The discussion went on late into the night.

They all agreed that the Lyon area would be the last place to start a restaurant. 'Your father's region South of Le Puy would be ideal for a small place. Even into the Lot. More and more tourists are going to that area to seek quiet and rest. The government is giving grants to encourage business. You might get some help to renovate a cottage, to make a small restaurant'.

'I've a good mind to go and help them for the first few months!' Like many people in France, Madame Bentley loved preparing food, and the whole idea was beginning to appeal to her. The thought of earning a living doing what we love is the dream of most of us. Still, cooking for a captive audience is not the same as cooking for a public only too ready to criticise, and who may not like half the dishes you prepare.

Burgundy

Burgundy means great wine to the world; but there is another world in Burgundy. Between Dijon and Beaune, vineyards that bear the greatest names in wine crowd in upon one another. Here the wonderful country description of drinking Burgundy holds good: 'when you drink fine wine it's as if the Good Lord were going down your throat with velvet breeches on!'

After the *Hospices de Beaune* introduced the world to the great wines of this region, the *Côtes* increased wine production, while the other parts of the region turned to mixed farming and animal husbandry. This is an area of good soils and a mild climate. It is made up of the valley of the Saone and the plateaux that lie between the Jura to the east and the *Massif Central* to the west.

The centre of the area, the Saone valley, consists in fact of a series of broad valleys separated by hills, the *Côtes*. Away from the main vineyards, cattle graze in lush pastures. Fields of wheat and oats show golden in the late sun of August. Maize is important for animal fodder, and fruit trees bring their harvest to the kitchen.

To the east, the countryside begins to climb towards the Jura mountains. Green lakes nestle into natural hollows between rocky slopes. On the good volcanic soils of the *Doubs* cattle fatten on high pastures. Forests provide game. When we add the fish of the rivers, it seems superfluous to say that the Burgundy is a land of plenty. No wonder people like the Graf family came to the area, to evolve an industry out of the dairy products, and the pigs that are still in plentiful supply.

Man has eaten well here for centuries. The tables of the Dukes of Burgundy foreshadowed the famous *haute cuisine* of France. Their palace at Dijon still stands, under its pointed roofs, among the industry that came with the railroad. The cooking of the ordinary folk lives on wherever people take the trouble to make good dishes.

All over Burgundy people cook well. A good kitchen needs hard work, good planning and imagination, and imagination is well to the fore in this region. Who else would have thought of cooking a frog's legs, and snails in their shells? New ideas from north, south, east and west have always come easily into Burgundy. It is the very hub of the routes from Paris and the north to the Mediterranean. Rivers have cut valleys from the east and opened up routes to the Rhine. The *Canal de Bourgogne* eases the way. The *Massif*

Central has disgorged its peasantry over the short descent, onto the Burgundian plain.

As in all areas where people work hard, we look for good, plain, rich dishes that nourish and sustain. Here, as well as this type of cooking, we may expect imaginative use of products, and unexpected dishes. These last are not for every day, but experiences for special occasions. Basically they are still simple dishes, but a good deal of work has to go on before the final product is accomplished.

Wine will be used in our Burgundy kitchen, naturally; it is used lavishly in the region. If you have not a bottle of good Beaune in which to cook 3 lb. of beef, try cooking with ordinary stock or water, and adding a glass of good wine just before you serve. This is the way to make the most of wine flavour. After all, if you can make your guests think that you have cooked it all in wine, you will have achieved a certain success before you start!

It is always useful to have a substitute for bread. In Burgundy the substitute is a flat, biscuity type of cake, cooked on a griddle. It was made, generally, with oatmeal; but as most of us have wheat flour, let us use that. The cake must be simple, so that you can do other things at the same time, and it must be quick to prepare.

GRIDDLE CAKE

8 oz. (1½ cups) plain flour
6 oz. (¾ cup) sugar
pinch of salt
2 oz. (4 tablespoons) softened butter

½ pint (1¼ cups) cream, whipped thick
yolk of 1 egg
tablespoon of milk

In a bowl, mix the flour, sugar, and salt. Rub in the butter. Add the cream and mix well, forming a ball of dough. Flour your board and roll out to ½ inch thickness. Brush with the yolk of egg, mixed with a little milk. Decorate with incised lines. Bake in a hot oven (mark 7; 425°F.) for 15 minutes. Serve while still warm with butter or jam. Or spread with cream cheese.

FLAMICHE (Leek tart)

One of the staple dishes of the area is the *flamiche*, a tart with a leek filling. (The original Flamiche was really a pie).

2 lb. of leeks
yolks of 3 eggs
1 lb. shortcrust pastry (see page 24)

oil and butter
salt and pepper

Cut all the green from the leeks. Make several cuts in the white from the top to the root. Don't sever completely. Soak for 10 minutes and wash well. Powdered earth tends to work from the green leaves into the root, hence this opening up of the white to wash all the dirt away. Heat some oil and butter in a pan and gently cook the leeks, whole or sliced in two, adding water as the cooking progresses. Line a tart tin with half the pastry, and fill with the leeks, mixed with the egg yolks. Season well. Cover the tart with the other half of the pastry and bake in a hot oven (mark 7; 425°F.) until the pastry is cooked; about ½ an hour.

Alternatively, you can bake pastry lined in the tart tin. (Remember to prick the pastry well and to sprinkle in a few white beans to stop it from bubbling up). Place the cooked leeks in the cooked pastry case and cover with a white sauce enriched with cream. Sprinkle grated cheese over the top and brown in a hot oven.

MENU

The covered Flamiche is the finer dish and would make a good main dish for a short menu that has no meat course.

SALADE PANACHÉE	MIXED SALAD
FLAMICHE	LEEK PIE
ÉPINARDS EN BRANCHE	WHOLE SPINACH
POIRES POCHÉES AU SIROP	PEARS POACHED IN SYRUP

MIXED SALAD. SPINACH.   Try sliced celery, radish, and cucumber salad. Toss in a bowl with a vinaigrette sauce. Tie the spinach in bunches after washing in three or four waters. Simmer with very little water and add a large knob of butter. Cut the bunches open before you serve.

PEARS POACHED IN SYRUP.   Pears are plentiful in Burgundy and they are often cooked in red wine. But let us suppose that our budget is limited and our wine is only to drink. Peel the pears and cut into two. Carefully take out the fibre and pips from the centre. Poach in well sugared water with half a lemon. Remove the pears when cooked; for ripe fruit this should be 15 minutes. Reduce the syrup until it will coat the back of a spoon. Remove from the heat and add $\frac{1}{2}$ a glass of dry white wine. Chill, and pour over the pears on serving.

BEEF COOKED IN RED WINE

Distinctive meat dishes are a feature of cooking in Burgundy. Let us imagine ourselves in this great wine region with some beef to cook.

We shall use chuck steak. You can use cheaper cuts for the dish but you will not get such good results. We have plenty of fresh thyme and parsley in the kitchen. Make a *bouquet garni*; bunch up parsley, thyme, bayleaf and two stalks of celery, and tie it with kitchen thread. (A large ball of strong thread is very useful in the kitchen).

Trim the meat well and cut into small steaks. Sear in a pan with some oil. Put in a large earthenware casserole with carrots cut in thick rounds, a few whole onions, not too large, and some chopped mushrooms, with their stalks. Mix together well, and add the *bouquet garni*. Sprinkle a good tablespoon of flour into the mixture, and turn several times. Just cover with red wine; but only just. Allow the wine to soak into the meat for several hours, and cook then in a cool oven (mark 1; 300°F.) for 2–3 hours, or until the meat is tender.

In the last hour of cooking add a handful of button mushrooms. The dish looks better if you drain the meat and put it into a deep serving dish. Sprinkle the cooked vegetables over the top and add some sauce. Reduce the sauce in a saucepan and check the flavouring. Add a glass of wine and serve in a sauce boat.

This dish should be cooked in red wine, but you could use a mixture of wine and water. If you can only use water, you still get a good beef casserole. Before serving, drain off some of the stock and heat quickly in a saucepan with a glass of red wine. Reduce by a half and add a large knob of butter. Pour over the meat and vegetables before serving. What a wonderful smell of wine!

POTÉE

Like the other regions of France, Burgundy has its version of the *potée*.

1 lb. piece of fat streaky bacon	½ lb. leeks, white only
3-4 lb. boiling pork, cut from the shoulder	2 lb. potatoes
	piece of celeriac *or* celery
1 firm cabbage, chopped	pepper, salt,
1 lb. carrots	garlic
½ lb. turnips	cloves
1 large onion	*bouquet garni*

Boil the bacon and the pork in plenty of water for 2 hours. Skim, and add the vegetables except potatoes; stick two cloves in the onion, before adding it to the pot. Add pepper, salt and garlic, and *bouquet garni*. Simmer for an hour or until the meat is tender. Put in the potatoes in the last half hour of cooking. Cook until the potatoes are ready. Check seasoning.

Serve the soup separately. Slice the meat, and serve with the vegetables.

Yveline Picot remembered her restaurant days with M. et Mme. Grasset with great pleasure. The couple had taken her, an orphan girl, into their home and trained her in the kitchen. After three years with them she could manage the cooking by herself and at the end, when M. Grasset was so ill, she had been *chef* for three months.

Now she was *gérante* of the same homely little place, not far from Macon. That is, she was in complete control and made any profits to be had. In return she paid a small rent every month to the Grassets. She was often sent customers by the jovial M. Grasset and he himself came to see her now and again when the transport of wine took him to Macon. But she had never been sent staff before!

Paul and Serge, whom we last met in Lyon, still wanted to have a restaurant. Madame Grasset thought it a good idea if they worked for a season in a small place similar to the one they had in mind. Her old restaurant, with that wonderful girl Yveline, was ideal.

Yveline and her husband Denis thought it a good idea as well. They were busy from June until October and sometimes later, depending on the hunting season. They were ready to expand the business a little, and the boys would fit in well, as they left the navy in June.

'Like your friends the Grassets, we plan to keep the restaurant like home. No 'great palace' stuff for us. We cook country dishes, and enjoy what we do'. 'Wonderful, that's just what we want ourselves'. Paul and Serge were overjoyed.

The Picots prepared a menu that they used for two or three days. The customers came for that menu, and did not expect anything else. Any violent dislikes could be catered for, as they had plenty of produce in the kitchen. It was just like cooking for a large family. Here we have the menu that Paul and Serge helped to prepare.

MENU

CRÈME DE VOLAILLE	CREAM OF CHICKEN SOUP
JAMBON PERSILLÉ	HAM AND PARSLEY MOULD
ESCARGOTS *ou* CARPE AU VIN BLANC	SNAILS *or* CARP IN WHITE WINE
SAUCE À LA DIABLE	SAUCE À LA DIABLE
POULET DE BRESSE SAUCE CRÉMEUSE	BRESSE CHICKEN WITH CREAM SAUCE
ou RÔTI DE BOEUF, SAUCE MOUTARDE	*or* ROAST BEEF WITH MUSTARD SAUCE
JARDINIÈRE DE LEGUMES	JARDINIERE OF VEGETABLES
SALADE	SALAD
FROMAGES DU PAYS	CHEESE
FRUITS *ou* RIGODON	FRUIT *or* RIGODON

One boy was to help in the kitchen, the other in the restaurant. But both helped with the preparations. 'The food will be as good as the preparation we put into it', Yveline told them.

CREAM OF CHICKEN SOUP.   Paul's first task was the *crème de volaille* soup.

old boiling hens	**bay leaf**
onions	**butter**
carrots	**flour**
thyme	**pepper and salt**
parsley	

He was shown how to clean the birds, by cutting the flesh just above the parson's nose and slipping his fingers round inside to free the guts. Very gently he pulled out the whole of the inside of the chicken. He pulled the heart and the windpipe out separately. The heart, liver and feed pouch, were put aside. He split the feed pouch and turned out the maize grains inside, washed them well and left them to soak in hot water. The cleaned hens were put into the vast stock pot together with onions, carrots, and the herbs tied together. The whole was well covered with water and boiled for two hours. Paul took out the birds, stripped the skin and took the meat from the bones.

You could keep the flesh in joints and keep it hot in the stock, with whole vegetables. In this way, you have *poule au pot*, a dinner dish in its own right. For the soup, however, Paul chopped the flesh and put it through a mincer. He melted the butter in a soup pot and sprinkled in flour until all the butter was absorbed. This he cooked for a few moments. Then a little at a time the strained stock was added to the butter and flour. Slowly the white sauce thinned and he was left, after adding all the stock, with a creamy white chicken soup to which he added the minced chicken.

Yveline checked the seasoning and just before serving whipped in some fresh cream. The giblets were simmered, and their stock added to the soup.

HAM AND PARSLEY MOULD.   Soak three pounds of smoked ham overnight. Drain, rinse, and cook for 1 hour in fresh boiling water. Simmer a knuckle of veal or pork with a calf's foot, onion, carrot and a *bouquet garni*. Season this stock, cover, and cook for an hour. Add a glass of dry white wine. Drain the stock and finish cooking the ham in it.

Drain the ham and remove all the skin, leaving a good layer of fat. Pass it through a mincer, or electric blender. Press the minced ham into a glass salad bowl.

Clarify the stock. This is an important process in the kitchen and both Serge and Paul were eager to see it done. Yveline first strained into a basin enough stock to form a ½-inch layer on top of the chopped ham. She cracked an egg-white into a pan and beat a little of the cooled stock with it. Over a low gas she slowly whipped in the rest of the stock that she needed. The pan was brought to the boil and left to stand. The egg white gradually rose to the top. This was skimmed off and the clear stock was strained off to cool.

When the stock was beginning to turn to jelly, finely chopped parsley, a little vinegar, and half a glass of white wine were mixed with it. The resulting jelly was poured on top of the ham and allowed to set.

There is a short cut that still gives a very presentable dish. Cook the ham right through with the herbs, vegetables and wine. Remove and mince the ham as before. Strain the stock. Add gelatine from a packet following the instructions given. Usually 1 oz. (3 envelopes) gelatine sets 1 pint (2½ cups) of stock. Allow to cool, whip in plenty of chopped parsley and pour over the ham as you would the natural jelly.

SNAILS.   The boys were fascinated by the idea of preparing snails for the table. 'Snails from tins are often used and as it is the butter that gives the overpowering flavour, they are quite successful. Let's start with the butter'.

Yveline whipped softened butter in a bowl and added chopped parsley, a tablespoon of very finely chopped shallot, pepper, salt and lemon juice, and plenty of crushed garlic. This preparation was well mixed together, and a knob of it was pushed into a clean snail shell. The snail was replaced on top of the savoury butter and the end was sealed with more butter. The snails were put in a medium oven for 15 minutes. 'But snails are much better when you cook them freshly yourself'.

Many snails in Europe are edible, but those most often used are about 1½ inches long, and yellowish, with broad black bands. An extra luxury from the vineyards are the snails that feed there. These are the best.

Choose snails that are hibernating. The opening to the shell is sealed with a hard substance. Remove this. Starve them for 5 to 6 days, sprinkling them with oatmeal. Wash well with salted water and vinegar. Sprinkle with salt, and leave for an hour. The snails will begin to foam slightly. Wash well in fresh water, and cook for 5 minutes in boiling water. Remove, cool, and take the snails from their shells with a pin.

Simmer the snails, out of their shells, in a *court bouillon* (see page 30), until tender. Wash the shells and dry them. Stuff the shells with butter as before, replace the snails and seal with butter. Heat as before in a moderate oven (mark 4; 350°F.). (Illustrated p. 134.)

CARP IN WHITE WINE. Freshwater fish are used extensively in the kitchens of Burgundy, and indeed all over France. They are not as well flavoured as fish from the sea and need added flavouring.

Butter an oven dish, and sprinkle a little chopped shallot in the bottom. Lay small carp, about 12 oz. each, in the dish after cleaning and scaling (see page 70). Pour some dry white wine over the fish. Sprinkle on some sliced mushrooms and add plenty of butter. Cook in a moderate oven (mark 4; 350°F.) for 15 minutes. Baste frequently, and serve with a sauce when cooked.

SAUCE DIABLE (Devil's sauce). This is a good accompaniment to food that needs some extra flavour. Boil chopped shallot, thyme, bayleaf and freshly ground pepper in white wine and water with some vinegar added. After a few minutes strain the liquid and add butter. Whip until butter has blended into the mixture. Season with cayenne pepper.

CHICKEN WITH CREAM SAUCE. Later Paul and Serge had a chance to go to the famous market of Bourg-en-Bresse where once a year the chickens of Bresse are judged. Winning a prize at the competition might mean great financial gain for a poultry farmer. The *chapon*, a cockerel neutered and fattened, is the most famous of these birds.

In the Picots' restaurant, after careful cleaning they were roasted with a little butter and oil. Yveline stuffed each bird with a bunch of thyme and parsley and used a hot oven (mark 7; 425°F.). When the breasts were brown she turned each bird upside down and continued roasting until the underside of the bird was brown. Then for 5 minutes she left the bird the right way up, for the breast to become crisp and plump again.

The chickens were jointed, the breasts carved and the cream sauce served separately.

SAUCE À LA CREME (Cream sauce). Melt butter in a pan and absorb all of it with flour. Stir and cook for a few minutes. (You will find that you need a slightly greater weight of flour than butter). Add, drop by drop at first, stock from a boiled chicken; thin down until you have a light, creamy consistency. (At home, the giblets from the chicken you are roasting, simmered for two hours in salted water, will make enough stock for a sauce). Check the seasoning and add thick cream just before serving.

Serve the sauce in a bowl, as Yveline did, and let the guests help themselves. For a good quality chicken this is the ideal accompaniment. Most chickens are improved by roasting with a piece of fatty bacon tied over the top. Yveline thought that the chickens of Bresse, with their own generous fat, did not need this help in cooking.

ROAST BEEF. Sirloin or topside are two good cuts for roasting. Rib has a delicious flavour but tends to be very fatty and wasteful. A 2½ lb. piece of topside would feed six people. In France the meat is always boned and rolled for roasting.

Make sure that you have a good wedge of fat tied round the rolled meat. Without this the meat will not be tender. Press in cloves of garlic to your own taste. Roast in a hot oven (mark 7; 425°F.). Allow fifteen minutes to the pound. You will find that after roasting a few joints you will be able to judge when the meat is still rare. The time varies with the quality of meat and the thickness of the joint. You will spoil the meat if you start sticking a knife in to test it.

SAUCE MOUTARDE (Mustard sauce).   Serge remembered his mother's condemnation of a certain restaurant, 'They served a sauce with flour in it for the meat'. But his new teacher also used a thickened mustard sauce to serve with the roast!

Starting with melted butter and flour in a saucepan she thinned with hot water until she had the usual creamy sauce. In a bowl, she beat egg yolks with wine vinegar, Dijon mustard, salt, pepper and melted butter. This was added to the creamy sauce and the two were well blended over a very low heat. The sauce was served warmed in a *bain marie* (a water-bath).

Serge tried a variation without the thickening. He preferred the taste but found it difficult to get a large enough quantity. It was an ideal quick sauce, made to order. He softened chopped shallots in butter and added vinegar and white wine and more butter. The sauce was tastier when reduced to about a third.

MIXED VEGETABLES.   In the restaurant the two boys quickly found that the vegetables, with slight variations, were always prepared in the same way; as a jardinière. This consisted of three or four vegetables mixed together. The vegetables were cooked separately. Yveline used carrots, peas, turnips and cauliflower. The carrots and turnips were shaped into small, nearly oval chunks, and cooked with a very little water, butter, sugar and salt. The cauliflower was cooked gently in salted water, and drained. Although the vegetables were cooked separately they could be mixed with some melted butter and kept together in a casserole, warm in the oven, ready to serve. The peas were cooked in this way:

PEAS COOKED WITH LETTUCE

shelled peas	**butter**
lettuce leaves	**sugar**
small onions	**salt**
bunch of parsley and chervil	

Put the peas in the pan with butter, shredded lettuce, the onions and herbs, sugar and salt, and cover them with water. Simmer them gently for 20 minutes, strain them, remove the herbs, and toss the peas in a little butter.

CHEESE.   Yveline and Denis were never satisfied unless they had a good cheese board. They often had a ripe Camembert on the board, and the boys learned how to store a Camembert on its side, if it had been cut into, to avoid the cheese running away – literally. There were plenty of regional cheeses. Their particular favourite was the blue from Bresse, but the others all had their charm; Gruyère, made in the Dombes area, and Passin, a type of Gruyère, Morvan goat cheese, cream cheeses from all over the region, and another type of blue from Gex.

RIGODON. The secret of the first sweet dish they helped to prepare is a good, freshly made custard.

½ pint (1¼ cups) milk	1 teaspoon (1¼) cornflour
3 oz. (3 tablespoons) sugar	vanilla essence
yolks of 3 eggs	1 stale sweet bun

Heat the milk until it starts to boil. Remove from the stove. Beat the egg yolks and the sugar together. Sprinkle in the cornflour and add the hot milk, whipping all the time. Keep whipping over a gentle heat until the custard begins to froth up. Remove from the stove and add the vanilla. (The best way to use vanilla for sweets is to have two pods of vanilla split in two kept in a jar of caster sugar. If you have this vanilla sugar prepared, no essence is needed).

Take the crust from a stale sweet bun, cut up the remaining centre, and mix it with the cooling custard, together with some chopped walnuts. Stir once or twice as the custard is setting, so that the nuts stay in the custard and do not sink to the bottom. Top with melted blackcurrant jam.

PUDDING DE FRAMBOISES (Raspberry pudding)

Another quick sweet they learned was a *pudding de framboises*.

Cut a sweet *brioche* bun into strips. (An ordinary sweet bun or a light sponge would do). Line a basin with the strips of bun. Cover with whipped cream, then raspberries. Repeat several layers of bun, fruit and cream. Finish with a layer of bun, put a plate over the top and a weight. Leave with the weight in the top to chill in the refrigerator.

TO CHOP ONIONS

The next few months sped by and Serge's notebook was soon full, and a second one started. Both he and Paul liked this type of cooking. Above all it was honest. The raw materials were the best that could be bought locally and there was no 'over preparation'.

Perhaps the most useful thing they learned was the way to chop onions. We've noticed how many onions go into the preparation of French country food. Paul and Serge spent many an hour crying bitter tears over strong onions. Yveline let them cry for a while and then gave her magic formula: 'As you start to cut the onions, sprinkle them with a little wine vinegar'. They did. It worked!

RECIPES FROM BURGUNDY

Here are a few of the dishes noted in Serge's first book.

GOUGÈRE

This is a cheese-flavoured bun. Make a *pâte a choux* (see page 37). For a 4-egg mixture use 2 oz. Gruyère cheese diced very finely. Mix the cheese into the pastry. Add pepper and salt.

Shape the mixture into balls about 2 inches across and bake on a greased baking sheet in a fairly hot oven (mark 6; 400°F.) for 30 minutes. The *gougères* are cooked when they are brittle on the surface.

This is a good first dish to a meal, especially before fish.

FROGS' LEGS

Fortunately the frogs' legs were bought from a wholesaler, already prepared. Serge could not see how he could face the little creatures alive. He learned to soak the legs in fresh water with some slices of lemon. The flesh went white, and swelled. They were then dusted with flour and cooked quickly in butter and oil. They looked appetizing, rather like small chicken legs, heaped on a plate with slices of lemon and pieces of parsley.

LA POCHOUSE

This needed a lot of preparation, but the cooking did not take a long time, like many fish dishes. Freshwater fish are used here, but a similar dish could be made from fish of the sea.

6–8 servings:

4 lb. mixed fish; eel, pike, carp, chub and bream	*bouquet garni*
	croûtons
4 oz. streaky bacon	**¼ pint (full ½ cup) cream**
2 oz. mushrooms	**2 oz. (4 tablespoons) butter**
4 oz. onion	**2 oz. (7 tablespoons) flour**
4 oz. carrot	**white wine**

Clean the fish, and cut off the heads. Oil a large pot, line with chopped onions and carrots, add pepper, salt and a *bouquet garni*. Cut the fish into chunks and put them in, on the vegetables. Cover with white wine (or white wine and water). Simmer for 20 minutes, or until the fish is cooked.

Drain the fish and place it in a deep serving dish. Strain the stock through a fine sieve. Knead together equal quantities of flour and butter. Stir into the stock while heating gently, to thicken. Add cream. Pour this hot sauce over the fish. Toss the bacon and chopped mushrooms in a little butter. Sprinkle over the top, and finish with parsley.

Eel is the problem in this dish as it takes longer to cook than the other fish. If the eel is of any size at all, put a meat hook through the head and hang it up. Cut the skin under the head, all the way round, and, using this as a start, skin the eel. Cut in half, and remove the backbone. Chunks cut from this filleted fish will cook much more quickly.

This method of thickening, using the flour and butter mixed together, is a good way for large quantities of sauce or soup. You will find that slightly more flour than butter is needed. Mix together with a fork in a basin. You can keep this preparation (*beurre manié*) wrapped in foil in the refrigerator until wanted.

SAUTÉD KIDNEYS

4 servings:

1¼ lb. kidneys	1 cup white wine
1 medium onion, chopped	sprinkle of tarragon, chopped
¼ lb. mushrooms, sliced	1 tablespoon (1¼) thick (heavy)
1 tablespoon (1¼) Dijon mustard	cream

Yveline often put kidneys on the menu. Veal kidneys are really the best, but she also used lambs' kidneys. She always insisted that her assistants trimmed all the fat and sinew from the kidney. 'Kidney will never cook properly with that rubbish on it'.

She sliced the prepared kidneys and tossed them in butter and oil with some finely chopped onion. Paul tossed some sliced mushrooms in another pan and these were added to the kidneys just as they were cooked. Then a good spoonful of Dijon mustard was added, and white wine stirred in. Tarragon was the herb used, and the dish was completed with a spoonful of thick cream.

ROAST PIGEON

When the hunting season came game was in plentiful supply. Serge had never liked game very much, and preferred pigeon, the way that Yveline cooked it. Pigeon is a good dish to serve at home because one bird feeds one person. The birds used are brown wood-pigeons.

Clean the birds and put the livers aside. Make a stuffing with chopped bacon, the chopped livers, and ham. Dry out with breadcrumbs. Toss sliced mushrooms in hot oil and add to the stuffing. Season well and add a little sage or thyme – experiment with the herbs you like. Cook the stuffing in some butter for a few minutes. Remember that the birds will cook quite quickly, and uncooked stuffing inside would not have enough time to cook right through.

The fondue made with Gruyère cheese (p. 104) is a typical dish from Dauphiné. Cubes of bread, held on a fork, are dipped into the mixture.

Stuff the pigeons. Wrap a slice of streaky bacon round each bird, and tie with twine to keep together. Roast in an oven dish in a hot oven (mark 7; 425°F.) for 15 minutes. When cooked, put in a warm serving dish. Drain the pan juices into a saucepan. Add red wine and butter. Reduce over low heat for 5 minutes. Pour over the pigeons before serving.

RED CURRANT TART

The red currants of the countryside make delicious tarts. Such a tart in fact was the first dish that Paul cooked by himself, on the first Sunday of their stay.

He lined a tart dish with shortcrust pastry (see page 24), and baked it until brown in a fairly hot oven (mark 6; 400°F.), being careful to prick the bottom of the pastry first, and weigh it down with a few white beans. He removed the stalks from the currants and filled the pastry case with the fruit. He made syrup by boiling water with plenty of sugar until it would coat the back of a spoon, and poured it over the fruit. He placed the tart in a moderate oven (mark 4; 350°F.) for long enough to warm the fruit; about 15 minutes.

PAIN D'ÉPICES (Spiced loaf)

Yveline thought that Serge needed a special sweet of his own. He did not have the advantages of Paul, who was brought up with his family in the country and, perhaps, if she taught him a real speciality he would feel that he could tackle anything.

¾ pint (scant 2 cups) water	1½ lb. (4½ cups) flour
1 teaspoon (1¼) aniseed	1 teaspoon (1¼) cinnamon
½ pint (1¼ cups) honey	1 teaspoon (1¼) grated nutmeg
10 oz. (full ½ cup) sugar	good pinch of salt
1 teaspoon (1¼) bicarbonate of soda	3 oz. mixed candied peel, chopped

Boil the water in a saucepan and add the aniseed. Dissolve the honey and sugar in the water. Remove from the heat, and add the soda.

Mix the flour with the spices, salt, and candied peel. Pour the dissolved honey and sugar into a mixing bowl. Add the flour mixture and make a dough. Be sure to mix well. Oil a baking tin, or tins, and fill to three-quarters full with the dough. Bake in a moderate oven (mark 4; 350°F.) for 1 hour. Test by sticking a needle into the cake.

Serge and Paul learned a lot during their period with the Picots. More important perhaps than the dishes, they learned how to plan the kitchen. The equipment needed every day was laid out where they could get to it. The produce for a particular meal was set out on racks. All waste was eliminated. Even the potato peelings were scrubbed and put into the stock pot. Most important, everything to be prepared was written down in order on a sheet of paper.

Snails as cooked in Burgundy (p. 127). They are stuffed with butter flavoured with garlic, parsley, and shallots.

Naturally, customers came to the little restaurant expecting good wines; this was the reputation of the region. Serge and Paul quickly learned that the great wines came from the area between Dijon and Chagny; the Côte de Nuits and the Côte de Beaune. There were one of two of these great wines on the list. *Richebourg*, from the Côte de Nuits and a Corton from the Côte de Beaune.

Denis Picot was particularly proud of his white wines from outside the main region and he always had fish on the menu so there was a demand for them. His favourite was a Chablis, from near Auxerre, and he thought that the name *Les Grenouilles* added something to the list.

From the Macon area he had a Pouilly (this is the name of a village), Château de Pouilly. Apart from these there were countless good honest wines round Chalon and Macon: *Mercurey (les Nogues) Buzy, Romanèche-Thorins, Saint-Amour.*

The regular customers did not want names: they wanted decent cheap wine. Denis bought a wine bottled at Saint-Amour without labels. 'If it's bottled you can keep it for three months in the cellar, and lose bottle sickness that detracts so much from the wine. Keep an ordinary wine like this and you will be surprised at the difference in quality'.

Paul and Serge took good note of all these little tips, and put them to good effect when they started their restaurant. Yes, they carried on with the plan and founded a small place in the Tarn. Both Madame Bentley and Madame Dupont helped them to start with. But that's another story.

Franche-Comté

To the east of Burgundy and up against the northern Swiss plain lies the land of the Franche-Comté. It consists of the Jura mountains, the plains, and the valley of the river Doube, with the valleys of the Loue and Ain to the south-west.

Although very near to the Alps it has an entirely different structure. The peaks even look different, with their blunt, rocky outlines. Square outcrops rear up to the sky. The valleys between the peaks are more like broad plains.

All the larger towns are at the edge of the Jura, for communications into the interior are difficult. Even the rivers will unexpectedly dive underground, or take a rough ride down rocky waterfalls.

Open to the humidity of the west, and encouraged by the action of man, the plains of the Franche-Comté are green and lush. Cattle feed well here and an abundant milk supply has given rise to one of the treasures of the area, cheese. A great industry has sprung up, helped by Swiss techniques and centred on the *fruitière*, which is a co-operative centre for the manufacture and ageing of cheese. This is the land of Gruyère cheeses, weighing 40 to 50 kilos each (85 to 110 lb.).

In the valleys, small fields are planted out with maize for cattle feed. Fruit and nut trees crowd round protectively. Wherever the vine can be grown the slopes, particularly to the west, are dark green in the sun. The wines of the Arbois are particularly famous with the *vin de garde*[1] a mystery to the non-initiate and, it must be confessed, sometimes to the expert cellar-master as well.

The other source of the wealth of Franche-Comté has always been the forest. Wood has been worked here from time immemorial, and the craft of carving has spread over into watchmaking, and the modern craft of working plastic.

Man's ability to adapt is here well evident. When wood lost its importance as fuel, and became less used in building, the people of the region turned to other skills. Besançon has become an important centre for watchmaking, and as plastic came into being the craftsmen quickly learned to turn, twist and bend the new material.

To build up a great dairy industry, the natural grass of the plains was insufficient. Artificial fertilizers and mechanical sowing helped to form the lush prairies of today. As

[1]A wine that is kept to mature. See *Vin Jaune* p. 143.

the few towns grew, the cultivation of vegetables became important, with the potato well to the fore. Many vegetables are grown in the smallholdings of the valley floors.

Cattle rearing has increased a great deal in recent years, so the kitchens of the area are well supplied with meat. Chickens are fattened for the table, and the pig is always at hand. Game of all varieties is in plentiful supply. Clear rivers pour forth their glistening horde.

When we add wine to all this we may be excused a pang of envy. But this envy should not last long, because we can all benefit from the French cookery that evolved in the midst of all these good things. One lesson we can learn is that perhaps we, in our own countries, do not use the natural gifts of the land and water to our advantage. We can do this by improving the scope of our cooking. As we noticed in Burgundy, even the humble snail can be turned into a delicious morsel!

Claud Blondet worked in insurance, and had once travelled the length and breadth of France. He kept a little book with details of hotels and restaurants, and was always ready to help a traveller. 'You must sleep in this place, but eat in the restaurant round the corner. Don't sleep there; I was eaten alive in 1950. But they do have a good kitchen, and it's still the best value in the region'. These strange directions were followed reverently by the young agents of the regional insurance office.

Claude was head of his office now and stayed safely at home, not far from Arbois. He ate well – 'better than all the restaurants of France' – slept well in the clear air of his region, and enjoyed watching his daughters, Elizabeth and Aline, grow up. 'What more could a man want?'

He loved to see a great slice of Comté Gruyère on the table, and was constantly amazed at the different ways his wife could use it. His particular weakness was a soft cheese dip that he used to enjoy with bread, and a glass of wine.

CANCOILLETTE

1 lb. finely grated Gruyère cheese   **garlic**
2 oz. (4 tablespoons) butter   **pepper**
½ glass (1 cup) dry white wine

Other hard cheeses can be used, but Gruyère is the best for this dish. Rub a saucepan round with a clove of garlic. Melt the butter in it. Add the cheese a little at a time. Add the wine and an equal quantity of water. Stir while the mixture melts and bubbles. *Cancoillette* can be used warm or cold.

CHEESE OMELET

Cheese flavoured omelets were those most eaten in the Blondet home, and are very easy to make. Beat up the eggs for an omelet (see p. 23). Season in the usual way, but add a sprinkle of grated cheese. Cook the omelet in the pan, and just before you fold it over add grated cheese to the taste you want, (try about 1 tablespoon per person).

CHEESE SOUFFLÉ

On special days his wife, Lucette, would often serve a cheese soufflé after the soup. Remember, it's the air trapped in a soufflé that enables it to rise in the oven.

2 oz. (4 tablespoons) butter	4 eggs
3 oz. (full $\frac{1}{2}$ cup) flour	salt and pepper
3 oz. ($\frac{1}{2}$ cup) grated cheese	nutmeg
1 pint ($2\frac{1}{2}$ cups) of milk	

Melt the butter in the pan. Add the flour and cook for a moment, stirring. Add the milk gradually, gently beating all the time. You will have a thick béchamel. Sift in the grated cheese until it dissolves. Add pepper, salt, and some grated nutmeg. Be careful! Not too much salt because of the cheese flavour. Separate the eggs. Add the yolks, and beat the whites solid. Fold the whites into the mixture. Carefully pour into a buttered soufflé dish, sprinkle with cheese, and bake in a moderate oven (mark 4; 350°F.). The soufflé will rise, so the dish should only be three-quarters full at the start. Bake until the top is brown and comes over the top of the dish, about 40 minutes.

Successful soufflés only come with practice. The middle of the dish must be cooked through or it will collapse as soon as it cools. The usual time is about 40 minutes, but be careful, there are so many variables. Eggs can be large, small or medium, ovens have their little idiosyncrasies. The list could go on. . . .

FOOLPROOF CHEESE SOUFFLÉ

Here is a method for a quick soufflé that cannot go wrong. Claude's wife showed him how to cook it, and even he succeeded!

4 eggs	salt
3 oz. ($\frac{1}{2}$ cup) grated cheese	white wine
pepper	

Separate the eggs. Add to the yolks the cheese, and a little white wine. Season well. Whip the whites until solid, and fold into the yolks. Heat oil and butter in the omelet pan until steaming. Pour in the mixture. Leave on the heat while you sprinkle more cheese over it. Brown under the grill, and dry out in a moderate oven (mark 4; 450°F.) for 5 minutes. Serve from the pan.

The resulting soufflé is very light, and it's up to you to judge the amount of flavour you want to put into it. If you do not possess an omelet pan that will go into the oven, heat a soufflé dish in the oven, oil it and pour the mixture into it from the pan. Finish the dish according to the recipe.

MENU

An easily prepared lunch menu would be:

SOUFFLÉ AU FROMAGE	CHEESE SOUFFLÉ
JAMBON AUX ÉPINARDS	HAM WITH SPINACH
SALADE	SALAD
FROMAGE BLANC FINES HERBES	WHITE CHEESE WITH HERBS
COMPOTE DE FRUITS	COMPOTE OF FRUIT

HAM WITH SPINACH. Spinach is very often served with cold ham, as a purée. Cook the spinach in the usual way (see page 29), but there is a difference, as for the purée you must break off the thick stems. Chop it and pass it through a vegetable mill or put in an electric blender. Reheat gently in a pan, and add fresh cream before serving.

WHITE CHEESE WITH HERBS. Try a variation from the usual cheese board. Take ordinary cooking cheese and beat it up with softened butter, about ¼ lb. (½ cup) of butter to 1 lb. of cheese. Divide into 4 small bowls and add a different herb to each bowl. You must add a lot of salt and pepper to the cheese. Try garlic and parsley, freshly ground black pepper, fresh thyme, paprika, and chopped shallot.

COMPOTE OF FRUIT. When fruit is plentiful a compote, chilled and served with cream, makes a refreshing end to a meal. Stone red plums and, with plenty of sugar, simmer in water. When soft pour into a bowl. Wipe round the pan, and cook apples, sliced fine, with sugar and lemon slices. Apricots or peaches cooked in the same way would be a good addition to the compote. Whip a fork through the mixed fruit and serve it roughly mashed with fresh cream.

GÂTEAU DE POTIRON (Pumpkin tart)

It always gave Lucette Blondet a thrill when she was put on her mettle as a cook. In the same way that Olympic champions get nervous before an event, but put their nervous energy towards the explosion of performing, so a cook needs to be tried and challenged. Most of us are content to plod along and do quite well, but if you want to improve and hit a few high spots, accept any challenge that is going. Don't run to the delicatessen in horror when those unexpected guests are invited for 'a little something'. Dive for the pantry and the fridge, plan a menu and cook it!

Lucette was not to be taken by surprise on this occasion; but M. Jeunet of the *Hostellerie de Paris* was coming to supper one Sunday. 'Don't worry, he's very nice. He's coming to the pool in Arbois to watch the girls swim'. Elizabeth and Aline were very keen swimmers and they spent all the time they could in the Olympic-standard pool. 'We'll be home about eight'. M. Foudrier a neighbour was also invited, and his wife, Nicole, gave a hand in the kitchen.

Lucette decided to make one of her specialities, a *gâteau de potiron*, made from pumpkins. She cut a small pumpkin into pieces and cooked it until soft in boiling water. The pumpkin was drained and put into a bowl. This is how she continued:

8 servings.

1 pumpkin, cooked	vanilla flavouring
1 pint (2½ cups) milk	**2 oz. (4 tablespoons) butter**
6 oz. (6 tablespoons) sugar	**flaky pastry** (see page 72)
4 eggs	

Lucette made the pastry and left it to rest in the refrigerator. She mashed the cooked pumpkin finely and added the butter. It was still quite warm, so the butter melted and blended in well. This mixture was allowed to cool, then the milk, the sugar, and the 4 eggs, beaten, were blended in.

Lucette lined a tart tin with the pastry and filled it with the pumpkin mixture. The tart was covered with pastry, brushed with beaten egg and decorated. The gâteau took 45 minutes to cook in a hot oven (mark 7; 425°F.). A useful hint here; Lucette covered the tart with metal foil as soon as the top of the pastry began to brown. She left it like this for 30 minutes to allow the bottom of the gâteau to cook. Uncovered again, the top took 5 minutes to turn golden brown.

This important item of the menu was cooked in the morning, crusted over with sugar, and left in a cool place, but not the refrigerator.

MENU

As soon as the party had left for the swimming pool, Lucette and Mme. Foudrier started work. Here is the full menu they had to cook.

SOUPE AUX CERISES	CHERRY SOUP
LIÈVRE RÔTI, SAUCE DE LA VIEILLE CHARLOTTE	ROAST HARE, SAUCE LA VIEILLE CHARLOTTE
POMMES BOULANGÈRES	BOULANGÈRE POTATOES
FRICASSÉE DE CHAMPIGNONS	FRICASSÉE OF MUSHROOMS
SALADE	SALAD
FROMAGES	CHEESE
GÂTEAU DE POTIRON	PUMPKIN TART

ROAST HARE. Two large saddles of hare had been soaking overnight in wine, lemon juice and freshly ground black pepper. This marinating makes all the difference to the tenderness and taste of the game. To cut the saddle, M. Blondet had chopped through the body just under the rib cage and taken off the back legs. The lower part of the body with the spine constituted the saddle.

Larding with fat bacon helps in cooking hare, which has no fat of its own. Mme. Foudrier was quite an expert at this and she made two neat rows of stitches on either side of the spine (see page 32). Now it was ready, and later would be put to roast in a hot oven (mark 7; 425°F.) for 50 minutes. The sauce, too, would be made later (see page 142).

BOULANGÈRE POTATOES. These potatoes were prepared next. Lucette sliced potatoes finely, buttered an oven dish and laid in a layer of potatoes, added chopped onions, then another layer of potatoes. This was repeated until the dish was full. She dotted butter on top and filled the dish with water. Salt, pepper and garlic were added. Lucette tasted the water in the dish to make sure it was salty. A few rashers of streaky bacon were placed on top. The dish would take about three hours in a cool oven (mark 2; 300°F.).

CHERRY SOUP. Let us see what the two ladies had ready. The sweet dish was made, the hare was ready for roasting, and the potatoes were in the oven. It was 6 o'clock. They had to allow 50 minutes in the oven for the hare. The soup was next.

'I've never seen or tasted this soup before. Seems funny to make a soup with cherries'. Mme. Foudrier had slight doubts in her mind about the success of the soup. It is in fact a good soup to serve before game.

2 oz. (4 tablespoons) butter	3 lb. stoned cherries
3 oz. (full $\frac{1}{2}$ cup) flour	sugar
about 3 pints (7$\frac{1}{2}$ cups) water	kirsch

Melt the butter in a pot and sprinkle in the flour. Cook for a few moments. Gradually add the water, stirring all the time. Pour in the stoned cherries (black cherries are usually used) and cook them gently in the liquid for half an hour. Add sugar and kirsch to flavour. Serve with *croûtons* fried in butter.

FRICASSÉE OF MUSHROOMS. Lucette wanted to prepare the fricassée at the very last moment. Here is the method. Toss in oil chopped lean bacon, sliced mushrooms and chopped onions. Add salt, pepper, grated nutmeg and tarragon. Moisten with white wine and water. Add some butter.

The swimming party came in very hungry. Lucette was glad that she had laid out nuts, crisps and little squares of cheese to eat with the *aperitifs*. In fact they all chose a *macoin*, which is a fortified wine often chilled and taken before meals. This one was flavoured with vanilla.

M. Jeunet was the first to congratulate Lucette on the soup. 'It's a marvel, Madame. One does not often have the chance to taste such a soup'. What a kind man he was!

SAUCE DE LA VIEILLE CHARLOTTE. This sauce is one often served with hare. Lucette melted 2 oz. (4 tablespoons) butter in a saucepan and absorbed it with 1 oz. (3$\frac{1}{2}$ tablespoons) of flour. She added finely 1 oz. chopped shallots, salt, pepper, and wine vinegar. The sauce became too thick so she used about a glass of white wine to moisten it.

The wines were chosen by Claude with great care. 'Shall I give a red Bugey with the hare?' In the end he decided to serve a rosé from Arbois with the meat, and the red with the cheeses – a blue cheese from Gex, Vachelin (a type of Gruyère from the region), little pyramids of goat cheese, and a pot of flavoured cream cheese. With the gâteau he chose a sparkling Seyssel. What better to follow than a dram of local *marc*.[1]

[1] See footnote p. 112.

With the coffee M. Jeunet entertained them with stories of the kitchen. He told of the Corsican who tore up his wages to prove that he did not really need the money; the Algerian who went into a trance at ten every night; and the assistant who whipped up the cream with salt. Later Madame Foudrier remarked on a wonderful dish that she had tried in the *Hostellerie de Paris* and, very kindly, he told her how it was cooked.

COQ AU VIN JAUNE ET AUX MORILLES (Chicken in yellow wine with morels).

1 chicken, about 3 lb.	**½ bottle 'yellow' or white wine**
½ lb. butter	**3½ oz. morels**
2 oz. flour	**¼ pint of cream**

Cut the chicken into 4 portions, 2 legs and 2 wings. Flour the pieces and fry gently in a little oil and butter. Cover the pan, and cook for twenty minutes over very low heat. Don't let the chicken colour. Take from the heat and pour in the wine. Add the morels and the cream. Cook very gently. Add salt and pepper. Serve in a warm dish, with *croûtons* fried in butter.

The dish could be cooked with mushrooms, but try to get morels if you want the true flavour of the dish. You can use dried morels that you have soaked and washed the night before. Also, outside the Arbois *vin jaune* is in very short supply. Dry Graves would be a possible substitute.

VIN JAUNE (Yellow wine)

M. Jeunet explained what exactly was meant by *vin jaune*. 'Yellow obviously refers to the colour. The other name for this wine, 'vin de garde' is more explanatory. The wine starts life as white wine, probably made from the *Gamay blanc* grape. This young wine is put into barrels already dosed with yellow wine, and allowed to evaporate in the wood for 6 years. A scum of natural yeasts forms on the surface. Gradually the nutty flavour and the colour grows in the wine. Because this transformation cannot be chemically described the process is never absolutely sure. Even the experienced cellar master can go wrong'.

ROAST THRUSH

The eighth guest was a young bachelor from Claude's office, Yves Marie. He was the proud possessor of a new flat and was determined not to live out of tins. Like countless thousands in France he was keen on shooting, and as thrushes made up the bulk of his bag he wanted to know how to make the most of this bird in the kitchen.

M. Jeunet, who always encouraged people to try new dishes and was never afraid to share his great knowledge of the kitchen, obliged with a local recipe. 'You must accept the fact that the thrush should be cooked uncleaned, except for drawing out the gizzard. If you feel that you must clean the bird, do so. In any case, the heads are left on in cooking, but the eyes are cut out. I take it for granted that you pluck the birds first. Season them, and set them to roast in a little butter.'

While the birds are roasting you take grapes, plunge them in boiling water and remove the skins and the pips. Skin 6 grapes per bird. When the birds are nearly cooked you add the grapes to the pan and leave to cook a while. Finish with a few drops of *vin jaune* or a little brandy. Serve on croûtons and garnish with *pommes gaufrettes* and bunches of cress.

POMMES GAUFRETTES   (Chipped potatoes)

Deep fried potatoes are certainly over-used commercially. Chips are a commonplace, and are often badly cooked. Great care is needed in preparation. Old potatoes are good for this way of cooking and should be carefully peeled, sliced to about ¼-inch thickness, and then cut again into chips.

Beef dripping, or oil, is heated until it begins to steam. Try the temperature of the fat by dropping in one chip. It should immediately sizzle. Dry the chips well, and drop into the oil in a chip basket. Don't overload the pan. When the potatoes are nearly cooked, test by breaking one. Drain them and leave until required. Just before serving, heat the oil to steaming and drop the chips in again. They will brown and tend to float as they puff up slightly. Drain and serve on a paper serviette.

Try cutting different shapes from the slices of potato. Pastry cutters are good for this. These potatoes get their name *gaufrettes* from the wafer shape, and they are cut with a wire cutter called a *mandoline*.

MENU

Afterwards Yves Marie tried to work out whether it was the brandy or the benevolent attitude of M. Jeunet that encouraged him to invite the whole company along to his batchelor flat for dinner. 'My sister is soon to start at university and I would like to give her a send-off'. After extracting from him a promise that they could all help, they agreed to come, except M. Jeunet who was very busy. Instead he donated some bottles of real *vin jaune* for the occasion. Lucette Blondet went into conference with Yves Marie and they decided on the menu.

POTAGES AUX NOISETTES	WALNUT SOUP
TRUITE ROSE, SAUCE MAYONNAISE	SALMON TROUT MAYONNAISE
COULIS DE POULET AUX CHAMPIGNONS	COULIS OF CHICKEN WITH MUSHROOMS
POMMES DUCHESSE	DUCHESSE POTATOES
PURÉE DE CAROTTES	CARROT PURÉE
SALADE DE CRESSON	CRESS SALAD
FROMAGES	CHEESE
TARTE AU SUCRE	TARTE AU SUCRE

Fortunately Yves Marie's kitchen was a large one, as his flat was in one of the old houses on the outskirts of Arbois. Madame Blondet, her two daughters, and Madame Foudrier came to help. His sister Sylvie was simply invited to dinner with her fiancé and no mention was made of the special occasion.

TARTE AU SUCRE. Elizabeth and Aline were set to work. The tart was one of the first things they had learned from their mother.

1 oz. yeast
3 tablespoons (3¾) warm milk
10 oz. (scant 2 cups) flour
4 oz. (½ cup) butter

3 eggs
3 oz. (3 tablespoons) sugar
pinch of salt

Cream the yeast with the warm milk. Add a pinch of sugar. Mix the flour with the butter, eggs, pinch of salt and 2 oz. (2 tablespoons) of the sugar. Add the yeast mixture, and knead well. Cover with a cloth and leave to rise. When the dough has doubled its volume, after perhaps an hour, knead again and roll to a ¼-inch thickness. Oil a tart tin (in fact they used two tins) and line with the dough. Allow to rise in a warm place. Dot the surface of the pastry with butter and sprinkle over the rest of the sugar. Add more sugar if necessary. Bake in a hot oven (mark 7; 425°F.) for 25 minutes.

SALMON TROUT MAYONNAISE. Meanwhile Lucette and Nicole got to work on the trout. They had 5 salmon trout, about 1½ lbs. each. The fish were simmered in a *court bouillon* (see page 30) with a bottle of rosé wine added to the stock. When cooked, the fish were drained, skinned, and the bones removed as follows. The heads were left on. Each fish was split lengthwise in two, the heads being carefully split as well. The bones were removed. Five half fish were placed in a serving dish, with thinly sliced lemons along them, and each remaining half was put into position on top.

The *court bouilllon* was strained. Gelatine powder – 1 oz. (3 envelopes) to 1 pint (2½ cups) of liquid – was melted with a spoonful of this, and then added to the rest of the *court bouillon*. When the liquid was beginning to set, it was spooned over the fish. The dish was set in a cool place to form a jelly.

WALNUT SOUP. Yves Marie had started on the soup; Lucette had written out the instructions for him.

2 lb. mushrooms
6 cabbage lettuces
1 large onion
1 veal or pork knuckle
1 teaspoon (1¼) sugar
4 oz. (½ cup) butter
1 pint (2½ cups) milk

2 pints (5 cups) water
5 tablespoons (6¼) rice
4 oz. (1 cup) walnuts, shelled and
  skinned
yolks of 3 eggs
¼ pint (full ½ cup) cream
salt and pepper

Slice the mushrooms finely. Wash the lettuces, discard the outer leaves, shred and cook them in 2 oz. (4 tablespoons) butter, together with the mushrooms. Add salt, pepper, and sugar. Cover, and continue cooking for 30 minutes. Add the veal or pork knuckle, the onion, the milk and the water. Scald the rice in very little water, and cook it for a moment. Stir well and add to the soup. Season. Simmer for 2 hours.

Remove the bone, and strain the soup into a bowl. Remove any vegetables from the pot and pour back the soup. Keep on a low heat. Grind the nuts and blend with the rest of the butter. Put the nut purée into a warm soup tureen. Stir in the egg yolks and cream, and blend with a cup of the soup. Add another cup of soup and mix thoroughly. Pour in the rest of the soup, stirring all the time.

COULIS OF CHICKEN WITH MUSHROOMS. The *coulis* is a very special way of preparing chicken and adds variety to that time-honoured bird. Lucette used two medium boiling fowls. She cooked them in water with carrot, onion, and a *bouquet garni*, for one hour. This time will, of course, depend upon the age and quality of the bird.

The birds were taken from the stock, skinned and boned, and the meat was chopped finely and minced. Again an electric blender is a very useful instrument to have. Some of the stock was mixed with the chicken, which was set aside in the warm.

Slice mushrooms, (Lucette used 2 lb.), and toss in a frying pan with some oil. Add chopped shallots, a *bouquet garni*, lemon juice, salt and pepper. Cook gently for 10 minutes. Make a white sauce with the stock of the chicken, butter and flour. Mix this into the mushrooms. Keep hot. Pour the mushroom sauce on to a hot serving dish and cover with the chicken. Season with salt, pepper, grated lemon peel and grated nutmeg.

POMMES DUCHESSE. 2 lb. of potatoes were cooked until soft in boiling water. Then they were cut into small pieces in the pan, with most of the water drained off, and cooked again gently until the last of the water had evaporated. They were then mashed. This way you are able to get mashed potatoes with no lumps.

Add 1 oz. (2 tablespoons) of butter and 3 egg yolks. Season well with salt and pepper. Use a bag with a wide nozzle and pipe the potato mixture onto a greased oven tray. Elizabeth made little mounds by going backward and forward with the nozzle. They were cooked for 5 minutes in a hot oven (mark 7; 425°F.), then coated with beaten egg, and cooked for another 5 minutes.

CARROT PURÉE. Carrots were sliced and cooked with little water with a nob of butter, salt and sugar. When very soft Aline mashed them and added butter.

CRESS SALAD. The cress was dressed, in a long dish, with oil, vinegar, salt, pepper and just a touch of garlic. Each guest was given a bunch.

Sylvie wondered what all the activity was, when she rang the bell. Her brother was such a quiet fellow. 'I do hope you will get on together', she whispered to her fiancé. 'Remember he's all the family I have'. Their mother and father had escaped the dangers of the revolution in Algeria only to be killed in a car accident. Their other relations were scattered over the world.

Yves Marie was proud of his sister and her fiancé, who was already at the *Faculté* as a medical student, proud that his boss and his family had come to help him out, and proud of the meal. 'Remember I can only claim the soup. Do you like it?'

It was a good menu! A little of the rich, fragrant soup took the edge from their hunger. The sharpness in the trout dish prepared the way for the softness of the chicken and vegetable purées. What a sight the main dish was! The cream and white of the mushroom and chicken was rimmed with golden brown potato tracery and the whole was set off by the deep red glint of the carrot purée. Magnificent!

Again a sharpness, this time of the cress, heralding a rich display of cheeses. That was truly the end of the meal but a crisp wedge of sugary crust accentuated the amber, luscious wine and brought about a sudden crescendo at the end of the meal. The surprise ending lingered with them well into the first cup of coffee.

TRIPE

'I often see wonderful tripe in the windows but don't have the courage to cook it myself', complained Yves Marie. Lucette gave him a recipe that is quite simple.

Cut the tripe into pieces, about 2 inches square. Simmer in salted water for 2 hours with carrot, onion, (with a clove stuck in it), and a *bouquet garni*. Make a sauce with chopped onion softened in plenty of butter and sprinkled with vinegar. Cook for a few minutes and add cream. When the tripe is soft toss the squares gently in some hot butter. Turn out into a deep serving dish and cover with the sauce.

TARTE AU FROMAGE

The Festival of Biou is an important occasion in Arbois. A great bunch of grapes is decorated and carried to church as an offering to the Virgin Mary. It starts on September 3rd and, like most happy festivals in France, goes on for several days. It is a time for mother to be out with the family. The time for everyone to help in the kitchen and prepare dishes such as *tarte au fromage*.

shortcrust pastry	2 oz. ($\frac{1}{2}$ cup) grated cheese
3 eggs	pepper
1 pint (2$\frac{1}{2}$ cups) of milk	nutmeg

Make the pastry (see page 24). Line a large tart tin. (The amounts for filling will make a tart 10 inches across). Beat the eggs in a bowl and add the milk and cheese. Grind a little white pepper into the mixture. Cook the pastry blind in a fairly hot oven (mark 6; 400°F.) until light brown. If you do not follow this method the bottom of the tart will not cook right through. Pour the mixture into the case and mix to spread the cheese. Dot with butter and sprinkle nutmeg on the top. Bake in a hot oven (mark 7; 425°F.) until the mixture is set and brown on top.

It is a mistake to cook these tarts, or *quiches*, until the egg mixture is hard. Remember that cooking will continue after the dish is taken from the oven, as it will remain hot for some time. Remove the tart while the egg still feels quite soft. Test it with your finger.

As M. Jeunet demonstrated, cooking should be a team effort and is much more fun in the home if it is so. Good cooks are always ready to share some of their dishes with you and love to have people in their kitchen, when they are not preparing a meal.

Yves Marie often helped Madame Blondet to prepare dinner and always offered to help with the washing up afterwards. Perhaps that's why the eldest Blondet girl, Elizabeth, came to like him so much.

Alsace-Lorraine

Why take these two great regions together? Because they make up a large area of eastern France that is firmly wedded to the continental land mass. Most other parts of France are influenced by the Atlantic and the Mediterranean. Not so Alsace and Lorraine.

Alsace in particular is shielded from the west by the Vosges Mountains. The air here is clear, and the reddish stone of the houses seems to radiate light in the spring and summer. With its steady warmth this continental summer brings the crops to life, and the grapes to fruition. These grapes pour their goodness into the excellent vintages.

The plain of Alsace, that ends at the Rhine, has industrial activity, but also agricultural richness. Vegetables and a great variety of fruit ripen in the clear, warm air. Peaches make luscious crunchy tarts. Bunches of prize asparagus decorate many a glistening *pâté de foie* in aspic.

Animals thrive too. Beef, veal and pork are served at the long tables, under high pointed roofs. The storks among the great warm chimneys are sacroscant, but their lesser cousins of the mountain forests and valley hedges are not. Large game – stag, deer and roebuck – is to be had, while grouse, partridge and woodcock test the eye of the marksman and the skill of the cook.

Lorraine shares the benefits of that great natural backbone, the Vosges, but is less fortunate in its weather. The mountains that shield Alsace cause the winds to spill their moisture in Lorraine, which is often grey and dull in both winter and summer.

The kitchens of this land of the Moselle are, however, full of good cheer and bright ideas. To the west, towards the Meuse, man has worked hard to make the most of the land and its crops. As in many parts of France the religious orders have paved the way to prosperity. The monks first drained land near to the Meuse to start the open field system where wheat now sways in the breeze.

On the slopes of the Meuse the vine has always been grown, but the low sunshine figures have meant a low yield, and thus a poor return. So in Lorraine the farmer planted plum trees, of the Mirabelle variety, to supply much needed cash.

Alsace and Lorraine are both famed for their pastrycooks. Pastries, sponges and puddings have been mixed, pummelled and rolled here for centuries. Voltaire could say, over two hundred years ago, that Metz had twenty pastrycooks but only one library.

(We might take issue with the philosopher of Vernay, who linked intellectual ability with libraries but not with pastrycooks).

This is the great industrial area of France. Being France, the kitchen does not suffer, perhaps because the links between country and town still exist here. Rural villages lie beside stream and copse, while tall chimneys stand just over the top of the next hill. The steelmill foreman will take his leisure fishing for his supper in some lake not far from Nancy.

Besides the great wine production of Alsace, it is also here that the beer-brewing industry of France thrives. With all the other crops that grow in the east, hops have not been left out. Neither, by the way, has the tobacco plant.

All the fresh water fish possible swim in the fast-flowing waters of the Vosges streams, and the slower-moving waters of the Moselle and the Meuse. Particularly the less common fish – carp, pike, perch, roach and bream – find their way into the fish stews of this area.

It seems strange to mention water again; but mineral waters are bottled by the thousand gallons in these regions. Vittel and Contrexeville find a place on the finest tables in the world. There can be nothing wrong with the business acumen of the French if they can make a fortune out of selling water!

TARTE ALSACIENNE   (Apple tart from Alsace)

Many of the dishes of the pastrycooks in this eastern area of France are too rich and filling to have at the end of a good meal. Perhaps they were created to be eaten by themselves, with a glass or two of fine Alsace wine. If they create opportunities to taste wine such as a Reisling from Riquewihr, then they can only be applauded. But the first dish we discuss would fit into a menu, for it is a variation of apple tart.

shortcrust pastry
cooking apples
2 eggs
1 tablespoon of flour

3 tablespoons of sugar
$\frac{1}{4}$ pint (full $\frac{1}{2}$ cup) milk or cream
kirsch

Make enough pastry to line a tart tin (see page 24). Peel cooking apples, and slice them thinly. Roll out the pastry and line the tin. Arrange the slices of apple on the pastry. Sprinkle with sugar and bake for ten minutes in a hot oven (mark 7; 425°F.). Whip the eggs and mix in the flour. Add the milk or cream stirring all the time, and the sugar. Sprinkle into this mixture some kirsch or brandy. Pour onto the hot, partly cooked tart, and bake for a further 20 minutes at the same temperature until the top is cooked and the pastry golden brown. The tart can also be made with stoned cherries. (Illustrated on p. 151.)

SHANKELAS

These are a type of almond fritter. Pastry is nearly always cooked in the oven but with this dish try the traditional way, frying it in a pan.

4 oz. ($\frac{1}{2}$ cup) butter
4 oz. ($\frac{3}{4}$ cup) flour
6 oz. (6 tablespoons) sugar

4 oz. (1 cup) ground almonds
5 eggs

Rub the butter and flour together. Add the sugar and ground almonds, and mix in the eggs. Blend well, form into a ball and roll out on a floured surface to about a $\frac{1}{2}$-inch thickness. Cut into fingers. Heat butter and oil in a frying pan to steaming. The fingers will be very crumbly so lift them carefully, one at a time, with a slice, and cook quickly in the pan. Brown both sides, drain, and serve on a white paper napkin. Ground almonds are readily available, but the fritters are much improved if you use fresh almonds, grated.

KUGELHOPF

A very distinctive cake from Alsace. It gets its shape from the special mould in which it is baked. This rather like a large jelly mould. If you don't feel like buying such a specialised tin, why not try a metal jelly mould. You will not get the true Kugelhopf shape, but you will be very near it.

12 oz. ($2\frac{1}{4}$ cups) flour
4 oz. ($\frac{1}{4}$ cup) sugar
4 oz. ($1\frac{1}{2}$ cups) butter
$\frac{1}{2}$ oz. yeast
2 tablespoons ($2\frac{1}{2}$) warm water
warm milk

rind of lemon
2 eggs
4 oz. raisins
4 oz. sultanas
icing sugar

Warm a mixing bowl in the oven. In it, rub the butter into the flour. Add the sugar, raisins, sultanas, and lemon peel. Mix well. Dissolve the yeast in warm water and add a teaspoon of sugar. Make a well in the cake-mix and pour in the yeast. Beat in the eggs. Mix well, and make up the cake dough with milk. Knead for ten minutes – the dough should be moist but not wet. Fill the mould half full. (You may need more than one mould if they are small). Allow to rise to fill three-quarters of the mould. Bake for 45 minutes in a moderate oven (mark 4; 350°F.). The mould will be full when the cake is baked. Allow to cool, and turn out. Sprinkle with icing sugar.

Cherry and apple tarts (p. 149) from Alsace, which is famous for its pastries, and a vacherin *(p. 160), meringue and pastry filled with fruit and cream.*

KNEPFI

Perhaps it would be a good idea to talk about a dish that comes into the province of the pastrycook but is a savoury dish. It is a type of dumpling, and would make a nourishing main dish.

1 lb. (3 cups) flour	**4 oz. ($\frac{1}{2}$ cup) butter**
3 eggs	**salt**
1 cup ($1\frac{1}{4}$) of milk	

Make a mixture of the flour, eggs, milk and a pinch of salt. Proceed as for a batter. Mix the eggs into the flour and add the milk, drop by drop at first. Dry a little with flour as necessary. Roll into a ball and leave to stand for 2 hours.

Dust your hands well with flour and form the dough into small balls, about the size of a golf ball. Drop carefully into a deep pan full of boiling water, and cook for ten minutes. Drain, and serve with squares of bread fried in butter, melted butter, and grated cheese or a fresh tomato sauce (see page 53).

MENU

Let's devise a simple menu, with this dish as the main part of the meal.

POINTES D'ASPERGES, SAUCE VINAIGRETTE	ASPARAGUS VINAIGRETTE
KNEPFI AUX BEURRE	KNEPFI WITH BUTTER
CÔTES DE PORC	PORK CHOPS
ABRICOTS AU FOUR	APRICOTS WITH KIRSCH

Cook the asparagus (see page 34) and serve with a sauce vinaigrette (see page 82). The dumplings are to be served, this time, with melted butter and cheese. You could serve them with the meat; pork chops grilled or fried in a little butter and oil.

ABRICOTS AU FOUR. Choose ripe apricots, halve them, and take out the stones. Place the fruit in an oven dish, and for 1 lb. of fruit add $\frac{1}{2}$ wine glass of water and 3 oz. (3 tablespoons) sugar. Cover, and cook in a moderate oven (mark 4; 350°F.). When the moisture is absorbed the fruit is cooked. Serve sprinkled with kirsch and sugar.

PORK CHOPS. See page 16.

Civet de lièvre (*p.* 168); *jugged hare. Deliciously rich, the dish is here served with a red cabbage salad.*

POT AU FEU

Knepfi made a very useful dish for Madame Ulrich. Her husband was a doctor and he would often be home late, after visiting a patient in one of the villages, or in the hospital at Colmar, the nearest town. On these occasions she might leave some meat and sauce from a *pot au feu* in a bowl, with a few knepfi. Popped in the oven they easily heated up.

Pot au feu is the very simplest dish of meat boiled with vegetables. If it is eaten directly after cooking the meat can be used as a main dish. The stock may be kept as a soup, or to add to other dishes.

You must have some bones in a *pot au feu*. Use beef on the bone, top rib, shin or even oxtail. Chop the meat and bones into manageable pieces. If you want a good main dish add some chuck steak. Sear the pieces of meat in a frying pan, but don't worry about the meat on the bone.

Put the meat and bones into a large pot, cover with water, and boil for five minutes. Skim to clear the stock. Add carrots, turnips, leeks, and celery. Season with salt and pepper, and add a *bouquet garni*. Simmer for three hours. If the meat for the main dish cooks quickly, remove it from the stock and put it aside to reheat just before serving.

You will have plenty of ready-cooked vegetables to serve from the *pot au feu*. Garnish with potatoes or *knepfi*. Take off some of the stock to serve as a soup at the start of the meal. Here is a meal that Madame Uhlrich served to her husband and two hungry boys one cold November evening.

MENU

SOUPE DU POT AU FEU	SOUP FROM POT AU FEU
PERCHES, SAUCE HOLLANDAISE	PERCH, SAUCE HOLLANDAISE
POT AU FEU	POT AU FEU
POMMES DE TERRE	BOILED POTATOES
SALADE	SALAD
FROMAGES	CHEESE
TARTE AUX POIRES	PEAR TART

Madame added the *knepfi* to the soup from the *pot au feu*. She drained off the amount of stock necessary, put it into a pot, and cooked the dumplings (rolled very small, not much bigger than marbles) in the stock, for ten minutes. (See page 153.)

PERCH WITH SAUCE HOLLANDAISE. The perch had been caught by a friend of the family; Monsieur Asterix was a wonderful fisherman. The perch he brought were beautiful shining creatures. Madame Uhlrich was careful to avoid the spikes on the back. She cleaned them carefully and cooked them in a *court bouillon* (see page 30) flavoured with white wine and vinegar. In about 15 minutes they were cooked. Madame removed them from the *bouillon*, scraped the scales off, and plunged them back again to make sure that all the fish were quite clean. She drained them again and arranged them on a warm serving dish.

SAUCE HOLLANDAISE.   This is a very fine sauce for all fish.

¼ lb. (½ cup) butter
yolks of 3 eggs

juice of 1 lemon
1 tablespoon water

Melt the butter in the double boiler, or in a bowl over a saucepan of boiling water. Put the egg yolks in another bowl and whip gently. Still whipping, pour in some of the melted butter. The eggs will thicken as they begin to cook on contact with the hot butter. Slowly beat all the butter into the yolks. You will have a thick sauce in the bowl. Transfer this sauce to the double boiler and whip in, drop by drop, the juice of a lemon heated with a tablespoon of hot water. The butter sauce will thin, but should not separate. Whip well and remove from the heat. Allow to cool in a sauce boat.

This sauce seems complicated, but after a few attempts it will become second nature. If you lose the nice creamy consistency at any time, particularly when adding the lemon juice and water, remove from the heat at once and whip in an extra egg yolk. If you need to thin, add some more hot water. Serve the sauce separately in a sauce boat.

PEAR TART.   The pastry for large soft fruit like pears can with advantage be more biscuity; that is, shorter. Use ½ lb. (1½ cups) flour, ¼ lb. (½ cup) butter or margarine, a pinch of salt and a teaspoon of sugar. Add two egg yolks before you use any water. The egg may be enough by itself to bind the mixture.

Peel and halve the pears, taking care to remove all pips and hard fibre. Stew them gently in a little water and plenty of sugar. When tender remove from the water. Make a sauce, with a large spoon of apricot jam and the syrup the pears were cooked in.

Roll out the pastry. You will probably have to lift it with a slice, as it will be very crumbly. Line a buttered tart tin and prick the pastry well. Cover with a circle of foil weighed down with a few white beans. Bake in a fairly hot oven (mark 6; 400°F.) for 20 minutes or until the pastry is cooked. Remove from the oven and allow to cool.

Arrange the cooked pears on the pastry and spoon the apricot sauce over them. Leave to cool.

You could add a meringue top to the cooked tart. Use four egg whites and 8 oz. (½ cup) of sugar. Beat 4 oz. (¼ cup) sugar and the whites together. When solid, fold in the other 4 oz. of sugar. Spread over the top of the pears and bake in a very cool oven (mark ½; 275°F.) until the meringue is set and beginning to brown; about 1 hour.

Everything on this menu was prepared some time before the meal. Madame Uhlrich even added the potatoes to the *pot au feu* and cooked them for 20 minutes in the stock. The *knepfi* were made two hours before the meal, and left in the refrigerator on a floured plate, ready to add to the soup.

A cook preparing a meal has many variables to deal with. Products vary; and so does the time needed to cook them. A piece of chuck steak from one animal will take 1½ hours to braise, from another it will take 2 hours. Human beings (the guests) are variable as well, and Madame Uhlrich had her husband, who might be delayed, and M. Asterix, who might not bring the fish.

He did bring the fish and, moreover, prepared the *court bouillon* and cooked those beautiful 6 oz. bream. Madame prepared the sauce. Henri, the erring husband, arrived with some fresh cheese, a Munster and a Romatour. The wine – Tokay, a white, dry deliciously light wine, and a red from Wissembourg – was in the cellar.

AN APERITIF

M. Asterix always enjoyed being with the Uhlrichs. Madame was so sympathetic and *Monsieur le médecin* was delightfully light-hearted with his friends. 'Hey, Asterix, what about the magic potion?' This was a standing joke with the family for M. Asterix often made his own version of the potion that is said to have given such strength to the Gauls of long ago. 'It's really an aperitif, but if you wish . . .'

Simmer 1 pint (2½ cups) of clear plum juice with the juice of a lemon, and a *bouquet* made of a piece of fresh mint and ½ a bay leaf, for five minutes. Allow to cool, and add ½ bottle dry white wine and a glass of calvados or brandy. Take out the *bouquet* and allow any sediment to settle. Decant into any strange-shaped bottle and keep chilled.

ALMOND TART

They all thought that the tart was a great success. The two boys, Yves and Pierre, finished off the morsel that was left. M. Asterix had a good recipe for a tart which came from Nancy. He wrote it down for Madame.

shortcrust pastry with eggs (see Pear Tart, p. 155)
7 oz. (7 tablespoons) sugar
2 eggs, separated
whites of 2 eggs
4 tablespoons (5) milk
8 tablespoons (10) apricot jam
4 oz. (1 cup) ground almonds
almond essence

Make the pastry, roll out, and line a tart tin. In a warm bowl, whip the egg yolks with the sugar. Add the milk, the apricot jam and the ground almonds. Beat the 2 egg whites and fold into the filling. Whip thoroughly, over hot water if possible. Fold in the last two egg whites, whipped solid. Add a few drops of almond essence. Trickle some molten jam into the tart case and put in the filling. Bake in a hot oven (mark 7; 425°F.) for 35 minutes.

CHOUCROÛTE GARNIE

'Come along to my house next Saturday and sample a *choucroûte* with me'. The Uhlrichs were very pleased. It was the first of many visits. Their fisherman friend always cooked his own bag of fish or game, but the specialities of the region were the province of his sister, Odette. She, like her brother, had retired from the education service a few years before. She was a great cook. Her fiancé had been killed during the war, and she had never thought again of marriage.

For this special dinner she was going to cook a *choucroûte garnie*. This Alsatian dish has been transformed by luxury restaurants all over the world. It is basically a simple country dish with pickled white cabbage as the base.

Most *choucroûte* (the German name is *sauerkraut*) seems to appear out of tins, but Odette Dax always pickled her own. She was lucky enough to have a small barrel but it could be pickled in an earthenware jar or an enamel bucket.

She chose firm, nearly white, cabbages. She cleaned off the outside leaves, cut out the stem, and sliced them very finely with a large sharp knife. The cabbage was then washed thoroughly and dried.

Next, she lined the barrel with vine leaves, and laid down a layer of cabbage. On top of this went coarse salt and sprinkled caraway seeds. These layers were repeated until just below the top of the barrel, about four inches from the rim. Then the cabbage was pressed down well and just covered with water. On top went a thick clean cloth, then a round wooden lid that fitted loosely inside the barrel. This was weighed down with a heavy stone.

Odette used 5 oz. (full ½ cup) of salt to 20 lb. of cabbage. Sometimes she used juniper berries instead of caraway seeds. After 24 hours the salt water rose above the lid, and it would be kept like this for the whole time of pickling. Once a week the cover was removed, and the surface skimmed. The moisture lost was replaced with fresh salt water. After 3–4 weeks foam no longer rose to the top of the cabbage, and it was ready.

They would be six at table, and the boys were sure to be hungry, so she took 2½ lb. of *choucroûte* from the barrel and rinsed it in fresh water.

6 servings:

2 onions, chopped
2½ lb. pickled cabbage
1½ lb. of streaky bacon
6 pork cutlets
12 frankfurter sausages

½ bottle of dry white wine
1 cooking apple, sliced
about ½ oz. caraway seeds
salt and pepper

In a large pan, soften the chopped onions in goose dripping, or oil. Pour in the *choucroûte* and stir well. Add the white wine and enough water to moisten the *choucroûte* well. Put in the apple, sliced, and the caraway seeds in a bag. Add salt and pepper. Cook for 2 hours. Put in the bacon, top up with water (or stock if you have some) and cook for another hour. When the *choucroûte* and the bacon are tender, put the sausages in carefully and cook for 10 minutes.

Grill the pork chops separately and keep them warm. Boil potatoes, drain off the water, and leave covered in the hot saucepan.

Odette used a vast old china serving dish. This was warmed and piled with the *choucroûte*. She sliced the bacon, and arranged the slices on top. The chops were arranged at the side of the dish with the sausages. Some of the potatoes were arranged here and there in the *choucroûte*, and the rest served in a bowl.

MENU

Choucroûte garnie is a copious dish but, as we have found in all the regions, the cook likes to make up a menu so that his or her central dish is framed by lesser dishes.

CRÈME DE CÉLERI	CREAM OF CELERY SOUP
LA CHOUCROÛTE GARNIE	PICKLED CABBAGE WITH PORK AND SAUSAGES
SALADE	SALADE
FROMAGES	CHEESE
QUICHE AUX MIRABELLES	PLUM FLAN

CRÈME DE CÉLERI (Cream of celery soup)

3 oz. ($\frac{1}{2}$ cup) ground rice

1$\frac{1}{2}$ pints (3$\frac{3}{4}$ cups) milk

bouquet garni

salt

pepper

small onion stuck with a clove

purée:

12 oz. celeriac

butter

Mix the ground rice smoothly with a little cold milk. Pour the rest of the milk into a pan with the *bouquet*, onion, salt and pepper. Simmer for a few moments. Pour some of the hot milk onto the ground rice and milk, mix, stirring well. Transfer to the rest of the milk and simmer for 20 minutes. Strain, pressing through the remains of the onion and ground rice.

Cut the celeriac into small pieces and cook in boiling salted water. When tender drain, and cook gently in plenty of butter in a frying pan. Mash into a purée or pass through an electric blender. Add this purée to the rice cream stock and warm through. Croûtons fried in butter make a good addition to this soup.

QUICHE AUX MIRABELLES (Plum flan). The *quiche* is a dish that comes typically from Alsace and Lorraine, although it appears in other regions as well. It is a flan with an egg and cream filling; the filling garnished with a multiplicity of products. So with a basic preparation you can make a variety of dishes. This *quiche* is made with Mirabelle plums.

$\frac{1}{2}$ lb. shortcrust pastry (see page 24)

2 lb. Mirabelle plums

sugar to taste

1 tablespoon (1$\frac{1}{4}$) butter

3 eggs

1 pint (2$\frac{1}{2}$ cups) cream or milk

Make the pastry and line a 10-inch tart tin. Put in a layer of plums and sprinkle with sugar. Cook in a hot oven (mark 7; 425°F.) for ten minutes. Whip the eggs with the cream, or milk, and add sugar; the mixture should taste sweet. Take the tart from the oven (after the 10 minutes) and pour in the egg and cream mixture. Dot with butter and replace in the oven for $\frac{1}{2}$ an hour.

The dish is much finer if made with cream, but you can use milk or a mixture of cream and milk. The famous *quiche lorraine* is a savoury variation of this dish.

QUICHE LORRAINE.   Make your pastry, line a baking tin, and cover the bottom with streaky bacon lightly fried in butter. Pour over the cream and eggs as above, but add a little salt and pepper. Grate nutmeg over the top and dot with butter. Cook in a hot oven (mark 7; 425°F.) for $\frac{1}{2}$ an hour.

Naturally they started their feast with Asterix's 'potion'. To follow he had selected some wines from the region. With the *choucroûte* there were bottles of *Gewurtztraminer* from Sigolsheim. For the cheese he had found some red from Pagny, in the Moselle, and the *quiche* was accompanied by a *vin de paille* from Colmar.

After dinner the men began a heated discussion on the Alsace dialect, *Hochdeutsch*. The ladies quietly made the coffee and discussed things of importance such as the price of a leg of lamb, the long hair of the male youths, the short skirts of the females, and the lack of feminine influence in the Cabinet. 'Only one woman in the Government in the last ten years'.

TERRINE DE FOIE DE PORC (Pig's liver terrine)

Madame Uhlrich invited the charming brother and sister back to dinner the following week. She wanted them to meet her sister, who was coming to stay until Christmas, and who made the most wonderful *terrine*.

1 lb. pig's liver
1 lb. lean pork, minced
1 lb. bacon
½ lb. (3 cups) breadcrumbs, soaked in water
2 eggs

1 large onion
handful of parsley
2 tablespoons (2½) salt
pepper
mixed spice
brandy (optional)

Chop the liver and the bacon finely. Mix with the minced pork. (Make sure that all the rind is off the bacon, and that there are no pieces of gristle). Line an earthenware casserole with thin slices of fat bacon. Mix the meat with the breadcrumbs, the eggs, the onion finely chopped, spices and seasoning. Add the brandy if you have some, and press everything down into the casserole. Cover with slices of fat bacon, and a bayleaf and some thyme. Seal the lid with flour and water, and cook for 2 hours in a moderate oven (mark 4; 350°F.).

Allow the casserole to cool, after cooking, and then chill it. Remove the herbs. Heat the bottom of the casserole over boiling water and turn out the *terrine*. Serve with *croûtons*.

MENU

Madame and her sister Rose sat down on the Thursday before the great event and planned the dinner. 'As there are two of us why don't we make that wonderful sweet, *Vacherin*?' Their mother and grandmother used to make this sweet dish. Madame Uhlrich was a little nervous about it, but knew that it alone could make the evening memorable.

TERRINE DE FOIE DE PORC	PIG'S LIVER TERRINE
PURÉE DE LENTILLES	CREAM OF LENTIL SOUP
RIS DE VEAU	SWEETBREADS
NOUILLES	NOODLES
POIREAUX BRAISÉS	BRAISED LEAKS
SALADE	SALAD
FROMAGES	CHEESE
VACHERIN	VACHERIN

When they looked at this ambitious menu they were both a bit nervous. But after they had divided the menu into sections, and shared out the work, they felt better. Here is the way they did it.

FRIDAY
Cook the terrine
Prepare the meringue crown for the vacherin

Rose
Annie

SATURDAY MORNING
Make the soup, prepare the sweetbreads   Rose and Annie

AFTERNOON
Braise the leeks. Finish the *Vacherin*   Annie

BEFORE DINNER
Cook the sweetbreads and prepare the noodles   Rose

VACHERIN.   Annie was to do the meringue for the *vacherin*. She also needed sweet
pastry, as this is a type of *gâteau* with a pastry base, and sides made of meringue. The
centre is filled with cream and fruit.

pastry:

8 oz. (1½ cups) flour	yolk of 1 egg
4 oz. (½ cup) butter	pinch of salt
2 oz. (4 tablespoons) sugar	

meringue:

4 eggs	1 bare tablespoon (1) cornflour
8 tablespoons (10) caster sugar	teaspoon of wine vinegar
pinch of cream of tartar	

filling:

1½ pints cream, whipped	frozen raspberries
vanilla sugar or vanilla essence	

Put the flour into the mixing bowl. Make a well in the centre and put all the pastry
ingredients into it. Mix the centre – of egg, sugar and butter – first, then incorporate
with the flour. Knead well to ensure a good mixture. Leave to rest for an hour, roll out
and line a 9-inch tart tin. Bake in a fairly hot oven (mark 6; 400°F.), weighed down with
a circle of foil and some beans or pieces of bread, until golden brown, (15 minutes).
Cool, and loosen from the tin. The pastry is half cooked.

To make the meringue, whip the egg whites until they start to go white. Add 4
tablespoons of sugar and whip again. Sprinkle in the cream of tartar and the cornflour.
Whip until solid. Add the rest of the sugar, and the vinegar. Finish the whipping. The
mixture will be very thick and difficult to turn.

Note. If you prefer to use your own meringue mixture, then just alter the cooking
time and temperature to suit it.

To make the meringue 'basket', take two baking sheets. Oil them lightly and sprinkle
with flour. Trace a circle on each, of about 8-inch diameter. Put a third of the meringue
mixture in an icing bag with a large nozzle, and within the traced pattern build up a
circle of meringue on each sheet. The mixture will be very thick and will stand up above
the metal of the baking sheets by about ¾ inch.

In an oven preheated to very cool (mark ¼; 250°F.), place the two baking sheets with
the meringue rings. Keep the oven door ajar with a wedge of paper, and bake for 1 hour,

or until the meringue has completely dried out. Allow to cool, and loosen from the base with a long thin knife.

Using the final one-third of the meringue mixture, put a ring round the edge of the pastry base. Place on this uncooked meringue one of the cooked circles of meringue. Put another ring of uncooked meringue on top of this and place on top the second cooked ring. With the remaining mixture in the bag, run round the inside and outside of the 'basket'. Cook in the same oven with the door ajar, for two hours. Allow to cool, and place this pastry and meringue on a flat dish.

Rose whipped cream, and added a little vanilla sugar. (Essence would do). There was no small fruit about, so she bought some frozen raspberries, mixed them with the cream, and filled the *vacherin*. (Illustrated on p. 151.)

CREAM OF LENTIL SOUP. By Friday night the team had the terrine cooked, as well as the *vacherin*, and all the shopping was done. On Saturday morning it was the turn of the soup.

1 lb. lentils	parsley
2 oz. bacon	small bay leaf
1 carrot	salt
1 onion	butter

Soak the lentils overnight. Rinse, and simmer in fresh water for 30 minutes in a large pot. Chop the bacon, carrot, onion, and parsley and toss in butter in a frying pan. Add this to the lentils, with salt and pepper to taste. Simmer until the lentils are cooked, about another $\frac{1}{2}$ hour. Strain the soup into the bowl and crush the lentils and vegetables through the wire sieve or liquidise in an electric blender. Pour back into the large pot with enough of the liquid to make a thick soup. Melt some butter into the soup and check the seasoning. Serve with *croûtons*.

MENU

Unfortunately the business of the day does not stop for a special dinner. The boys were home on the Saturday because it was raining and, to cap it all, brought a friend home to lunch. Rose cooked the lunch and made it quick and simple. She made the boys help and jokingly ordered them round the kitchen. They first went out and bought some tender loin of pork. They already had potatoes and turnips. This was their meal.

PAUPIETTES DE PORC	PAUPIETTES OF PORK
POMMES SAUTÉES	SAUTÉ POTATOES
NAVETS BRAISÉS	BRAISED TURNIPS
OMELETTE SUCRÉE	SWEET OMELET

PAUPIETTES OF PORK. The boys' aunt cut the tender loin of pork into slices and hammered it out flat. The boys were set to work chopping parsley and onions very finely. Oil was heated in a large pan. Each hammered-out slice of pork had its spoonful of chopped parsley and onion. This stuffing was seasoned well, and the pork was rolled and tied with some thin kitchen twine. Into the sizzling pot went each roll. The heat was lowered, and they were left to cook slowly.

SAUTÉ POTATOES; BRAISED TURNIPS. Potatoes were peeled, cut into chunks, and tossed in oil. The turnips were peeled and trimmed. They were all quite small, otherwise they would have been cut into chunks of roughly the same size. Madame cooked some of the chopped onion in another pan, and when this was soft she added the turnips, mixed them thoroughly with the oil and onions, and left them to braise with a cup of water. They were seasoned well and served with melted butter.

SWEET OMELET. 'To the table'. They had a litre of red wine from the supermarket, and it went down well with the homely meal. Before she sat down, Madame Uhlrich tossed some apples in butter and left them to cook until tender. 'Who's going to cook the omelet?' 'Jules?' Their friend Jules Rouvier was a student of philosophy, who thought deeply and long about everything he did. He took 15 minutes to stir the eggs ready for the omelet (see page 23). He was to add sugar and a few dots of butter to the eggs. Rose showed him how to draw the eggs up into a thick wedge and, feeling sorry for his confusion, added the apples, some more sugar, and a sprinkle of kirsch to complete the dish.

CHRISTMAS GOOSE

1 goose, ready for the oven

stuffing:

½ lb. sausage meat
1 tablespoon (1¼) parsley, chopped

1 tablespoon (1¼) butter
1 tablespoon (1¼) thyme, chopped

braised choucroûte:

1 onion, chopped
½ lb. chopped bacon and ham, mixed

1½ lb. choucroûte
1 lb. Strasbourg sausages

Christmas was coming along, and of course that meant goose. Rose usually took over the goose and this was her method. She stuffed the bird with sausage meat, mixed with chopped parsley and thyme, rubbed the back with butter, and roasted it in a hot oven (mark 7; 425°F.). From time to time she drained off some of the fat that is given off during cooking. The goose was served on a bed of braised *choucroûte* (see page 156 for *choucroûte*).

In a large pan she softened some chopped onion, then added chopped bacon and ham. The washed *choucroûte* was placed on top and stirred well to mix it with the onions, bacon and ham. Water was added, and the *choucroûte* was left to cook slowly until tender. As an extra garnish some Strasbourg sausages were cooked for ten minutes with the *choucroûte*.

CHOCOLATE GÂTEAU

There was a very simple chocolate gâteau from Lorraine that they always made at Christmas.

$\frac{1}{4}$ lb. ($\frac{1}{2}$ cup) butter
$\frac{1}{4}$ lb. chocolate
4 eggs
4 oz. ($\frac{1}{4}$ cup) sugar

1 tablespoon ($1\frac{1}{4}$) flour
vanilla
1 teaspoon ($1\frac{1}{4}$) grated almonds

Separate the eggs. Cream the butter with a fork. Soften the chocolate in a saucepan with a teaspoon of water. Mix the chocolate and butter in a bowl. Stir in the egg yolks. Add the sugar and the flour. Flavour with the almonds and the vanilla. Whip the egg whites and fold in. Butter a cake tin and pour in the mixture. Bake in a warm oven (mark 3; 325°F.) until cooked; about $1\frac{1}{2}$ hours. Test with a sharp knife; if it comes out clean the cake is cooked.

M. Asterix often came to see them. At Christmas time he came bearing champagne 'This is a wine that's good for you. What do you say, Doctor?'

The wine reminded Doctor Uhlrich of a cousin of his who lived in the Champagne district. When he went to visit this cousin for the first time, in his new house, he had been treated to a complete survey of the district. As a civil engineer, Bernard Mesnier did not miss much.

Champagne and
the North

Bernard Mesnier, engineer, product of one of the great schools of Paris, had been all over the world, but 'his' country was the Champagne and its extension to the north. He had decided to settle in the district of his birth near Troyes, and his frequent surveying expeditions took him through the Champagne, into the Ardennes and on to the sea.

'Where else can you get the finest wine in the world, the most peaceful countryside, busy towns that still have a sense of history about them, and a coast that gives the best fish in great abundance'.

As a student he had studied the way in which this north-eastern part of France gathers itself as though to descend upon Paris. Like the ripples on a pool, the heights of the Ardennes and the Champagne circle the Paris basin. The sheep of the Ardennes graze on soft slopes protected by elms, oaks, and larch trees that still stand in spite of the depredations of man. The 'mountain' of Reims slopes away into the vineyards of Pinot and Chardonnay, that give their fruit to the old skills of Dom Perignon.[1]

Farther north, the land was rich long before industry came. On the vast rolling farm-lands wheat, oats, beet and hops all give their riches to man. The land was already there to feed the cities; and in these cities textiles were made and still are. The machines of Lille, Arras, and Cambrai are new, but the skills are old.

On the coast, Boulogne is the first fishing port of France. Sole, cod, hake, mackerel, herring are ready for the cook's eager hand. Again, the machines and the boats are new but you cannot escape a feeling of the past in the work of the fisherman.

As he went about his work observing, measuring, sampling, M. Mesnier had a good chance to judge the richness and variety of this part of France. There were the forests and old rock of the Argonne; the open sloping plateaux of the great wine area about Reims and Epernay; the vast rich farm lands of the Artois; the canals and lagoons of Flanders; and the chalk cliffs and flint pebble beaches of the coast.

The people he met seemed solid and dependable. They were not discouraged by storm or rain, for their roots went deep; and if a crop was spoilt one day, it would surely thrive the next. Those crops, and the farm animals were used to good effect in kitchens all over the area. He ate well everywhere.

[1] A 17th-century Benedictine monk who discovered the process for making sparkling Champagne.

The dishes he found were often simple, and he felt that there was a direct line to other centuries. The housewife in her kitchen was not interested in the latest dish from North Africa, China or the smartest restaurant in Paris. She only wanted to take the products of the land and turn them into nourishing food. The food in farmhouses and country inns was tasty, well presented, but simple. He could recognise what went into them; and my goodness they were filling!

If the products available to the cook were varied, so were the drinks on the table. Sparkling and still wines from Champagne added a rich glow to many a feast. In the Ardennes, rosy apples filled the cider press, and in the north – Picardy, Artois, Flanders – strong beer went the rounds under fragrant pipe smoke. Beer? They even cooked with it! And mineral water came from neighbouring Lorraine.

Imagination did seem to flow strongly in one section of the kitchen. Sweet pastries, cakes and puddings were much in evidence. They were the natural result of plentiful butter, eggs and cream and the finest wheat lands of France. Again, many of these sweet things were simple to make.

BREAD

The greatest product of wheat is bread, and bread is very much in evidence on the French table. The best known loaf in France is, of course, long and crusty; but many people in country districts make their own bread in round loaves. It is not difficult to make, and can even save you money.

3 lb. (9 cups) plain flour	1 teaspoon (1¼) sugar
6 level teaspoons (7½) salt	about 1½ pints (3¾ cups) warm water
1 oz. baker's yeast	

Make sure that all your materials are warm before you start. Mix the yeast with a little warm water in a bowl. When it is completely dissolved add the sugar, and ¾ pint (scant 2 cups) of the warm water. Put the flour in a mixing bowl, and sift in the salt. Make a well in the centre and pour in the yeast mixture. Sprinkle flour lightly over the liquid and leave for ½ an hour. The yeast should foam on the top. Pour in the other ¾ pint (scant 2 cups)of water and mix thoroughly. The mixture will make a solid mass of dough which should be very pliable but not wet. Dry out with a little flour if necessary. Knead for 15 minutes. *This is very important* as you must distribute the yeast through the dough. Cover and leave to rise for perhaps two hours. The dough should double its size.

When the dough has risen, knead for 5 minutes. Cut into 4 pieces, and shape into round loaves. Oil oven sheets and place the four loaves on them. Leave to rise in a warm place for ½ an hour and bake in a very hot oven (mark 9; 475°F.) for 15 minutes. Lower the oven to hot (mark 7; 425°F.) and bake until the bread is brown and sounds hollow when tapped. Cool on a wire rack.

Fresh bread like this will keep much better if you rub some fat into the flour before adding the yeast. Try different flours. Mix wholemeal with plain flour (following the same method but using more salt) and try rubbing in ¼ lb. (½ cup) of fat. Using all wholemeal flour, you need 1 oz. (1 tablespoon) of salt and ¼ lb. (½ cup) of butter or margarine.

From this staple part of our diet let us move to those sweet fancy things that M. Mesnier noted in the cooking of this part of France.

CROQUANTS

8 oz. (2 cups) ground almonds   vanilla
1 lb. (1 cup) castor sugar   brown sugar
whites of 4 eggs

Mix the ground almonds and sugar. Add the egg whites, a little at a time. Drop in some almond essence or use almond sugar if you prefer. Blend ingredients well. Roll into small boat-shapes and bake on oiled oven sheets in a moderate oven (mark 4; 350°F.) for 20 minutes.

MACARONS D'AMIENS

12 oz. (3 cups) ground almonds   3 tablespoons (4) clear apricot jam
8 oz. (full $\frac{1}{2}$ cup) icing sugar   vanilla essence
white of 1 egg, beaten

Mix the almonds and the sugar. Add the beaten egg white, the jam, and the vanilla. Blend well and allow to stand overnight. Roll out into a long rectangle about $\frac{1}{4}$ inch thickness and cut into slices.

Oil the oven trays and lay on them sheets of thin white kitchen paper. Oil the top of the paper and arrange the almond slices on top.

Bake in a moderate oven (mark 4; 350°F.) for 20 minutes. Allow to cool on the paper. Remove, and turn over the paper. The macaroons will be stuck fast. Soak the back with a clean sponge and the macaroons will loosen.

TUILES

These take their name from the shape. They look rather like curved roof tiles.

2 eggs   pinch of salt
8 oz. (full $\frac{1}{2}$ cup) sugar   12 oz. (3 cups) oatmeal

Beat the eggs and sugar together. Add the salt and oatmeal. Heat oven trays in the oven and coat with melted butter. Drop teaspoons of the mixture onto the trays, making sure to leave a space between each to allow for spreading. Bake for 5 minutes in a moderate oven (mark 4; 350°F.). When cooked, lift off with a thin knife or spatula, and rest on a rolling pin to cool. This gives the distinctive shape to the 'tiles'.

TÔT FAIT AUX POMMES

5½ oz. (1 cup) flour
1 oz. (1 tablespoon) sugar
3 eggs
2 medium apples, peeled

1 pint (2½ cups) milk
vanilla essence
rum (optional)

Mix the sugar and the flour in the mixing bowl. Add the eggs one at a time. Grate in the peeled apples. Add the milk, starting with a few drops and whipping it in slowly. Drop in some vanilla, and a glass of rum if you want a more luxurious dish.

Butter a pancake pan and when steaming drop in a spoonful of the mixture. Roll the pan to spread the mixture over the bottom. When this has set, loosen with a spatula and slip into a hot buttered oven-dish of roughly the same diameter. Pour the rest of the mixture on top. Cook in a fairly hot oven (mark 5; 375°F) for 12 minutes. Serve hot, sprinkled with sugar.

RABOTES (Baked apple dumplings)

1½ lb. flaky pastry (see page 72)
6 cooking apples

sugar
mixed spice

The apples should not be too large; about 4 oz. each. Core them. Roll out the pastry until quite thin. Place an apple on the pastry, well in from the edge. Stuff the apple with sugar and a sprinkle of spice. Cut round it, leaving a margin of pastry to fold over. Fold over the top of the fruit, damp the edges with milk and crimp together. Repeat with each apple. Brush with milk and bake on a buttered dish in a warm oven (mark 3; 325°F.) for 30 minutes or until the pastry is cooked. Sift with sugar and serve hot or cold.

MENU

On one journey, Bernard went into the Ardennes near the Belgian border. He was not far from Montherme in the beautiful countryside of the Meuse Valley. The broad sweep of the river between wooded slopes seemed so still from high up on a hillside. His survey was a real pleasure that day, but he wondered if the motorway he was working on would spoil the landscape.

Often, when in that region, he would stay with old friends, the Barbières. For supper one night they shared this simple meal.

SALADE DE CHOU ROUGE AU JAMBON
CIVET DE LIÈVRE
POMMES DE TERRE
RABOTES

RED CABBAGE SALAD WITH HAM
JUGGED HARE
BOILED POTATOES
BAKED APPLE DUMPLINGS

RED CABBAGE SALAD. Quarter the red cabbage, cut out the stalk, trim off the outer leaves and slice very finely. Heat a wine glass of vinegar, and pour it over the sliced cabbage. Turn, and leave to soak for 6 hours.

Slice raw mushrooms and dress with vinaigrette (see page 82). Arrange the cabbage in a flat dish, in two long mounds. Place the mushrooms in the centre and sprinkle vinaigrette over the whole. Dot clumps of parsley over the sliced cabbage salad, and serve with slices of ham. (Illustrated p. 152.)

JUGGED HARE. The hare stew was a wonderful dish on that clear autumn evening. This again is a straightforward dish, and its success depends on good preparation.

Hang the hare by the back legs, not skinned or cleaned, with a container below the muzzle to catch the blood. Hang for 4–5 days and drain off any blood each day into a covered container. The hanging improves and tenderizes the meat.

After hanging, skin and clean the hare. Most of the blood will be in the chest cavity so make sure you do not spill this. Drain out the blood, and put with the other blood in a covered container. Keep the liver.

Chop the hare into portions: back legs, front legs and back (saddle). Cut the saddle into two or four, depending on the size of the animal. Marinate these portions in red wine with chopped carrot, onion, and *bouquet garni*. The wine does not have to cover the hare, but will soak into the meat if left overnight.

Drain off the portions of hare, dry, and brown in hot dripping. Place in a large casserole, and sprinkle in a good tablespoon of flour. (The dish can be cooked on top of the stove or in the oven so choose your cooking pot accordingly). Grind in fresh black pepper and add salt. Add a *bouquet garni* and a few medium sized onions. Pour in the wine used for marinating (without the vegetables) and top up so that the meat is just covered.

Cook gently until the meat is tender, for about 2 hours, either on the stove or in a cool oven (mark 2; 300°F.). Just at the end add the liver, chopped small, and the blood to thicken and flavour the sauce. Do not boil the sauce after you have added the blood.

Madame Berbière served the *civet* with boiled potatoes, onions roast in the oven and whole carrots cooked in salted water with a spoonful of butter and a little sugar. (Illustrated p. 152.)

At the end of the meal they had rabotes very lightly sugared, with whipped cream. Bernard had brought with him some red wine from the Aube – which is the region about Troyes – called *Riceys* from the name of the vineyards. With coffee, black and strong, a brandy from the same area aided digestion. It seemed to aid conversation as well for they talked long into the night.

MENU

Two or three times a year Bernard and his wife would be invited to eat with his uncle who lived in St. Ménéhould. Those meals were real feasts and always in the tradition of the Argonne, a wonderful area of rocks, forest, caves and lakes. Here is one meal they had with Uncle Georges.

TÊTE DE VEAU, SAUCE GRIBICHE	CALF'S HEAD WITH SAUCE GRIBICHE
POTAGE DE POMMES DE TERRE	POTATO SOUP
JAMBON EN CROÛTE	FLAKY HAM SLICE
MOUTON ST. MÉNÉHOULD	STUFFED, BRAISED SHOULDER OF MUTTON
POMMES CROQUETTES	CROQUETTE POTATOES
PETITS POIS AUX CAROTTES	GARDEN PEAS WITH CARROTS
SALADE DE PISSENLIT	DANDELION SALAD
FROMAGES	CHEESE
MELON	MELON

What a feast it was! And how fortunate that Aunt Pauline had plenty of help in the kitchen.

CALF'S HEAD. Calf's head is increasingly difficult to get outside France but if you can get one, cleaned and scalded, the effort is worthwhile.

All French recipes use only the outer skin of the head and ears. Skin the head, working from the back towards the muzzle. Soak the skin in well salted water, and wash well. Wash in fresh water and dry.

Cut the skin into narrow strips and slice the ears. Cook in a *court bouillon* dosed with plenty of vinegar until tender, about 30 minutes.

SAUCE GRIBICHE. Aunt Pauline served the dish with a *sauce gribiche* which was made with yolks of 4 hard-boiled eggs, and 1 teaspoon ($1\frac{1}{4}$) each of mustard, gherkins, oil, vinegar, parsley, and capers. She creamed the yolks with mustard and oil, added the vinegar, sliced gherkins, chopped parsley and capers. The head could also be served with a sauce vinaigrette (see page 82) with plenty of chopped parsley added.

POTATO SOUP. The soup that evening was one of the simplest to make and is prepared for supper all over France. It is often the *soup du jour* in small restaurants.

4 oz. ($\frac{1}{4}$ cup) butter	1 cup of cream or milk
$1\frac{1}{2}$ lb. of potatoes	3 pints ($7\frac{1}{2}$ cups) of water
2 leeks	salt and pepper

Wash the leeks well, trim the green part off, and slice finely. Soften them in 1 oz. (2 tablespoons) of butter, in a large pot, and add the potatoes cut in small chunks. Mix well and add the water and salt and pepper. Simmer until the potatoes are soft. Remove the potatoes and mash them. Press through a sieve and put back into the stock. Heat and mix well. Check the seasoning and add cream or milk to get the right consistency. Add the rest of the butter. You can serve this soup with *croûtons*, or cook some spaghetti, broken into small pieces, and add it to the soup.

FLAKY HAM SLICE. The next dish was simply a slice of ham in flaky pastry – but with a difference.

6 servings:

1 lb. flaky pastry (see page 72)	**½ pint (1¼ cups) béchamel sauce**
6 slices of ham	**½ lb. mushrooms**

'Of course' said Aunt Pauline, 'the dish depends on how good your flaky pastry is. I always use at least 1 lb. of flour, because if there is some over you can use it another day for a tart or a small pie'.

Use slices of cooked ham from a shop, or cook a piece of ham yourself (see page 44). Allow to cool and cut into the required number of slices. The thickness needed is the one you usually cut for serving with a salad.

Roll the pastry out a ¼-inch thick, and cut rectangles slightly larger than the size of the ham slices. Make a sandwich of the ham between two rectangles of pastry. Moisten the edges and crimp together well. Trace a circle in the top with a very sharp knife. Bake in a hot oven (mark 7; 425°F.) for 15 minutes.

While the ham is baking, toss some sliced mushrooms in hot butter until tender. Make some béchamel sauce (see page 95) and stir the mushrooms into the sauce. Season well. Keep hot.

After baking, cut round the circle in the top of the pastry and lift it out, being careful to take the pastry underneath. Fill the hole with the creamy mushroom sauce, and replace the cap of pastry.

STUFFED, BRAISED SHOULDER OF MUTTON. The method of coating meat with butter and breadcrumbs is called 'a la Sainte Ménéhould'. It can be used very well for chicken, veal, pork and lamb. Aunt Pauline used a piece of mutton for the dish. She boned a shoulder of mutton and stuffed it, securing it carefully with thin kitchen thread looped round four or five times.

1 shoulder of mutton, boned

stuffing:

1 large onion, chopped	**¼ lb. chicken liver, chopped**
1 clove garlic	**parsley**
2 tablespoons (2½) butter	**mixed spice**
1 glass Champagne or white wine	**salt and pepper**
½ lb. sausage meat	

She softened the chopped onion in butter, added some garlic and poured in a glass of Champagne. We could use dry white wine. If you do use Champagne make sure that it is really dry. Only wine marked '*brut*' is really dry. She reduced this preparation by half over a low heat. The sausage meat, chopped chicken liver, parsley, salt, pepper, and spice were added to the pan and cooked gently for a few moments. This was the stuffing for the shoulder of mutton.

Aunt Pauline liked braising meat because she could use cheaper cuts of meat and still cook them tenderly with plenty of flavour. She chopped bacon, onion, carrots, celery, very small, and sizzled the bacon pieces first in a large thick pot. Then in went some butter and oil, and the vegetables, together with a *bouquet garni* and a large onion with one or two cloves stuck into it. She mixed the lot together, and allowed the vegetables to absorb the butter and oil.

In went the shoulder, stuffed and tied, on top of the vegetables and bacon. She let the meat brown for ten minutes in the pot and then added some water. The shoulder was not covered; the water came up about half way. Salt and pepper, and the meat was covered and left to braise for 2 hours. When tender, it was taken out and dried, and coated with melted butter and plenty of breadcrumbs. This coating was browned in a hot oven (mark 7; 425°F.) for 15 minutes. The thread was removed and the meat carved at the table.

CROQUETTE POTATOES

2 lb. potatoes	1 egg
3 oz. (scant ½ cup) butter	yolk of 1 egg
salt	flour
pepper	breadcrumbs
nutmeg	egg for coating

Cut up the potatoes and cook them in salted water. When cooked, mash well. If there are any lumps pass through a sieve. Add the butter, salt, pepper, whole egg and egg yolk. Blend well. Make small cakes with the mixture. Dust with flour, dip in beaten egg, roll in breadcrumbs, and fry in butter until crisp.

GARDEN PEAS WITH CARROTS. Cooking more than one vegetable in the same pan is typical of the north-east of France. In this case Aunt Pauline cooked peas and carrots together. The only thing to remember if you want to try this, is that vegetables cook at different rates.

Cut carrots into thin sticks and start cooking them in water with ½ oz. (1 tablespoon) butter, salt, and pepper. When half cooked, after about 10 minutes, add the peas and cook together. You will need to add some more boiling water. Dress with butter and chopped parsley.

DANDELION SALAD. A neighbour of Uncle George's cultivated dandelions for use in salad. The leaves of the plant under cultivation improve in size and flavour. This salad was George's speciality; he was also interested in the infusions of leaves and herbs used by country folk.

He diced bacon and fried it until crisp. To the bacon he added a tablespoon of vinegar, and this mixture was poured over the dandelion leaves in a warm salad bowl. No further seasoning was needed.

CHEESE. For cheese they had a deep golden Brie in its fine brown crust, *maroilles* (small hard cheeses matured in beer), and cream cheese mixed with softened butter and tarragon. 'It's amazing to think that 7 litres of milk go into making one little *maroille*'. 'That must be why they are so expensive' said the thrifty Aunt Pauline.

They drank champagne *brut* all through the meal. Uncle Georges always finished his wine before the fruit. 'For me the acidity of the wine does not go with the acidity of the fruit'.

MENU

Because he had good friends there, Bernard had no need to stay in hotels in the north of France. Those meals, eaten within sound of the shifting flint-pebble beaches! Fish of course influenced the whole style of cooking. Here was a menu that he noted in his little book, and which was graven into his memory.

TOMATES FARCIES	TOMATOES STUFFED WITH MUSSELS
MAQUEREAUX À LA CRÈME	MACKEREL IN WHITE SAUCE
CARBONNADE DE BOEUF	CARBONNADE OF BEEF
SALSIFIS	SALSIFY
SALADE	SALAD
FROMAGES	CHEESE
TARTE AUX POMMES	APPLE TART

TOMATOES STUFFED WITH MUSSELS. There are many ways of serving tomatoes but the sea has a hand in this method. Halve the tomatoes, take out the pips, and scoop away a little of the flesh. Heat scrubbed mussels in a pan with a very little water, or white wine, and some parsley. When the shells open, take out the mussels and allow them to cool. Mix the shell fish with some mayonnaise (see page 85) and stuff the tomatoes with this mixture.

MACKEREL IN WHITE SAUCE. The dish of mackerel was very well presented and this added a lot to its appeal. The fish were cleaned carefully, with the heads discarded, and cut into thick chunks across the body. These chunks were cooked in a *court bouillon* with plenty of vinegar. When cooked, the pieces of fish were skinned, and arranged on a serving dish warmed in the oven. A white sauce made with the stock was poured over the fish.

The dish was surrounded with mussels, and slices of roe coated with egg and bread-crumbs and fried in butter. Bunches of parsley and cress completed the presentation.

CARBONNADE OF BEEF. The carbonnade is a dish that is found right through into Belgium. It is a casserole of beef cooked in beer.

3 lb. beef	1 tablespoon ($1\frac{1}{4}$) flour
dripping	bayleaf
$\frac{1}{2}$ lb. onions, finely sliced	1 tablespoon ($1\frac{1}{4}$) brown sugar
2 pints beer	

Brown the meat in dripping. Place in a casserole, and cook the sliced onions in the same fat and add them to the meat. Clean the pieces from the frying pan with beer (bitter or light ale), then add the rest of the beer to the frying pan and bring to the boil. Mix the flour with the meat and onions in the casserole, and pour on the beer. Season well, and add the bayleaf and the brown sugar, and cook gently for $1\frac{1}{2}$ hours, until the beef is tender.

Braised turnips make a good accompaniment.

SALSIFY. This is a root vegetable much used in the north of France. It must be scraped well and washed. Cook in salted water, drain and toss in some cream.

APPLE TART. This is an apple tart with a difference. Spread roughly-mashed, cooked apples over the uncooked pastry, then carefully arrange uncooked apples in slices on top. Cook as for Apple Tart (see page 24). The tart is thus very moist. It is served with unsweetened cream.

RECIPES FROM NORTH-EASTERN FRANCE

Bernard's notebook was well supplied with fish dishes from the region about Boulogne and Dunkirk. Here are a few:

SALADE DE HARENGS (Herring salad)

Use smoked herring, with soft roes. Fillet the fish or buy fillets. Soak in milk for $\frac{1}{2}$ an hour, and then in olive oil. Make a sauce from the roes crushed with, to each roe, 1 teaspoon ($1\frac{1}{4}$) mustard, a twist of white pepper and 2 teaspoons ($2\frac{1}{2}$) oil. Spread the fillets with this sauce, and serve with a dish of hot potatoes, beetroot, parsley and chives. Sprinkle a few chopped gherkins over the top.

MOULES À LA BOULONNAISE (Mussels in the Boulogne style)

Clean the mussels and open with a little wine (see page 172). Take out of the shells, keeping the liquor aside, and toss gently with chopped shallot, butter and parsley. Thicken the mussel liquor with some bread crumbs, and pour over the cooked mussels. Stir, and serve with slices of lemon.

CABILLAUD (Cod in white wine)

Season thick cod cutlets with salt, pepper and grated nutmeg. Fry in butter and sprinkle chopped shallots into the pan. Turn out into an oven dish and barely cover with white wine, or wine and water. Place beside the fish a *bouquet garni*, season well, and poach for 10 minutes on a gentle heat on top of the stove.

When poaching fish in this way, remember to use liquid very sparingly. Take the fish from the liquid when cooked, and stir in cream or some béchamel sauce. Use this creamy preparation as a sauce.

SOUPE DE POISSON (Fish soup)

Not only is this a good dish to start a meal, it is also a good way of using fish pieces that the fishmonger practically gives away. Use heads, tails, and pieces such as collar of cod, and a few whiting. Simmer with some chopped carrot, onion and a *bouquet garni*. Season well. (If you have any heads in the stock, make sure that you cut out the eyes, as these add a bitter flavour to the soup).

After $\frac{1}{2}$ an hour's cooking, remove from the stove and strain the stock. Put this into another pot. Make thickening with some cornflour (or rice flour) mixed with cold water to a smooth paste. Add this to the soup, heat, and stir until it thickens. Serve in a soup tureen with some shelled shrimps and parsley.

GRILLED SOLE

Madame Jouvet, who was the wife of a harbour official in Boulogne, had a bee in her bonnet about sole. 'This wonderful fish is disguised, swamped with sauce, and generally messed about in restaurants. It has such a flavour that it needs no addition'.

She always grilled her sole with butter and lemon juice. 'It's all so simple, but you must prepare your fish well. Cut the heads off diagonally, clean and trim off the tail and the fins. Make a small cut across the base of the tail in the dark skin. Work some of the skin back and then grasp with a cloth and pull off the whole skin. Cut along the backbone from the head to the tail; cut in about $\frac{1}{2}$ an inch and ease away the flesh from the backbone. This lets the heat of the grill into the thickest part. Slash the fish over its surface perhaps six times with a very sharp knife. The fish is now ready for the grill. Don't cook very fast if you have a large fish, and have a little bowl of melted butter ready to spoon over it.'

HOCHEPOT

It was Madame Jouvet who gave Bernard the recipe for the *Hochepot*, a Flemish dish.

8 servings:

1 lb. salted topside of beef	4 leeks, trimmed and cleaned
$\frac{1}{2}$ a shoulder of mutton	4 medium turnips
1 lb. lean pork	1 large parsnip, cut in quarters
1 lb. streaky bacon	*bouquet garni*
a piece of boiling sausage	salt and pepper
$\frac{1}{2}$ lb. carrots	juniper berries (optional)
$\frac{1}{2}$ lb. onions, medium sized	

The butcher will sell salt beef, or will salt it for you. (Allow 4 days for this). Use the thick half of a shoulder of mutton; about 2 lb. Any lean cut will do for the pork. Boil all the meat together in the pot, and skim. Add the vegetables whole, and the *bouquet*, and season well. A few juniper berries, crushed, are a good addition to the flavour. Boil until the meats are cooked. As each takes a different time per pound, they will come out in this order: salt pork; lean pork; sausage; beef; and then mutton. (Mutton 20 minutes per lb. plus 20 minutes; beef and pork 25 minutes per lb. plus 25 minutes). As each is taken out, arrange on a serving dish, cover, and keep warm. Serve with the vegetables, plus cabbage braised in large pieces (see page 30) and boiled potatoes.

ONION SAUCE. There was a very good sauce that went well with the *Hochepot*. Madame made a béchamel, and dropped into it onions sliced very thin. While these were cooking she added salt, pepper, and vinegar. The sauce was then simmered for an hour.

GALOPINS

After serving one memorable *hochepot* she set the guests to make *galopins*. They had to soak ½ lb. bread without a crust in boiling milk, and mash it up well. 3 egg yolks were added. Some of the very liquid mixture was poured onto smoking butter in a pan and cooked like a pancake. These were eaten straight from the pan with plenty of sugar. 'It's good to sit down sometimes and let the guests cook for you'. What about a 'bring-your-own-recipe-and-cook-it' party?

MATELOTE OF FISH

Bernard obtained the recipe for the *hochepot* from Madame Jouvet in exchange for a *matelote* recipe from the Marne.

1 lb. eel	**tarragon**
1 lb. pike	**garlic**
1 lb. carp or bream	**2 oz. (4 tablespoons) butter**
white wine	**1 oz. (3¼ tablespoons) flour**
3 oz. shallots, finely chopped	**salt and pepper**

Scale, clean and trim the fish. Cut into chunks across the body. Butter the bottom of the pot, put in the fish, and cover with wine and water. Add the shallots, chopped, and the herbs; season well. Simmer for ten minutes. Knead the flour and butter together, drop into the stock, and stir while the dish thickens, about 10 minutes.

MENU

Here is a meal that Bernard had with his friends in the Ardennes.

OEUFS POCHÉS À LA CRÈME	EGGS POACHED IN CREAM
MATELOTE DE VEAU	MATELOTE OF VEAL
CHOU ROUGE	RED CABBAGE
SALADE	SALAD
FROMAGES	CHEESE
CIGARETTES DE MIEL	HONEY 'CIGARETTES'

EGGS POACHED IN CREAM.   The eggs were cooked in a deep poacher. (If you don't possess a poacher you could use individual ovenware pots). Put the poachers into boiling water. Pour some cream into each. When the cream is scalding hot, crack an egg into each, and cook until the egg is firm and glazed.

MATELOTE OF VEAL

1½ lb. veal	garlic
2 onions	2 oz. (4 tablespoons) butter
bouquet garni	1 oz. (3¼ tablespoons) flour
red wine	

Chop the onions. Cut the veal into small pieces. Brown in a pan with the onions. Add the *bouquet*, garlic, and red wine. Simmer for 15 minutes and add some water or light stock. Season. When the meat is tender knead the butter and flour together and stir into the stock, thickening it. Serve with small onions and mushrooms as with the fish *matelote* (see page 175).

RED CABBAGE.   Slice red cabbage finely and put it into a pot with a liberal sprinkling of vinegar. Add red wine, salt, pepper, grated nutmeg, and a tablespoon of brown sugar. Simmer the cabbage, and when it is nearly cooked add sliced apple.

The secret of good red cabbage is to get a balance between the sweet and sour elements of the preparation. The cabbage cooks slowly so that you have the opportunity to taste and check the ingredients. You might need more salt, vinegar or sugar. Pop them in, and don't worry too much about the measured amounts.

HONEY 'CIGARETTES'.   Madame Barbière was very proud of her 'cigarettes'. They always ate in the large roomy kitchen with its stone floor, scoured almost white, and large inglenook fireplace, complete with benches. If M. Barbière wanted to smoke his pipe he had to go out of that kitchen! This is her recipe for 'cigarettes' and it was a good way to use the wonderful honey of the region.

1 egg	3 oz. (6 tablespoons) butter
2 tablespoons (2½) sugar	8 oz. (1½ cups) flour
2 tablespoons (2½) honey	1 teaspoon (1¼) baking powder

Mix the egg and sugar together. Beat in the butter. Add the honey, flour and baking powder. Mix well. Roll out as thin as possible into a rectangle, 3 inches wide. Cut into 4-inch pieces, and roll up each piece. Bake on an oven tray until golden brown, which will be about 15 minutes in a moderate oven (mark 4; 350°F.).

It was always a wonder to Bernard Mesnier that people from the other regions of France were slightly condescending about cooking done in the north, although they respected the great wine, Champagne. He drank very little Champagne himself, only on special occasions, as it is just as expensive in the region as out of it. It was the cooking of the area that fascinated him. 'We have everything here. It is literally a land of milk and honey'. Perhaps it was the fish of the Artois, Boulonnais and Flanders that appealed to him most. These places made him think of that other region of France famed for fish – and many other things besides – Normandy.

Normandy

So near to Paris; and yet, for the most part, Normandy keeps its country character. Its products feed Paris and the whole countryside about. Creamy butter from Normandy finds its way across the Channel and makes a conquest of English cooks, just as nine hundred years ago the Normans came to conquer the English – and their kitchen.

The influence of the sea unifies the area. Over the rocky hills of the Orne, among the high hedges of the upland stock farm, over the Seine and on to the great wheat farms of the Vexin, the skies are the same. Warm blue gives way to dark rain clouds. Winters are not severe and cattle can stay in the fields all winter through.

The Scandinavians who settled in this area centuries ago must have found the land a friendly place. They called the valleys *dals* and the streams *becs*. They probably gave their determined character to the Normans of today. The people here are proud of their hard heads and their power of endurance. Anyone who can eat half a good meal, then take a couple of glasses of apple brandy and continue the meal to the bitter end must be resistant. This custom is called making 'Le trou Normand'.[1] And what meals they are!

To the west, near Brittany, farms sheltered from the winds nurture some of the finest stock in the world. Sheep have given way to cattle for beef and milk. Pigs with a suspicious eye watch farmers' wives only too ready and eager to turn them into *terrines* and sausages. Poultry scratch a rich living, and are fattened for the market or kept for laying. We must not forget that great working animal the Percheron[2] horse, that takes its name from a district of Normandy.

From Caen great open fields stretch towards the Seine. Here wheat and flax flourish. The orchards skirt the edges, in their turn protected by beech woods. The area has no domestic wine but the cider apple makes up this deficiency. Cider in Normandy has all the variety of wine. The valley d'Auge produces different flavours from the districts of the Ouche. The cider varies from year to year, and its treatment by cellar masters is also of great importance. From cider a famous brandy is distilled that has its own

---

[1] A rough translation might be 'The Norman Space-maker.'

[2] One of the great breeds of working horse, the Percheron compares with the English Shire horses, and the Scottish Clydesdales.

appellation contrôlée.[1] Coffee without Calvados is like Adam without Eve to the farmer of Normandy. This wonderful liquor also has an important influence in the kitchen.

In the south the land gets higher and there are still forests – Alençon draws the Forest of Perseigne around her like a skirt. The people live farther apart, but still reap the benefit of good stock and farmyard animals although there is less cultivated land.

We have spoken of the influence of Calvados in the kitchen, but cream, butter and eggs play a far more important part; indeed it is very easy in this region to overdo the cream sauce and thicken too often with rich butter. Not only do we want menus that are not over-rich but there must be variety in a meal, variety of texture as well as taste.

The coast of Normandy is very well supplied with fish. The Norman cook does not rely on great fishing ports, like Boulogne to the east, but there are innumerable small fishing havens where good catches tumble onto the quay-side. Most of the salt water fish are to be had, but it is the so-called lower quality fish that is much prized in the Norman kitchen. Herring, mackerel, skate, eel, even the lowly whiting, turn up in one marvellous dish after another. 'Marvellous', by the way, does not mean complicated; sea fish has so much flavour that it should be cooked as simply as possible.

Let us start work in a Norman kitchen beside the sea. The catch is good, and fresh. Moreover the fish is cheap!

Fish can be fried, braised or boiled, just as meat can. Fried in the pan, it is usually dusted with flour and cooked in butter. Deep-fried fish is coated with batter, and dropped into hot oil. When you are braising, use very little liquid; boiled fish should be only just covered, and simmered gently, not really boiled at all.

HARENGS SALÉS   (Salt herrings)

Herring is the first fish we shall deal with. This fish is economical and full of nutriment. Clean it carefully, try to pull the gut through one of the gills.

Lay the fresh herrings in an oven dish and pour over them an equal mixture of white wine and water, with a good dose of vinegar. Salt and whole black peppercorns flavour the stock, together with finely sliced onions and carrots. Do not cover the fish completely with liquid. Cook for 20 minutes in a moderate oven (mark 4; 350°F.), spooning some of the stock over the fish from time to time. The herrings can be eaten hot with potatoes, as a main course, or cold as an hors d'oeuvre.

MAQUEREAUX DE COTENTIN (Mackerel, stuffed and baked)

Mackerel, in particular, should be very fresh. Look for a clear bright eye and a skin that has not become oily. This is an ordinary fish; it is interesting to see how Norman cooking makes it into a fine dish.

Chop shallots very finely and soften them in butter. Take them off the heat and mix in some breadcrumbs that have been soaked in milk and squeezed dry. Add tender young fennel leaves, chopped, and some gooseberries that have been plunged into boiling water for a few moments. (Capers could replace the gooseberries). Season well.

[1] In France, there are regulations which apply to the denomination and labelling of wines and spirits.

Stuff the cleaned mackerel with this mixture. (Choose fish weighing about ¾ lb. each). Wrap them in fennel leaves and tie with fine thread. You can then, if you like, wrap each fish in foil, lightly oiled, and with a few fennel seeds sprinkled over it. Bake in an oven dish with butter in a fairly hot oven (mark 5; 375°F.) for 15 minutes. Unwrap and serve with melted butter and thick cream, mixed with some more simmered gooseberries or capers.

MERLAN (Whiting)

For most people, whiting is a fish to serve to the cat. Cleaned and scaled, tossed in flour and cooked in butter, it is a worthy addition to a meal. As a change from flour, try sprinkling the fish with oatmeal. (Trout is particularly good like this).

When you serve the fish, sprinkle more butter into the pan and squeeze in half a lemon. Pour this sauce over it.

CONGRE À LA CRÈME   (Conger eel in cream sauce)

Make a *court bouillon* (see page 30). Cook 1-inch thick slices of conger eel in this for 20 minutes. Drain off the fish, skin, and take out the bones. Keep in a warm place.

Melt 1 oz. (2 tablespoons) of butter in a pan and sprinkle in 1 oz. (3½ tablespoons) of flour. Cook for a few moments. Add some of the *court bouillon* in which the eel has been cooked. Add a little at a time until the sauce is quite thin. Make sure it cooks for at least 20 minutes to avoid any taste of flour. Add cream. Serve the eel pieces with the creamy sauce poured over them, and a sprinkle of finely chopped spring onions.

QUICHE DE MORUE   (Cod flan)

Soak a thick piece of salt cod overnight. Drain, and simmer in fresh water for 10 minutes. Remove all the skin and bones. Fry slices of mushroom lightly in butter. Add pepper, salt, and lemon juice.

Make a shortcrust pastry (see page 24). Line a tart tin, cover with a piece of foil weighed down with beans, and cook for 15 minutes in a moderate oven (mark 4; 350°F.). Remove from the oven and take off the foil.

Make some béchamel sauce (see page 95) and mix into it the salt cod pieces and the mushrooms. Pour this mixture into the tart. Dot the top with butter, and cook for 15 minutes in a hot oven (mark 7; 425°F.).

CARRELET MAÎTRE D'HÔTEL   (Plaice with butter and parsley)

Fillet the plaice. Flour the fillets and fry them quickly in butter. Mix finely chopped parsley into softened butter and sprinkle on the juice of a lemon. Season well. Form into tiny balls and keep firm in the fridge until needed. Place on top of the fish on serving.

MENU

There was great excitement at the Trédoulat home. Jean Claude's cousins from the country were coming on a visit to Caen. 'I bet they bring some of that wonderful cider with them'. Jean Claude was a laboratory technician in a college at Caen. His childhood had been spent with his parents on the farm in the Orne and he still remembered the wonderful tastes and smells of his mother's country kitchen.

'I shall have to think of what to give them to eat'. His wife, Solange, began to plan the meals for the four-day visit. 'Maman, can you remember your old recipe for braised tongue?' Jean Claude's mother had lived with them since the death of his father. She adored her little grandson Jean Jacques and got on very well with her daughter-in-law. The two of them put their heads together, and this was the menu for the first festive dinner.

6 servings:

SOUPE	SOUP
OEUFS DURS AUX MOULES	HARD-BOILED EGGS WITH MUSSELS
COTELETTES D'AGNEAU	LAMB CHOPS
POMMES DE TERRE	FRIED POTATOES
MANGE-TOUT	SUGAR PEAS
SALADE	SALAD
FROMAGES	CHEESE
MIRLITONS	MIRLITONS

VEGETABLE SOUP. The soup was very simple. Madame Trédoulat – Grandmère – made it, and managed to get a wonderful flavour into it. Potatoes cut into pieces, and the white of leeks, sliced, were cooked in boiling water for half an hour. Then a cabbage cut into 8 pieces was added to the soup, together with green beans sliced thin, chopped celery, and parsley.

She seasoned the soup well, and cooked it for an hour. In the last $\frac{1}{2}$ hour of cooking she poured into the pot some melted pork dripping.

HARD-BOILED EGGS WITH MUSSELS. Solange opened a quart of mussels in the usual way and took them from the shells. She hard-boiled 6 large eggs and cut them in half. Half eggs were laid in an oven dish, with the mussels on top, together with $\frac{1}{4}$ lb. sliced mushrooms cooked with butter. The other half eggs were placed, yolk down, on the mussels and mushrooms.

The next job was to make a white sauce. Solange started with 1 large sliced onion, softened in 1 oz. (2 tablespoons) of butter. She sprinkled 1 oz. ($3\frac{1}{2}$ tablespoons) of flour into the pan, and added $\frac{1}{2}$ pint ($1\frac{1}{4}$ cups) of milk. This sauce was cooked for 20 minutes. She then added a glass of cider, a tablespoon of butter, salt, pepper and 1 tablespoon of cream. She covered the egg preparation with the cream sauce and put the dish into a moderate oven (mark 4; 350°F.) for 8 minutes.

MIRLITONS. As usual it was much better to plan the cooking of the meal. Naturally the soup was cooked first (in the morning in fact); and the eggs were prepared, and the sauce kept separate, ready to reheat and add to the dish. Solange enjoyed making the *mirlitons*, which were tartlets of puff pastry with a special filling.

She made the puff pastry (see page 72) the day before and kept it in the fridge. The filling she would make just before dinner, so that she could serve the *mirlitons* fresh and hot at the end of the meal.

filling:

3 eggs
6 oz. (6 tablespoons) sugar

4 oz. ($\frac{1}{2}$ cup) butter
vanilla essence

Beat the eggs and sugar together until well blended. Turn out into a double boiler. Add the butter and heat gently, stirring all the time, until the ingredients have melted. Remove from the heat and add vanilla essence. Cool. (For a variation, add juice and grated peel from a lemon, instead of the vanilla essence).

Solange made tartlet cases with the puff pastry. (You could make a large tart). She pricked the pastry well and poured in the filling, not quite to the top. The tarts were baked in a fairly hot oven (mark 5; 375°F.) for 15 minutes.

POTATOES FRIED IN EGG AND BREADCRUMBS. They used potatoes already cooked. This is a good idea because there are often cold potatoes in the fridge. They gave Jean Claude the job of cooking the dish. He always put on a chef's hat for the occasion, and looked a real expert, flourishing thin slices of potato, dipping them in egg then covering them with breadcrumbs before frying them.

LAMB CHOPS WITH CALVADOS SAUCE. The main dish and its attendant vegetables were the only things to cook at dinner time. The *mange tout*, sugar peas, were cooked in salted water with a knob of butter. Cooking the chops was simple but the sauce needed some attention.
Grandmère seared lamb chops in a pan, and then lowered the heat so that they should cook slowly. She added the chopped onions and shallots and let them cook with the chops. She made a rich sauce by crushing the chicken livers, and heating them for 15 minutes in a saucepan with the butter and the *calvados*. This mixture finally formed a rich purée.

The chops were served on a warm serving dish separated by bread slices fried in butter. The sauce was spooned over the top.

GRAISSE

The cousins from the country arrived and were taken on a tour of Caen to get their appetites started. Caen had been nearly destroyed during the war and Jean Claude showed them the old part of the city first and then the new blocks towards the sea. 'Fortunately we kept our churches'.

Back home, to start things off, they had a glass of Calvados. The soup continued the warming process. 'But it would taste better if I had had some *graisse*!' This *graisse* is a preparation that can be added to dishes to give extra flavour, rather like the *confit d'oie* in the Pyrenees (see page 50). Grandmère had her own recipe, but did not often have the chance to make it in her son's home, as the young people were rather against the very strong, rich flavour. Here is her recipe.

6 lb. beef suet	6 carrots
2 lb. pork suet	4 onions
2 lb. lean beef	*bouquet garni*

The beef and pork suet used is fresh fat from about the kidneys of the animal. Cut the fat and the meat into small pieces and melt all together in the pot over a low heat. Add the vegetables, finely sliced, and the herbs. When the vegetables are cooked (in about 1 hour), and the mixture has become creamy, season well. Cover, and cook very slowly for 10 hours. Drain off, and strain the liquid into small pots. Chilled, this will keep for a long time.

TORD GOULE (Rice pudding with cinnamon)

The cider bottle circulated while they spoke of the old life of the country. The boy, Jean Jacques, ate with them that night but did not share in the cider, which came from the farm and was very potent. To make up for this he had his favourite sweet, rice with cinnamon. 'We call that *Tord goule* on the farm', one of his uncles informed him.

Solange put $1\frac{1}{2}$ tablespoons ($2\frac{1}{4}$) of rice and $1\frac{1}{2}$ tablespoons ($2\frac{1}{4}$) sugar into an oven dish. She then poured on $1\frac{1}{2}$ pints ($3\frac{3}{4}$ cups) of milk flavoured with cinnamon, dotted butter on top, and cooked it in a moderate oven (mark 4; 350°F.) for $1\frac{1}{2}$ hours.

OMELETTE MÈRE POULARD

During the visit, meals were very simple as the cousins wanted to visit the coast and the port of Caen, go shopping, see films – in short, all the things that people do on a visit.

The omelet again comes into its own in Norman cooking and there are some interesting variations of the basic dish. Perhaps the most famous was created by a wonderful cook, Mère Poulard. Legendary in the area of Mont St Michel, she came from the Niverne, but was adopted as queen of cooking on the Norman coast by the tourists who came to her restaurant at the turn of the century.

Separate the eggs. Salt the yolks well, add pepper, and beat them for a few moments. Whip the whites until solid, and mix them into the yolks. This mixture will have at least doubled the volume of the eggs as prepared for an ordinary omelet. Heat butter to sizzling in a pan, and pour in the eggs. Cook for a moment, without stirring, so that the centre is still soft. Fold in two.

SWEET OMELET

Omelettes are also prepared as a sweet in Normandy. Cook slices of apple in butter until soft. Add sugar and *calvados*. Make an omelette (see page 23), and before folding it over add this mixture as a filling. Sprinkle the dish with sugar before serving. This is a very good ending to a meal that has fish as a main course.

MENU

RAIE À LA CRÈME	SKATE IN CREAM
SALADE CAUCHOISE	POTATO, CELERY AND HAM SALAD
FROMAGES	CHEESE
OMELETTE AUX POMMES	SWEET OMELET

SKATE IN CREAM.   Only the wing pieces of the skate are used in the kitchen, and it is only these that are found on the fishmonger's slab. Note for fishermen; the whole fish must have its wings cut from it and these must be washed well, the extremities chopped away and the fish skinned on both sides.

Soak the wing pieces in salted water for an hour. Simmer in a *court bouillon* until tender. If the skin has been left on, remove it. Serve on a warm dish, covered with boiling cream. Or you could make a thickened white sauce with butter, flour and the stock in which the fish was cooked. This would be a cheaper dish.

POTATO, CELERY AND HAM SALAD.   The type of salad for the meal that Solange and her mother-in-law prepared could be served as an hors d'oeuvre. Here it supplemented the fish very well.

Boil potatoes in their jackets. Let them cool, and remove the skins. Cut the potatoes into strips, together with celery, and place in a salad bowl. Dress with equal parts of lemon juice and vinegar to which is slowly added thick (heavy) cream. (The cream must not be whipped first. It will not curdle if added very slowly.) Sprinkle chopped cooked ham on top of the dressed salad.

CHEESE.   Jean Claud had bought a good selection of cheeses at the beginning of the visit. Their usual cheese was a Camembert, supplemented by a slice of Gruyère for Jean Jacques. In honour of their cousins he carefully chose two Pont l'Evêque cheeses, some creamy Petit Buchy and a good piece of Neufchâtel. So that the boy would not feel left out, he also took a box of the Petit Suisse cheeses that are eaten with sugar.

TONGUE

For supper one night they had Grandmère's famous recipe for tongue. She always liked to use sheep's tongues. But ox tongue still makes a good dish. (Only one would be needed).

2 sheep's tongues	**½ lb. leeks**
chopped carrot, onion and turnip	**1 oz. (2 tablespoons) butter**
bouquet garni	**1 oz. (3½ tablespoons) flour**
pepper	**cream**
salt	**breadcrumbs**
1 lb. whole button mushrooms	

Tongues are usually pickled in brine, and need soaking overnight. After soaking, wash the tongues and put them into a large pot, full of water to cover them well. Add chopped onion, carrot, turnip, the *bouquet garni*, and seasoning. Boil until tender, skimming frequently. (About 45 minutes. An ox tongue would take 3–4 hours). Drain and remove the skin, taking care to take out any bone or gristle that there may be.

Chop the white part of the leeks, and cook in butter until tender. Sprinkle in the flour, mix, and add stock from the pot. Slice the tongue and arrange on the serving dish. Sprinkle over the mushrooms, already cooked in stock. Add cream to the sauce and cover the dish with it. Sprinkle over some breadcrumbs and pass under a hot grill.

BISCUITS

At the end of the meal after a glass of cider, each one wanted something different. 'I'll have a petit Suisse'. 'A piece of Pont l'Evêque for me'. 'Any of those biscuits left, Solange?' The biscuits were a speciality of Caen; Solange always had a supply in a tin.

8 oz. (1½ cups) flour	**pinch of salt**
8 oz. (1 cup) butter	**3 hard boiled eggs**
4 oz. (¼ cup) castor sugar	**juice and grated peel of an orange**

Chop the hard-boiled eggs, and then pound them. Rub the butter into the flour. Add all the other ingredients, and mix well. Flour your hands and form the mixture into a ball. Roll out on a floured board about ¼-inch thick. Cut into rounds, and bake on a buttered oven tray for 15 minutes in a moderate oven (mark 4; 350°F).

MATELOTE NORMANDE

One night they had a fish supper with fresh fish bought at the quayside. 'We don't eat a lot of fish on the farm so we thought this would be a change'. They had mussels, turbot and flounder plus a couple of beautiful crabs.

6–8 servings:

1 large onion	**1¾ lb. turbot**
2 tablespoons (2½) butter	**1¾ lb. flounder**
1 quart mussels	**1 oz. (2 tablespoons) butter**
about 1½ pints cider	**1 oz. (3½ tablespoons) flour**
1 tablespoon (1¼) chopped parsley	

In a large pot, Jean Claude fried some of the chopped onion in butter. Then he poured in the scrubbed mussels, and added a glass of cider. The pot was heated strongly until the mussels opened, then he poured out the mussels and wiped the pot. Marc was set to remove the mussels from their shells. Meanwhile Jean Claude softened some more chopped onion in the pot with butter and chopped parsley. The fish, cut into chunks across the body, were placed on top of the onions and set to simmer in a mixture of equal parts of cider and water for 10 minutes. The fish were then drained, put into an oven dish, covered with the stock, and left in a moderate oven (mark 4; 350°F.) for a further 10 minutes. The stock was drained from the fish and thickened with flour and butter . Mussels were sprinkled over the top of the fish and the thickened sauce added.

TARTINES À LA VIANDE DE CRABE (Crab-meat on toast)

They had also bought 2 crabs. These had been cooked by the fishermen, so all Jean Claude and his assistants had to do was to lift off the top of the main shell and crack the claws. The meat was taken out, together with the brown paste from the shell, and spread on slices of toast with plenty of butter. The smell was so good that Marc hurried to the grocer on the corner and bought a couple of bottles of Muscadet. 'I really prefer wine with fish'.

OMELETTE AUX MOULES (Mussel omelet)

They had plenty of mussels left over and these were used the next day as a filling for an omelet (see page 23). Solange made a thickened sauce with the stock from the mussels, and mixed in the mussels and a few pieces of fish that were left over. She started her omelet in the pan and poured over it the rich fish sauce. One fold and it was ready.

MENU

Two weeks later Jean Claude and his family visited the cousins on their farm. This was north west of Alençon, in an area of hilly country. They drove along roads protected by great bushy hedges. Once they passed several massive horses being led from one field to another. Jean Jacques was silent with admiration for these wonderful beasts. 'They are the true Percheron breed', his father told him. 'Your uncle has some on the farm'.

The farmhouse was very old, and beamed, with stone floors and tiny windows. The kitchen was the centre of the house, and there old Madame Druon rose from her chair to greet her sister affectionately. Jean Claude and Marc looked at their mothers sitting side by side and thought back to long ago when they played together in the old barn.

'Nothing special tonight'. This was Jeanette Druon's favourite opening gambit for a meal that was special. Marc grinned across at his wife. 'In that case I won't tap the special little barrel of cider'. He ducked the wooden spoon she threw at him and went to open the cider. Jean Claude went to help, sample, and give his opinion.

6 servings:

SOUPE DE CRESSON	CRESS SOUP
LAPIN EN COMPÔTE	RABBIT CASSEROLE
POULET À LA SAUCE DU PAYS D'AUGE	CHICKEN WITH SAUCE PAYS D'AUGE
POMMES DE TERRE BLANQUETTE	BLANQUETTE OF POTATOES
CHOUX DE BRUXELLES	BRUSSELS SPROUTS
SALADE	SALAD
FROMAGES	CHEESE
FOUACES	FOUACES

RABBIT CASSEROLE. The rabbit dish, really a kind of terrine, was made the day before. Here is the recipe.

1 rabbit	parsley
streaky bacon	chervil
carrots	salt
tarragon	pepper
thyme	small glass of Calvados

Cut the rabbit into pieces. Line a casserole with rashers of streaky bacon. Put pieces of rabbit on top, and cover with more bacon. Top with rabbit and cover again with bacon. Season well, and add all the herbs tied in a bunch. Lay on the carrots, cut in very thin round slices. Cover with more bacon. Cover the casserole with the lid, and cook in a warm oven (mark 3; 350°F.) for an hour. Pour in the Calvados, and replace in the oven for another hour, or until the rabbit is tender.

CRESS SOUP. Choose two large bunches of cress with very crisp leaves. Wash well, and take out any discoloured pieces. Cut off the larger stalks. Cut into strips, and soften with butter in a large pot. Add water, or preferably chicken stock, season, and cook for 15 minutes. Remove the cress, and chop very fine or purée in an electric blender.

Cut 1 lb. of potatoes into small pieces, and cook until soft in the cress stock. Remove and mash. Replace the cress and the mashed potatoes in the stock, stir well, and add some cream. Cook for a further 15 minutes. The soup is much improved if you use chicken stock. Chicken bouillon cubes would do, but add these after you have done all the cooking. Pour onto crisp *croûtons* sprinkled with grated Gruyère cheese.

186

BLANQUETTE OF POTATOES. The next thing Jeanette did was to prepare the potatoes. She cooked the white of 4 leeks in 2 tablespoons (2½) of butter, added 1½ tablespoons (scant 2) of flour and then 1 pint (2½ cups) of milk. She seasoned this thick sauce well and added 2 lb. potatoes cut into thin slices, and a *bouquet garni*. These were left to cook slowly on top of the oven for 20 minutes. Nearly all the liquid was absorbed, and a creamy fragrant 'cake' of potatoes was left.

CHICKEN WITH SAUCE PAYS D'AUGE. While the potato dish was cooking Jeanette started the chicken. She cut chickens into eight portions and slowly cooked them, lightly floured to protect the flesh, in butter. For the sauce, 2 egg-yolks were well whipped and blended with melted 2 oz. (4 tablespoons) of butter, in the same way as at the start of a *béarnaise* sauce (see page 62). This was thinned with ½ pint (1¼ cups) of cream with a flavouring of pepper and salt.

While she was finishing the sauce for the chickens, the cry '*à table*' was set up, and Jeanette reheated the soup. Solange and the two Grandmères had set the places and seen to the bread, salad and cheese. Marc and Jean Claude sang as they brought in the cider, and the meal started. As they were finishing the rabbit, Jeanette and her mother-in-law tossed in butter some brussels sprouts already cooked tender in boiling water, removed the chicken pieces from the warm oven, and poured over them the reheated sauce. The potatoes were turned out into a blue-decorated bowl. The main course was on the table in no time.

FOUACES. After the cheese, Jeanette had a real surprise for them – *Fouaces*. These hearth cakes were famed in the region centuries ago but are very difficult to find now. Jeanette had cooked some for them. She had no hearth, for the farm was centrally heated and the stove was gas; but the *fouaces* cooked very well in the oven.

1 lb. (3 cups) flour	**milk**
4 oz. (½ cup) butter	**saffron**
2 eggs	**mixed spice**

Jeanette rubbed the butter into the flour and added the eggs. She made a pliable pastry by adding some hot milk to which the spice and the saffron has been added. This was rolled out to a ¼-inch thickness and cut into small rounds about 3 inches across. She baked these in a moderate oven (mark 4; 350°F.) for 20 minutes, coated with some beaten egg. This pastry could also be cooked in a thick iron frying pan and would then be, perhaps, more authentic. They ate them in the farmhouse that night with hot apricot jam.

NORMAN RECIPES

That was a weekend to remember! Jean Jacques did not want to go back to the town. Jean Claude and his mother felt themselves truly at home in the country they knew so well, and Solange felt that she had so many dishes to learn from her cousin by marriage, Jeanette. Here are a few of the recipes she noted down.

PIEDS DE COCHON FARCIS (Stuffed pigs' trotters)

Cook the trotters in water, with herbs, carrot, and onion, until soft. Solange noticed that they had two large pressure cookers in the kitchen. 'They are wonderful for preparing meat like trotters. In the pressure cooker they take 40 minutes whereas on the gas it is three hours. I even do my *pot au feu* in the pressure cooker'.

When the trotters are tender, take out the bones, and stuff them. To make the stuffing, soften chopped onions in butter. Add parsley, thyme, and breadcrumbs. Stir to blend, then add any available pieces of cooked meat, minced. Tie each trotter with fine thread. Coat with egg and breadcrumbs, and brown under the grill. Serve with creamed potatoes.

DOUILLONS (Pear turnovers)

Simmer skinned, cored pears in water with plenty of sugar until tender. Drain, cover in an envelope of puff pastry, and bake in a warm oven (mark 3; 325°F.) for 30 minutes. This is a very similar dish to the *Rabotes* made in Champagne (see page 167).

BROCHETTES DE ROGNONS DE MOUTON (Lamb's kidneys, grilled)

Soak the kidneys for an hour, and skin them. If they are large, cut them in half. Pierce with a skewer, alternated with pieces of fatty bacon. Cook under the grill or in a fairly hot oven (mark 6; 400°F.). Serve on a bed of cress, sprinkled with chopped spring onion.

L'OIE EN DAUBE (Goose *en daube*)

This was the centrepiece of their farewell dinner.

1 goose	*for the pot:*
stuffing:	**bacon slices**
1 large onion, chopped	**carrot**
½ lb. belly of pork, chopped	**onion**
2 eggs	**leek**
1 apple, sliced	**celery**
breadcrumbs	**cider**
mixed spice	*garnish:*
pepper and salt	**apples roasted in the oven**

The goose should be ready for the oven. Set aside the giblets. Fry the chopped onion lightly in dripping, and add the rest of the ingredients to make the stuffing. Mix well. Add the eggs, and bind with the breadcrumbs. Add the chopped giblets. Stuff the bird and truss so that the legs are together and the stuffing is secure. Brown the goose in the oven for 20 minutes.

Brown the bacon, carrot, onion, leek and celery in dripping. Put in a large pot. Place the goose on top, and fill the pot with water and cider. Add a *bouquet garni*, season, and simmer for at least 2 hours. Test the meat for tenderness, and skim the surface of the liquid often.

JAMBON AU CIDRE (Ham in cider)

Simmer slices of cured ham in cider until tender. (About 25 minutes). Make a sauce. Soften sliced onions in butter, sprinkle in flour, and add some of the cider used to cook the ham. It is really better to serve the sauce separately, especially if you have good thick slices of ham.

TARTES AUX CERISES (Cherry tart)

Stone ripe cherries, and cook them gently in a saucepan with sugar and a spoonful of calvados. Cook until the cherries begin to stick together. Leave to cool. Make some flaky pastry (see page 72). Line a tart tin, weigh down with foil and a few beans, and cook blind in a moderate oven (mark 4; 350°F.) for 15 minutes.

Beat about 8 oz. (1 cup) white cream cheese with 4 oz. ($\frac{1}{4}$ cup) of castor sugar. Add 4 tablespoons (5) of whipped cream, and blend well together. Line the pastry case with the creamy sauce, and pour in the cooled cherries.

TRIPES À LA MODE DE CAEN

Solange was glad that she could give in return a recipe that they all wanted. It was her aunt's recipe for the famous '*Tripes à la Mode de Caen*'.

4–6 servings:

1½ lb. tripe	*bouquet garni*
1 calf's foot	cloves
¼ lb. fat bacon	salt
2 medium carrots	cayenne pepper
2 medium onions	about 1 quart of cider

Simmer the tripe in salted water for half an hour. Bone the calf's foot, and dice the meat from it. Drain the tripe and cut it into large square pieces. Wipe the pot in which the tripe was cooked. Line the bottom with the fat salt pork and pile on top the vegetables, diced, the bones of the calf's foot, and all the seasoning. Lay the tripe and meat from the calf's foot on top, and cover with cider. Cook over a gentle heat for 8 hours. Serve the tripe with the liquid in deep plates, such as old-fashioned soup plates.

MENU

It was interesting to work out a possible meal with the tripe as a main dish. 'We've always eaten the tripe with potatoes, and with fruit to follow'. In spite of this Marc worked out a menu.

TARTINES À LA VIANDE DE CRABE	CRAB MEAT ON TOAST
TRIPES À LA MODE DE CAEN	TRIPE À LA MODE DE CAEN
POMMES NOUVELLES	NEW POTATOES
SALADE CRESSON	CRESS SALAD
CAMEMBERT	CAMEMBERT CHEESE
PÊCHES AU CALVA	PEACHES IN CALVADOS

'I think you must have something very different from meat flavour to introduce the dish. It should be crusty but not too rich. Then comes the rich smoothness of the tripe eaten with fresh well-flavoured firm potatoes. (For the crab recipe see page 185.)

The tang of the salad cleans the mouth and the Camembert gives us a moment to ponder on strength of flavour and staying power. We are then ready for a rich but refreshing fruit sweet.

PEACHES IN CALVADOS. Skin the peaches by simmering for a few moments, and removing the skin with a sharp knife. Cut in two and remove the stone. Colour in sizzling butter, and pour a glass of *calvados* into the pan.

Driving back to Caen Jean Claude thought over the sights, sounds and smells, to say nothing of the tastes, of their stay on the farm. 'Solange, it would be very easy for us to eat too much and too richly. We could not stand dishes like those you have written down every day but, now and again, it is good to eat well'.

Like many of us, Jean Claude mistook 'eating a lot' for 'eating well'. The French menu looks long because of the salad and cheese course but, during a full meal, a sensible eater will take only a leaf of salad and a thin sliver of cheese. The other well chosen courses can also be tasted sparingly.

When you plan a meal, try Marc's technique. He was only thinking of the tastes and the quality of the dishes. But if you look at a diet sheet you will find that, strangely enough, his meal works out well from the calorie and carbohydrate point of view. But then is it so strange? A dietician works objectively, while Marc knew what he felt like inside.

The Loire Valley

The lands about the River Loire certainly have the right to be called the garden of France. The climate is controlled by the Atlantic, so there is a high rainfall all the year round and a marked absence of very low temperatures. Everything grows well here, and wherever there is a piece of high ground overlooking the river valley the vine appears in profusion. As if they sense that more good times are round the corner, the vines produce wine that is to be enjoyed at once. No need to store, there's plenty more to come!

The Loire is a great river but it has been saved the degradation of pollution by industry and river traffic. Above Nantes, the waterway is not navigable for boats of any size, and so river traffic is carried by a series of canals, leaving the river clear for the small boats of eager fishermen ready to profit from the clear water that is the home of succulent fish – trout, salmon, carp, pike, barbel plus a host of smaller fish.

There is plenty of water for irrigation, to supplement the soft rains. So yields of fruit and vegetables are high. The whole land seems to be under cultivation, protected from possible floods by defences standing high above the low banks. Each town has its speciality. Angers is famous for strawberries, Blois for asparagus and Orleans for market vegetables. Flowers are grown everywhere.

North of the great bend in the river guarded by Orleans, high land rises up to the Perche and Normandy. This is a land of sheep, cows that give creamy milk, pigs, geese, chickens. As if this were not enough, south of the river bend there are also supplies in plenty. On slopes that are the first steps up to the great mountain area of the *Massif Central*, sheep graze and so do beef cattle. Great stock-farms sprawl among woods of tall trees.

Winters are harder here because of the effect of the mountains to the south, but no harm comes to the vine of the Sancerre. The monks of Saint-Satur found this vantage point above the river long ago, and made wine in honour of their creator fit to make men feel like gods.

Deep in the curve of the great arc of water lies the Sologne, a vast place of lakes and low marshy land. Here a Napoleon, descendant of the great emperor, founded a farming school the first of its kind in France, and then together with a great number of the population left to seek a kinder place. Later man set to work on the environment. The lakes were sown with carp and pike, and also trout. When a lake has been fished for 5 years it is often drained and sown with crops. Later the fish may come back after calculated re-flooding.

Game of all sorts has always thrived in this bleak area. Birds and animals have multiplied with the protection of man, and plenty of people come to hunt for the benefit of the kitchen. All the game birds are here; in particular, good partridges. In the forests about Orleans royal game, the deer, fleet through the copses. Young wild pigs adorn many a wedding feast.

CERNEAUX AU VERJUS[1]   (Pickled walnuts)

Much produce from the Loire is sent to Paris. People also preserve much in their homes. This is a recipe for pickled walnuts that is often used near Tours. It is a good dish for an hors d'oeuvre.

Use green walnuts that are not quite ripe. Shell them and take out the kernel, leaving the white inner skin intact. Soak for three days in a very salty solution of water, well dosed with wine vinegar. The nuts could now be eaten, but it is better to continue the pickling by soaking them further in a savoury vinegar.

For about $2\frac{1}{2}$ lb. of nut kernels use 2 pints of wine vinegar; enough to cover the nuts. Make a muslin bag, and put into it a small teaspoon each of crushed mace, mixed spice, cloves, and cinnamon, and 6 peppercorns. Tie the bag up tightly and bring the vinegar to the boil with the aromatic bag in it. When it boils, remove the vinegar from the heat and allow to cool. Remove the herb bag. Rinse the walnuts, put them into a jar with a good screw top, and fill the jar with the herb vinegar and screw on the lid.

You can experiment and use different herbs with different produce. For example onions can be kept in the same way, but try long sprigs of fennel in the vinegar. Put a sprig into the jar before you close the lid.

MENU

The sharpness of the walnuts could make a good start to a main dish of game.

CERNEAUX AU VERJUS	PICKLED WALNUTS
FAISAN EN BARBOUILLE	CASSEROLE OF PHEASANT
FÈVES	BROAD BEANS
SALADE	SALAD
FROMAGES	CHEESE
CRÈMETS	CRÈMETS

CASSEROLE OF PHEASANT.   Pheasant is thought of as a luxury dish in areas not so well endowed with game as the Sologne. Here it is a simple country dish, and the meal could be a hunter's supper after a long day shooting or fishing among lonely creeks and stunted trees.

---

[1] *Verjus* is verjuice, or the juice of sour grapes.

Pluck and draw the pheasant (see page 27). Chop carrots and onions very finely, and slowly fry 1 tablespoon (1¼) of each in butter. Cut the bird into portions and brown these with the vegetables. Sprinkle in a tablespoon of flour and cook for a few minutes. Add thyme, bay leaf, and celery, tied in a bunch, garlic and plenty of salt and pepper. Light a spoonful of brandy and pour it over the pheasant. Blow out immediately. Pour in half a bottle of red wine. Stir well and simmer for 25 minutes.

Take out the pieces of game and place them in the bottom of a casserole. Add ¼ lb. of button mushrooms, ¼ lb. small onions and two good rashers of bacon, chopped.

Cover with the wine sauce, well strained. Cover, and cook in a low oven (mark 2; 300°F.) for 45 minutes or until the meat is tender.

BROAD BEANS. Cook the broad beans in salted water. When tender, drain off the water and add butter. Cook gently for a moment and add cream. You could place a sprig of savory in the cooking water, and serve the beans with a little of this herb, finely chopped.

SALAD. It would be an added touch to toss the salad in some walnut oil. Sprinkle some vinegar over it, and stir in finely crushed garlic. Cheese from Sainte Maure, and one or two small goat cheeses, would go down well at this stage.

CRÈMETS. Don't eat too much of the cheese because the *crèmets* are small sweet, creamy preparations.

Whip ¾ pint (scant 2 cups) of cream. Whip the white of one egg, and fold it into the whipped cream. Pour this mixture into small pots, cover each pot with muslin tied on firmly, and turn the pots upside down on a wire tray. Allow to drain for 2 to 3 hours. Turn over, take off the muslin, and top up with thick (heavy) unwhipped cream. Serve sprinkled with vanilla-flavoured sugar.

René Chamussy liked nothing better than to leave behind the grease and noise of the garage where he worked, to slip out onto the quiet waters of the Loire below Tours. Saturday afternoon was sacred; fishing day.

That particular day he was taking his new friend Bonnabel with him, and the two families were going to eat the proceeds of the afternoon's labours. 'If you only catch eels you can eat them yourself'. His wife Edwidge was quite adamant on the subject of eels. Bonnabel's wife was in complete agreement. 'And if I catch a pike?' 'Some chance!'

The two ladies, and the Chamussey's daughter, Claudie, prepared the rest of the meal and hoped that the two fishermen would be successful. 'If not, there are some eggs in the cupboard to make an omelet'.

SAVARIN. Edwidge decided to make a special gâteau, a *savarin*. Ghislaine Bonnabel was eager to learn the way to make it.

6 oz. (full cup) flour	**3 oz. (6 tablespoons) butter**
½ oz. yeast	
¼ pint (full ½ cup) milk	*syrup:*
1 teaspoon (1¼) sugar	**8 oz. (½ cup) sugar**
pinch of salt	**¾ pint (scant 2 cups) water**
2 eggs	**1 tablespoon (1¼) rum**

Warm a bowl and put in the flour. Dissolve the yeast in a little milk, and add a teaspoon of sugar. Mix the yeast solution with the rest of the milk.

Make a well in the flour, add the salt and pour in the yeast. Add the 2 eggs and mix the dough. Knead for 5 minutes. Cover, and leave to rise for 45 minutes. Knead again and beat in the softened butter. Continue kneading until the butter is worked into the dough. The dough should be very pliable but not sticky.

Butter a ring mould and lay in the dough, which should not come more than half way up the sides. Leave in a warm place, covered, to rise. After an hour the dough should fill the tin. Bake in a hot oven (mark 7; 425°F.) for 10 minutes. Reduce to moderate (mark 4; 350°F.) and bake for a further 25 minutes. Turn over onto a wire tray, cover with a cloth and leave to cool for 10 minutes. Run a sharp knife round the mould, and turn the *savarin* out.

To make the syrup, boil the sugar with the water in a saucepan until the solution will coat the back of a spoon. Add the rum.

Prick the *savarin* all over with a needle, and gently pour the syrup over it. Try to get all the syrup to soak into the *savarin*. You will have a ring of rum-flavoured cake. Fill the centre hole with cream, whipped with sugar flavoured with vanilla, and with crystallised fruit.

MENU

They were just about to fill the centre of the *savarin* when the men came in. René had brought a friend, Monsieur Albert, who sold papers and magazines in a little kiosk near the *lycée*. 'He seemed a bit lonely so I invited him and his catch to dinner'.

Eels, much to the ladies' horror, were very evident in the catch. But there were quite a few small fish, gudgeon and perch. 'They are too small', cried Madame Bonnabel. 'But Madame, the best things come in small packets', replied Monsieur Albert, who was five feet nothing in his large boots. They all collapsed! 'Good! To work!' René rubbed his hands at the thought of those eels. 'The men will cook the fish and the ladies look after the rest'.

MATELOTE D'ANGUILLES,	EEL STEW
ou FRITURE DE LA LOIRE	*or* FRIED LOIRE FISH
CÔTE DE VEAU	VEAL CHOPS
ASPERGES MORNAY	ASPARAGUS IN CHEESE SAUCE
SALADE	SALAD
FROMAGES	CHEESE
SAVARIN À LA CRÈME	SAVARIN WITH CREAM

EEL STEW.   Clean the eels and cut off the heads. (They were very small and did not need skinning). Cut into chunks across the body and fry in oil and butter, with a handful of chopped onions. Moisten with red wine (the eels should not be quite covered) and add a *bouquet garni*, salt and pepper. Simmer until the eels are tender, about 20 minutes. Remove the *bouquet garni* and whip in some butter to enrich the sauce. Simmer for a few minutes.

FRIED FISH.   Albert meanwhile was showing how he dealt with the small fish. He made a batter from $\frac{1}{4}$ lb. ($\frac{3}{4}$ cup) flour, 2 tablespoons ($2\frac{1}{2}$) of olive oil, salt, pepper and 8 tablespoons (10) of warm water. He blended these ingredients together and mixed in the white of a large egg, whipped until solid.

The small fish needed no cleaning. Albert just trimmed round them with a sharp knife, dipped them in batter, and fried them fast in plenty of oil. Arranged on a warm plate with lemon halves they looked splendid.

ASPARAGUS IN CHEESE SAUCE.   Edwidge had already cooked the asparagus in plenty of salted water after trimming the stems and rinsing it well. She was going to serve it with a sauce made from a béchamel base (see page 95), with butter and grated cheese added. The asparagus could be heated gently in the sauce.

The fish went down very well with a wine from the region of Loches. It was quite dry, and had been in the fridge since the morning. The eels were eaten with an ordinary red wine in a litre bottle, from the local grocer. Madame Bannobel was talked into tasting some eel and liked it. Edwidge and her daughter Claudie stuck to their guns and refused to try it.

VEAL CHOPS.   The chops took 15 minutes to cook while the conversation went round the table. Edwidge fried them in a large frying pan, adding sliced mushrooms. The chops were taken out when cooked, and kept warm while the mushrooms were finished. She had ready some braised onions, and these went in with the mushrooms to warm through. She added butter, then cream, and seasoned well. The chops were served with the rich sauce over them. The asparagus in its hot sauce was served at the same time, but they all finished the meat first and ate the vegetable afterwards.

MENU

They had a slightly sparkling Vouvray with the *savarin* and voted that they should all eat together again very shortly. 'What about a picnic?' 'Why not a café where we can take our own food?'

This sort of establishment is to be found all over France, and is very popular with large families. Monsieur Albert knew of such a place with a very sympathetic patron. 'It is tucked away among trees in a little valley. I would like to offer the wine for such a trip'.

They decided to go one Sunday, so Edwidge and Ghislaine set to work on Saturday morning to do some cooking. The menu was pretty substantial but they knew that they would be hungry after a morning in the fresh air. They called the menu *casse croûte* because that would be the name on the door of the café.

RILLETTES	POTTED MEAT
OEUFS	EGGS
PÂTÉ DE VEAU ET DE LAPIN	VEAL AND RABBIT PIE
SALADE AU FROMAGE	SALAD WITH CHEESE
GÂTEAU DE PITHIVIERS	GÂTEAU DE PITHIVIERS

VEAL AND RABBIT PIE

Pastry:
1½ lb. (4½ cups) flour
2 teaspoons (2½) salt
3 oz. (6 tablespoons) butter
3 oz. (6 tablespoons) dripping
⅓ pint (scant 1 cup) water
1 teaspoon olive oil
filling:
1 good sized rabbit

¾ lb. sausage meat
¾ lb. lean veal
slices of streaky bacon
chopped parsley
thyme
salt
pepper
2 oz. (1 cup) breadcrumbs

Edwidge wanted a pie that would stand all by itself on the table, pie tin discarded. She put the flour in the bowl and mixed in the salt. The fat (she used half butter and half lard) was melted in the water, hot from a pan. When it was dissolved she added 1 teaspoon of olive oil, and poured it into a well in the middle of the flour. The pastry was mixed well and kneaded.

The method of forming the pie was her own idea and Ghislaine was very curious. 'I never had the courage to make a pie and cook it in the oven without a tin. Once you have a heavy pie cooked in a tin it is very difficult to get it out'.

'A cake tin makes a good pie shape. The tin is smeared with butter inside. Then I cut two lengths of kitchen foil about two inches wide and lay them in the tin at right angles to one another. So there is the start of a basket of foil inside the tin, well tucked into the corners. A length of twine is laid on top of each piece of foil. I then lay two more pieces of foil on top of the two lengths of twine, and smear butter on top. In this way there is a sort of cradle by which the pie can be carefully lifted out.'

Ghislaine rolled out the pie crust, directed by Edwidge. She divided the pastry into two, and divided one part in half again. One of the small pieces was rolled out to form the base of the pie. The large piece, rolled into a rectangle the height of the tin, formed the sides. These were put in place. The joins were damped and pressed firmly with the back of a knife. The remaining small piece of pastry was kept to make the top when the crust was filled.

Bone the rabbit and cut out any sinews. In a mixing bowl, mix the sausage meat with the chopped parsley and the breadcrumbs. Season well and sprinkle in some thyme. Cut the veal into small chunks. Line the inside of the pie with a few pieces of bacon; don't completely cover the inside. Sprinkle in some of the sausage meat mixture. Lay on rabbit pieces, then some veal, then some more sausage meat. Continue these layers until the pie is full. Finish with sausage meat and two rashers of bacon. Lay on twigs of thyme and cover the pie with a pastry cap. Brush with egg yolk.

Decorate the pie with pieces of pastry, cut a small round hole in the top, and bake it in a moderate oven (mark 4; 350°F.) for $1\frac{1}{2}$ hours. After half the cooking time, cover the pie with a piece of foil. When some clear liquid starts to come out of the hole, the pie is cooked. (It is always better to test for tenderness with a skewer to make sure). Let the pie cool, and lift it from the tin by the foil and string handles.

RILLETTES

2 lb. pork belly
2 lb. pork kidney-fat
2 oz. (4 tablespoons) salt

pepper
1 teaspoon ($1\frac{1}{4}$) mixed spice

Cut the meat and fat into pieces. Slowly melt in a pot and cook gently for 4 hours. The mixture is ready when the meat flakes into pieces under the pressure of a fork. Mix well and season with salt, 4 turns of the peppermill, and the spices. Pour immediately into small glass pots (heated in the oven) and allow to set.

GÂTEAU DE PITHIVIERS.   This cake is a good one for picnics and to take on journeys, because it keeps well.

2 eggs, separated
6 oz. (6 tablespoons) sugar
1 teaspoon ($1\frac{1}{4}$) vanilla

3 oz. (6 tablespoons) butter
6 oz. ($1\frac{1}{2}$ cups) ground almonds

In a mixing bowl, beat egg yolks, sugar and vanilla together. In another bowl, mix the softened butter with the ground almonds. Beat all the ingredients together. Whip the egg whites solid and fold in. Grease an 8-inch square cake tin, and fill with the mixture. Bake in a warm oven (mark 3; 325°F.) for 20 minutes.

Cover with an icing made by stirring about 4 oz. ($\frac{1}{4}$ cup) of icing sugar into an egg white, lightly beaten, to make a spreading mixture. Sprinkle glazed fruit peel over the top.

BAKED SHAD

René and Patrice came back very excited because they had caught a shad. 'I do hope your supper goes with shad, Edwidge'. 'What makes you think there is any supper? I thought you would like to save your appetite for the pie tomorrow'. 'Don't joke about important things'. Edwidge remembered the time she had forgotten the cheese on a picnic, and her husband had not spoken to her for the rest of the day!

Claudie went out to get some sorrel, and they got to work on the shad. The fish weighed about 3 lb. so there would not be much between five people. René cleaned the fish, scraping inside one of the gills and drawing out the inside through this passage. Then he rinsed through with fresh water. The scales were scraped and the sides cut in four places with a sharp knife. The sorrel was chopped finely, and cooked gently in some butter. Three eggs were beaten into it, one at a time, and some breadcrumbs added to dry the mixture which then served to stuff the fish. Into the oven it went, on a flat dish with chopped shallots and plenty of butter. It took about 40 minutes in a moderate oven (mark 4; 350°F.).

Edwidge made a white butter sauce. She melted ½ lb. (1 cup) of butter, and added a tablespoon (1¼) of chopped shallots, a sprinkle of vinegar, salt, and pepper. The sauce was kept hot and served separately. They had some soup first.

POTAGE DE CRÉCY (Crécy soup)

Cook ¼ lb. carrots and ¼ lb. onions, thinly sliced, in butter. When they are tender, add salt, pepper and 4 oz. (⅔ cup) rice. Stir well and add water. Cook until the rice is soft (4 oz. (⅔ cup) of rice will take about 2 pints (5 cups) of water). Press the cooked rice and vegetables through a sieve, or purée in an electric blender. Replace in a pot, and add stock, or milk and water, until you have the right consistency for a soup. Melt in plenty of butter, and check the seasoning.

PORK WITH PRUNES

The fish came next and they all had to congratulate the fishermen. A white Saumur wine helped it down famously. They all felt ready for the pork.

Edwidge had pork cutlets, but tenderloin would do very well for this dish. She had soaked the prunes in tea until they were plump. The stones were removed, and the fruit simmered in some white wine for half an hour. The chops were fried in oil and butter, and a sauce made by mixing the juices in the pan with white wine, juice from the prunes, and cream. The prunes were arranged round the chops.

They had some *pommes duchesse* (see page 146) with the pork. Edwidge made the soft potato mixture and spread it thick on a buttered oven tray, coated the top with egg mixture and browned it in the oven. It looked good enough to be a dish in its own right. 'If I had a few truffles to sprinkle over it, this would indeed be a dish to be proud of'.

After supper they settled down with a map and talked about the outing with Monsieur Albert, and of course the menu that had been arranged. 'I've never eaten cheese with the salad before'. Patrice wanted to know if the cheese was put into the salad bowl. 'But of course' answered Edwidge. 'I use Gruyère cut into strips, very fine, like a wafer. The best salad for this is dandelion leaves but you could use any crisp salad. The dressing is mixed in, in the usual way'.

STRAWBERRY PANCAKES

Ghislaine wanted to know of a special dish made from strawberries. Her small nephews were coming from Paris to stay, and she wanted to add a sweet recipe to her kitchen repertoire. Edwidge told her the way to prepare this dish.

Make a rice pudding (see page 182) but add two egg yolks, whipping them into the milk. Use vanilla not cinnamon. When cool, use this with strawberries to stuff pancakes (see page 14). Stuff the pancakes, and warm them in the oven for ten minutes. Serve with a sauce made from crushed strawberries and whipped cream.

CRAYFISH SOUFFLÉ

Edwidge's great speciality was a soufflé made from crayfish. The basic idea is the same for all savoury soufflés. You add flavour from the crayfish (or whatever you are using) to a thick sauce, and introduce air by the addition of whipped egg whites. Pieces of the fish are enveloped in this 'air bed'. In cooking, the trapped air expands, and the dish increases in volume and lightness.

1 lb. crayfish
2 tablespoons (2½) chopped carrot
2 tablespoons (2½) chopped onion
** and shallot**
¼ lb. (½ cup) butter
thyme, bayleaf, tarragon

1 oz. (2 tablespoons) butter
1 oz. (3½ tablespoons) flour
white wine
cayenne pepper
6 eggs, separated

Clean the crayfish (see page 39). Chop the vegetables finely. In a large pot, melt the ¼ lb. of butter and soften the vegetables. Add the crayfish and cook for 5 minutes. Cover with white wine and water. Add the herbs in a bunch. Season, and simmer for 10 minutes. Take out the fish, crack the shells, and remove all the meat that you can. You now have a good stock, and the fish. Taste the stock and reduce, to strengthen the flavour if necessary.

Melt the 1 oz. of butter in a saucepan and mix in the flour. Thin with about ½ pint (1¼ cups) of crayfish stock. Cook this white sauce well and season with salt and cayenne pepper. Beat in the 6 egg-yolks. Whip the whites solid in a mixing bowl. Keep a little of the sauce aside and use to heat the flesh of the crayfish gently. Butter a soufflé dish. Fold the whites into the sauce, and pour some of this 'air bed' mixture into the dish. Lay on the crayfish flesh and cover with more 'air bed'. Smooth the top, and cook in a fairly hot oven (mark 5; 375°F.) for 25 minutes.

You can extend the height of your soufflé dish by a cylinder of stiff white paper tucked inside the top of the dish. Don't overdo this; a 2-inch extension is usually ample.

BRAINS IN BUTTER

The 'snack' in the café proved to be a tremendous success and they promised themselves another visit. Afterwards they all suggested prize dishes. Albert shocked the ladies by his choice of a favourite dish – brains. 'How could you, Monsieur Albert!' 'You wanted my dish in your quiz, so there it is. Here's the way to cook them'.

Calf's brains are the best. Make sure that the brains are not bruised or torn. Make a *court bouillon* in the usual way, adding plenty of vinegar. Bring this to the boil and carefully put in the brains, 6 sets for 6 people. Simmer for 15 minutes. Remove the brains and take off any dark pieces or loose skin. Allow to cool, and cut into slices. Flour these and cook gently in butter. Arrange on a plate, and serve with heated butter that is just turning brown. This makes a delicious course between the soup and the main dish.

BLANQUETTE DE VEAU

The quiz on food was a good idea while they rested under the trees, digesting the cold pie. Even Alain, Claudie's boy friend, had a dish.

4 servings:

1½ lb. veal	*bouquet garni*
3 oz. (6 tablespoons) butter	½ lb. button mushrooms
3 oz. (full ½ cup) flour	½ lb. small onions
1 carrot	yolks of 3 eggs
1 onion, stuck with a clove	lemon
	nutmeg

Use veal cut from the shoulder or the breast. Cut it into small chunks, simmer it in water for 3 minutes, and drain the pot. Replace the veal, and cover with water. Season, add a ½ lemon, sliced, and cook for 1½ hours. In a saucepan, melt the butter and add the flour. Cook for a moment and add about 3 pints (7½ cups) of veal stock. Add the onion with the clove and a few fine slivers of carrot, plus the *bouquet garni*. Simmer the sauce for 15 minutes and powder lightly with grated nutmeg. Cook the mushrooms whole in oil and butter. Braise the onions gently in the oven.

Carefully place the onions and mushrooms with the veal, and pour over the creamy stock. Mix very gently.

They were all so surprised that such a good volley-ball player should know such a recipe that they gave him the prize, the last piece of the *Gâteau de Pithiviers*.

QUICHE DE VIANDES (Meat flan)

Here was the dish chosen by Edwidge, which is an interesting variation on the *quiche*. Make some shortcrust pastry (see page 24) and line a tart tin. Prick the base well with a fork. Spread *rillettes* (see page 197) over the bottom of the tart, and add minced cooked pork scraps. Beat 4 eggs with $\frac{1}{2}$ pint (1$\frac{1}{4}$ cups) of milk and add $\frac{1}{2}$ pint (1$\frac{1}{4}$ cups) of cream. Season well, and pour into the tart. Cook for $\frac{1}{2}$ hour in a moderate oven (mark 4; 350°F.).

You must decide if you would prefer to cook the tart first, lightly, without the filling. It is more trouble, but Edwidge always did it and thought it worth the effort.

MUTTON RAGOÛT

Ghislaine had a very simple dish, but it was good for all that. Brown 2 lb. of diced shoulder of mutton in a pan with dripping. Sprinkle in 2 oz. (7 tablespoons) of flour and stir in 2 pints (5 cups) of boiling water. Season well and add a *bouquet garni*. Soften slices of onion in dripping, in another pan, and add chopped turnip. Flavour with a little crushed garlic, add to the meat and simmer for 1$\frac{1}{2}$ hours, or until the meat is tender.

POTAGE PAYSANNE

Claudie thought of a soup using the fresh vegetables of the Loire valley. Chop 1 lb. mixed carrots, onions, and leeks, with 3 sticks of celery and a turnip (about 3 oz.). Colour in 4 oz. ($\frac{1}{2}$ cup) of butter, in a large pot. Cover with twice the volume of water Season well and simmer for 10 minutes. Add peas, 2 spring onions, chopped, and 3 oz. (6 tablespoons) of butter. Check the seasoning and continue cooking. When all the vegetables are cooked, mix in some bechamel sauce (see page 95).

MENU

René and Patrice suggested fantastic dishes made from fish. They were mocked for their fantasy and praised for their courage. 'We must fit all this into a menu!'

POTAGE PAYSANNE	VEGETABLE SOUP
QUICHE DE VIANDES	MEAT FLAN
BLANQUETTE DE VEAU	BLANQUETTE OF VEAL
SALADE	SALAD
FROMAGES	CHEESE

MOUSSE AU CITRON (Lemon mousse)

Edwidge suggested a very light sweet. 'This one would do for your young nephews as well, Ghislaine'.

2 lemons	**3 tablespoons ($3\frac{3}{4}$) sugar**
4 eggs	**1 oz. (3 packets) gelatine**

Separate the eggs into two bowls. Mix the egg yolks and the sugar thoroughly. Add the juice of the two lemons, and the grated peel of one.

Whip the egg whites until solid. Melt the gelatine in the saucepan with a little hot water. Mix until clear. Pour this into the yolk mixture, whipping all the time. Fold in the beaten whites. Allow to set in the fridge. Serve with whipped cream.

VENISON CHOPS

The two families often went on visits to the Sologne. It was a very interesting area, and the two fishermen of the party took their rods. Now and again they caught pike and carp. The suppers on those occasions were very good.

In restaurants there they ate venison and young wild pig. They would probably never cook these meats at home, but amused themselves in collecting and researching ways of cooking game, to see if the great chefs used the same methods.

Game meat is dark and tasty. Meat from old animals needs to be left overnight in a mixture of red wine, herbs and peppercorns. Meat from young game can be cooked in the same way as beef or lamb. To show how simple it all is (except of course for procuring the game), here is a recipe for venison chops. These are cut from a young deer. Fry the chops gently in a pan, using butter and oil. Arrange on a warm serving dish. Pour some vinegar into the cooking pan. Stir well, to detach all the pan juices, and pour over the meat. Serve with *croûtons* fried in butter.

SAUCES FOR GAME

There are two sauces that are often served with game.

POIVRADE.   Cook chopped onion, chopped carrot and bacon gently in butter. Add a bunch of herbs: thyme, parsley, bay leaf. Pour in 1 pint ($2\frac{1}{2}$ cups) of wine vinegar. Simmer until the volume of the vinegar is reduced by half. Brown $\frac{1}{2}$ oz. (1 tablespoon) of butter and cook $\frac{1}{2}$ oz. ($1\frac{3}{4}$ tablespoons) of flour in it for a few moments. Pour a little of the vinegar stock into the flour and butter. Mix well, and pour this thickening into the stock. Add butter, and simmer for 10 minutes. Strain, and serve with the meat.

SAUCE AUX CERISES.   Stone $\frac{1}{2}$ lb. black cherries and simmer, just covered with sugared water. The cherries should become tender very quickly. Simmer 4 tablespoons (5) of redcurrant jelly with a glass of port, $\frac{1}{2}$ teaspoon of cinnamon, a clove, and the juice and grated peel of one orange. Cook until reduced by half. Strain this mixture onto the cherries and mix well. Serve hot with the meat.

The Tools of the Trade

As you may have guessed, Ghislaine was not a very experienced cook. In Paris she had always worked in an office, and did not seem to have the time to do much cooking. After a couple of months of helping Edwidge in the kitchen her husband noticed the difference at home.

When she had learned how to make pastry, a white sauce, and the egg mixture for a *quiche* it all seemed much simpler, because from these basic preparations many dishes came. Some dishes took time but others were very simple. She could save the longer preparations for the weekend.

Then, immediately, she felt that she did not have the right equipment at home. She found that she needed very few things in the kitchen but they had to be good. Patrice was surprised when he went with her to buy the things they really needed. The purchases did not break the bank.

BASIC KITCHEN EQUIPMENT

Let's have a look at the things really necessary in the kitchen, the things needed to cook the dishes that we have discovered together in the regions of France.

There are two things to think of when buying kitchen equipment. Only buy the things that are necessary; and buy good quality equipment, the best you can afford. Don't be tempted by cutters, mixers and graters, usually made of plastic, that are supposed to be the very latest on the market. Avoid cheap give-aways because, more often than not, they are useless, and clutter up the kitchen. Basic kitchen equipment has not changed for hundreds of years. And remember, we are only thinking of necessities.

1 wire whisk about 12 inches long
1 broad spatula or slice 12 inches long
1 metal grater
1 wire strainer, at least 6 inches in diameter
1 salad strainer

Ball of thin twine

Pouring jug to contain frying salad oil, with a small brush for coating surfaces or adding small amount of oil to a dish

Measuring jug, at least 2-pint (5 cup) capacity

Weighing machine

Knife sharpener

Brush for the surface of pastry

Cutting board, at least 20 inches × 12 inches

Pastry board (or better still a piece of marble) at least 20 inches × 24 inches

18-inch rolling pin (the straight-sided type)

KNIVES

1 10-inch slicing and chopping knife

1 7-inch paring knife

1 bread knife

SPOONS

2 tablespoons and 2 large forks

1 wooden spoon, 12 inches long, for savoury dishes

1 wooden spoon, 10 inches long, for sweet dishes

POTS AND PANS

Large soup pot, the larger the better

2 saucepans, about 8 inches in diameter

2 pans for sauces, about 6 inches in diameter

Deep sided frying pan made of iron or tinned copper, 12 inches in diameter

10-inch omelet/pancake pan

1 oven-proof casserole, at least 4-pint (10-cup) capacity

BOWLS

12-inch salad bowl

Large mixing bowl, at least 12 inches in diameter

1 bowl, 10 inches in diameter

1 small bowl, 8 inches in diameter

Try to get bowls that you could put into the oven. Oven-proof glass is very good.

DISHES AND TINS FOR THE OVEN

Sizes will depend upon the size of your oven but get the largest that will fit in

2 large oven trays (the type with a very low edge is the best for most purposes)

2 large roasting tins (one perhaps smaller than the other)

2 round tart tins, one 8 inches and one 9 inches in diameter

1 large cake tin. (Go for a round one if you are undecided)

Patty tin for baking tartlets. (For at least 12 tartlets)

2 oven dishes that would be presented at the table. One round and the other square.

At least one large oval serving plate

SEASONINGS

Containers for herbs: thyme, parsley, bayleaf, garlic
Pepper mill (for black peppercorns)
Pepper mill (for white pepper)
Pot for salt. Cooks rarely use a salt mill for they prefer to grab a handful of salt and throw
    it into the waiting dish. (Never get between a chef and his dish!)
Bottle for wine vinegar
Lemon squeezer

SOME USEFUL ADDITIONS

Extra knife for carving. Very long with a flexible blade
Extra whisk. This gives you a whisk for savoury sauces and another for sweet sauces
Electric mixer. This becomes less and less of a luxury. It is best to wait until you can
    afford a machine that will do as many jobs as possible; for instance, also liquidise fruit
Double boiler. It is possible to heat one saucepan over water boiling in another, but this
    purchase makes life so much easier
Rotary whisk. The kind that is turned by a geared wheel at the side. This is the best for
    whipping egg whites until really solid
Cherry pipper. This can also be used for stoning olives
Oyster knife
Steamer. As well as being able to cook over steam you can use the top as an extra strainer
Fish kettle. Your largest saucepan could be used for fish, but as your fish repertoire
    increases the fish kettle becomes very useful
Metal foil on large roller
Tin opener. (Even the French manage to open quite a lot of tins)

NOTE

This inventory of equipment could go on, but be careful! When making additions ask
yourself if that extra kitchen tool is necessary. Bear in mind that we have looked into
many kitchens all over France. You could attempt all the dishes in this book with the
utensils mentioned.

Index

Note:
Menus are given in French with an English translation and each individual recipe is then given under an English heading.
Most regional dishes not included in the menus will be found under a French heading.
Whenever possible dishes are included in both English and French indexes.

English

French